GOD LOVES EVERYONE

BY FRED BERT ITHURBURN

Order this book online at www.trafford.com
or email orders@trafford.com

Most Trafford titles are also available at major online book retailers.

Printed in the United States of America.

ISBN: 978-1-4669-5434-2 (sc)
ISBN: 978-1-4669-5433-5 (hc)
ISBN: 978-1-4669-5432-8 (e)

Library of Congress Control Number: 2012915347

Trafford rev. 08/28/2012

North America & international
toll-free: 1 888 232 4444 (USA & Canada)
phone: 250 383 6864 • fax: 812 355 4082

The Good News According to God

Six centuries before the life of *Jesus*, *God* designated "a prophet to the nations" while still in his mother's womb, and this prophet (*Jeremiah*) later handed on the prophecy of *God's New Covenant* (Jer 31:31-34) as follows:

> Behold the days shall come saith the Lord, and I will make a new covenant with the house of Israel and with the house of Judah: not according to the covenant which I made with their fathers, in the day that I took them by the hand to bring them out of the land of Egypt: the covenant which they made void, and I had dominion over them, saith the Lord. But this shall be the covenant that I will make with the house of Israel after those days, saith the Lord: I will give my law in their bowels, and I will write it in their hearts, and I will be their God, and they shall be my people. And they shall teach no more every man his neighbor, and every man his brother, saying: Know the Lord for all shall know me from the least of them even to the greatest, saith the Lord: for

> I will forgive their iniquity and I will remember their sin no more.

These things *God* accomplishes in *Jesus Christ's* death and resurrection to show us that the *New Covenant* is of *God's* design and awakens us with a figure of that new and eternal or everlasting covenant, to realize *Jesus Christ* ratified and fulfills *God's* unilateral deal, in that fuller revelation, which is given through *Jesus* the *Nazorean*. *God* solely institutes and performs this *New Covenant* of the *Old Testament* in the *New Testament*, that is to say, in *Jesus's Blood* (cf. 1 Cor 11:23-26) calling together all people created, making them *one*, not in the flesh but in the *spirit of God*. The *People of God* are all *God's* human creatures and are all saved solely by *God* in *Christ*, and from *God's* goodness even though unbeknownst to many, all people are beneficiaries and are saved for everlasting life. (*The Gospel before the Gospel*.)

Thus, hours before the sacrificial death of *Jesus* bleeding to death on the *cross* of his crucifixion, *Jesus* refers to this *New Covenant* and incorporates it by reference in his death and voices words of *God*, which he likely was instructed to say, at the paschal meal shared with his followers. *Jesus* after consuming the bread at supper, in a similar way, takes a cup of wine, gives thanks to *God*, his *Father*, and gives it to us, saying words, such as, the following:

> "All of you must drink from it, for this is my blood, the blood of the *covenant* to be poured out in behalf of many for the forgiveness of sins." (Mt 26:27-28); or, "This is my blood, the blood of the *covenant* to be poured out on behalf of many . . ." (Mk 14:24); or, "This cup is the *new covenant* in my blood, which will be shed for you." (Lk 22:20) (emphasis mine to *New Covenant* references).

Immediately after these words at supper, *Jesus* "walks the talk" to the death he foretells in context of fulfilling *God's* performance of the *New Covenant's* terms and promises "for you," meaning every created individual.

The words of the *Last Supper*, writes *Pope Benedict XVI*, are words that are "interdependent" with *Jesus's* death as without their meaning his death is a mere execution. "Interdependent" with his death are also the words instituting the *Eucharist* (thanksgiving to *God*) with memorial meals *Jesus* institutes to repeat and distribute *Eucharist* until the end of time and remission of all sin. By this action the "Sacrifice of the *Cross*" is continuously made present. Each meal is to be subject to the basic form of the *passover* but focused on the *cross* to remember *Jesus's* loving deed and give thanks and praise to *God* in remembrance of the love shown by *God* in *Jesus. Jesus* voluntarily sacrifices his life to baptize, in blood, every human being in *God's* fullness of forgiveness and salvation for our free *passover* to *God's* presence. *Jesus* fulfills also *God's New and Eternal Covenant* constantly in his Sacrifice of the *Cross at Mass*. The *paschal* mystery on *Christ's* death and resurrection seem foolish to us, but not to *God's* way of creation. The mystery of *Christ's* loving deed performing *God's* promises for our salvation is made present for us, for our redemption and transformation in faith and life at *calvary* and daily Masses memorialized worldwide, by *God's Spirit* of love for all humankind. Expressly the *Eucharist* is open to all humanity, unconditionally, as *God* wills it to be for us from the beginning of creation; thus, to have *God* actually and intimately within ourselves nourishing us and renewing us. Our faith is nourished, hope increased, and charity strengthened thereby. *God's* imperfect human creations are always being perfected in *Spirit* as *Jesus* constantly redeems them to be *People of God*. Conformance of *Jesus's* words at supper and *Jesus's* order for all to take is repeated at every one of these *suppers* of the *Lord* to allow *God* often to be within us. Also, we hear from the *risen Christ* in heaven these same words of the *Last Supper* and that the *Eucharistic* gifts are to be handed to all *Jews* and *Gentiles. Saint Paul* was the first to name the Sacrament and report in writing the words of the *Eucharist* (1 Cor 11:25), referring to *God's New Covenant*, in part, as follows:

> "This cup is the *new covenant* in my blood. Do this, whenever you drink it in remembrance of me." (Emphasis mine.)

In consequence of the words of *Jesus* at the *Last Supper*, repeated as *God* from *heaven*, all people on earth, created by *God* and baptized in the *Blood of the New Covenant*, are made "worthy" as beneficiaries of the *New Covenant*. We all should often take and consume *Jesus's* body and blood, especially if we sin often, for *God's Real Presence* to be in our "bowels," to thank *God*, to nourish our lives and faith, and to be transformed by *God* to love each other. *God* does not take dominion of us and make us take or love but leaves us freedom to choose. *Jesus*, however, ordered "you" all to take and eat, take and drink, of his flesh and blood.

We *Jews*, *Moslems*, and *Christians* are our father *Abraham's* children of the Book. When *Jerusalem* was destroyed, *Jeremiah* remained to utter the great oracle of the *New Covenant* (Jer 31:31-34) also known as "The Gospel before the Gospel," a landmark of our *book*. *Jeremiah*, like *Jesus*, was likely killed for disturbing his countrymen. During the exile, the *Old Testament* was published so that *Jews*, *Moslems*, and *Christians* had access to understand that Jesus of *Nazareth* referred to the *New Covenant* in context of his sacrifice in the *New Testament*, as *Son of God* and *Son of Man*, to save us all for everlasting life with *God*.

The qualities of the *New and Eternal Covenant*, unlike other covenants made as a common theme by the prophets, are imprinted in the hearts of all people to never be broken. The knowledge of *God's law* of loving each other, too, will be generally known in the life of all people that we will no longer need the *Bible*, the *Torah*, and the *Koran*. We have this prophecy, which is fulfilled only through the *Blood of the Lamb* sacrificed on the *Cross* (cf. Lk 22:20, 1 Cor 11:25) imprinting in our consciences *God's law*. We no longer need teaching; but men's traditions intervened and negated evidence of *God's Covenant*.

Jesus, our Lord God, wants us all to proclaim his work and thank his *Father*, especially at *Eucharist*. He wants each of us, on our own, to "take this, all of you," referring to the Eucharist, in hopes, that by considering *God's* love in *Jesus's* sacrificial love for us, we will reciprocate to love others. Focusing on *Jesus* within the following events: his scriptural life, journey to *Jerusalem*, *Last Supper*, *Gethsemani*, scourging, way of the *cross*, *crucifixion*, death, and resurrection, each of us may open our heart spontaneously and reciprocate by some loving response to *God*, *Jesus*, and others simply for the fact that *Jesus* and *God* love us that much. Actually, I am not competent to teach love as I have no greater competence than any of you. I love myself, but I suspect loving neighbors impartially, as *God* really wants us to do, takes *God's* assist to do and teach competently.

Saint Ambrose, later bishop of *Milan*, often received *Eucharist*. He, too, was an attorney who appreciated *God's* unilateral *Covenant*. *Ambrose* (d. 397) gave us the *Latin Mass*, which lasted several centuries, until Vatican II. He wrote it in *Latin* in order to have a common language to share *Eucharist*. It read in pertinent part:

Accipite, et bibite ex eo omnes.
HIC EST ENIM CALIX SANCUINIS MEI,
MOVI ET ÆTERBU TESTAMENTI:
MYSTERIUM FIDEL:
QUI PRO VOBIS
ET PRO MULTIS EFFUNDETUR
IN REMISSIONEM PECCATORUM
Hǽ quotiescúmque fecéritis, in mei
memóriam faciétis.

Which words are translated with my emphasis as follows:

Take ye all, and drink of this:

For this is the chalice of my blood
of the ***new and eternal covenant****:*
The mystery of faith,
Which shall be shed
For you and for many
Unto the forgivness of sins
As often as you shall do these things, in

Memory of Me shall you do them.

The *Mass* in *Latin* remained intact from about AD 400 until the *Second Vatican Council* changed it to the vernacular. *Ambrose* seems to use his expertise in law to correct *Scripture's Christology* by emphasis of the *New and Eternal Covenant*, the New Testament, instituted in *Christ's blood* (Jer 31:31-34, cf. 1 Cor 11:25). *Ambrose* interchanged "testament" for "covenant," perhaps because both are unilateral agreements to a lawyer. In *English* my *Holy Name Manual Missal* (1941) translated it to "covenant" which may have been more meaningful to the authors. Any lawyer appreciates *God's New Covenant* is a unilateral agreement, similar to a last will or testament, which gives things to beneficiaries freely and unconditionally. *Pope Benedict's* recent changes use *Ambrose's Chalice* (Calix) but not, *Jesus's Cup*, for some reason that escapes me. The mystery of *Christ's* death and resurrection is expressly celebrated at every *Mass*, presumably using *Christ's* loving terms, but *Pope Benedict* prefers traditional words. By *Jesus's* action the sacrifice of the *cross* is made present as is *God's real presence* at *Eucharist*, regardless of form in the vernacular. Its *spirit*, not form, is essentially the same as what *Jesus* said; but with the compliments of *Pope Benedict XVI*, I furnish with emphasis our newest version's pertinent part referring to the *New Covenant*:

"TAKE THIS, ALL OF YOU, AND DRINK
FROM IT,
FOR THIS IS THE CHALICE OF MY
BLOOD,
THE BLOOD OF **THE NEW AND
ETERNAL COVENANT**,
WHICH WILL BE POURED OUT FOR YOU
AND
FOR MANY
FOR THE FORGIVENESS OF SINS."

Ambrose also gave *Mariology* decisive direction in the *west*, but her closer relationship with us is mostly due to *Luke*. *Luke*, the most trustworthy gospel reporter, in my opinion, interviewed *Mary* a score of years after *Jesus's death*, and the *Greek* found her, even though presumably a biased mother, to be a good witness. *Mary,* the mother of *Jesus Christ,* reported all the things she experienced about the early life of *Jesus,* and at *Luke's* interview, she handed on to him the recollections she treasured. And he, accepting her sentimental reporting, wrote what she said to him in narrative form precisely as those events were transmitted. *Luke* carefully traced the whole sequence of events from the beginning and set it in writing, that we may see how reliable the information was that he received. And I submit, to show the trustworthiness of *Luke's* writings.

The *Virgin Mary* received the announcement of the birth of *Jesus* as follows: in the sixth month of her cousin, *Elizabeth's* pregnancy, the angel *Gabriel* was sent from *God* to a town of *Galilee* named *Nazareth* to the virgin betrothed to a man named *Joseph*, of the house of *David*. The virgin's name was *Mary*. Upon arriving, the angel said to her: "Rejoice, O highly favored daughter! The Lord is with you. Blessed are you among women." She was deeply troubled by his words and wondered what his greeting meant. The angel went on to say to her: "Do not fear, Mary. You have found favor with God. You shall conceive and bear a son and give him the name Jesus. Great will be his dignity and he will be called Son of the Most High. The Lord God will give him the throne of David his father. He will rule over the house of Jacob forever and his reign will be without end." *Mary* said to the angel, "How can this be since I do not know man?" The angel answered her. "The Holy Spirit will come upon you and the power of the Most High will overshadow you; hence the holy offspring to be born will be called Son of God. Know that Elizabeth, your kinswoman, has conceived a son in her old age; she who was thought to be sterile is now in her sixth month, for nothing is impossible with God." *Mary* said, "I am the servant of the Lord. Let it be done to me as you say." With that, the angel left her.

Thereupon, *Mary* set out proceeding in haste into the hill country to a town of *Judah* where she entered *Zechariah's* house and greeted *Elizabeth*. When *Elizabeth* heard *Mary's* greeting, the baby leapt in her womb. *Elizabeth* was filled with the *Holy Spirit* and cried out in a loud voice: “Blest are you among women and blest is the fruit of your womb. But who am I that the mother of my Lord should come to me? The moment your greeting sounded in my ears, the baby leapt in my womb for joy. Blest is she who trusted that the Lord’s words to her would be fulfilled.” Then *Mary* said, “My being proclaims the greatness of the Lord, my spirit finds joy in God my savior. For he has looked upon his servant in her lowliness; all ages to come shall call me blessed. God who is mighty has done great things for me. Holy is his name. His mercy is from age to age on those who fear him. He has shown might with his arm; he has confused the proud in their inmost thoughts. He has deposed the mighty, from their thrones and raised the lowly to high places. The hungry he has given every good thing, while the rich he has sent empty away. He has upheld Israel his servant, ever mindful of his mercy. Even as he promised our fathers, promised Abraham and his descendants forever.” *Mary* remained with *Elizabeth* about three months and then returned home.

About six months later, *Jesus* was born as follows: In those days, *Caesar Augustus* published a decree ordering a census of the whole world. This first census took place while *Quirinius* was governor of *Syria*. Everyone went to register, each to his own town. And so *Joseph* went from the town of *Nazareth* in *Galilee* to *Judea*, to *David’s* town of *Bethlehem*—because he was of the house and lineage of *David*—to register with *Mary*, his espoused wife, who was with child.

While they were there, the days of her confinement were completed. She gave birth to her first-born son and wrapped him in swaddling clothes and laid him in a manger because there was no room for them in the place where traveler's lodged. There were shepherds in that region living in the field and keeping night watch by turns over their flocks. The angel of the *Lord* appeared to them as the glory of the *Lord* shown around them, and they were very much afraid. The angel said to them: "You have nothing to fear I come to proclaim good news to you—tidings of great joy to be shared by the whole people. This day in David's city a savior has been born to you, the Messiah and Lord. Let this be a sign to you, in a manger you will find an infant wrapped in swaddling clothes." Suddenly, there was with the angels a multitude of the heavenly host, praising *God* and saying,

> "Glory to God in high heaven, peace on
> earth to those on whom his favor rests."

When the angels had returned to heaven, the shepherds said to one another: "Let us go over to Bethlehem and see this event which the Lord has made known to us." They went in haste and found *Mary* and *Joseph* and the baby lying in the manger; once they saw, they understood what had been told them concerning this child. All who heard of it were astonished at the report given them by the shepherds. *Mary* treasured all these things and reflected on them in her heart. The shepherds returned, glorifying and praising *God* for all they had heard and seen in accord with what had been told them. When the eighth day arrived for his circumcision, the name *Jesus* was given to the child, the name the angels had given him before he was conceived. When the day came to purify them according to the laws of *Moses*, the couple brought him up to *Jerusalem* so that he could be presented to the *Lord* for it is written in the law of the *Lord*, "Every first-born male shall be consecrated to the Lord." They came to offer in sacrifice "a pair of turtle doves or two young pigeons," in accordance with the dictates in the law of the *Lord*. There lived in *Jerusalem* at the time a certain man named *Simeon*. He was just and pious and awaited the consolation of *Israel*, and the *Holy Spirit* was upon him. It was revealed to him by the *Holy Spirit* that he would not experience death until he had seen the *anointed* of the *Lord*. He came to the temple now, inspired by the *Spirit*, and when the parents brought in the child *Jesus* to perform for him the customary ritual of the law, he took him in his arms and blessed *God* in these words: "Now, Master, you can dismiss your servant in peace; you have fulfilled your word. For my eyes have witnessed your saving deed displayed for all the peoples to see. *A revealing light to the Gentiles*, the glory of your people Israel" (emphasis mine). The child's father and mother were marveling at what was being said about him. *Simeon* blessed them and said to *Mary* his mother: "This child is destined to be the downfall and the rise of many in Israel, a sign that will be opposed—and yourself shall be pierced with a sword—so that the thoughts of many hearts may be laid bare." There was also a certain prophetess, *Anna* by name, daughter of *Phanuel* of the tribe of *Asher.* She had seen many days, having lived seven years with her husband after her marriage and then as a widow until she was eighty-four. She was constantly in the temple, worshipping day and night in fasting and prayer. Coming on the scene at this moment, she gave thanks to *God* and talked about the child to all who looked forward to the deliverance of *Jerusalem*. When the pair had fulfilled all the prescriptions of the law of the *Lord,* they returned to *Galilee* and their own town of *Nazareth*. The child grew in size and strength, filled with wisdom, and the grace of *God* was upon him.

His parents used to go every year to *Jerusalem* for the feast of the *Passover*, and when he was twelve, they went up for the celebration as was their custom. As they were returning at the end of the feast, the child *Jesus* remained behind unknown to his parents. Thinking he was in the party, they continued their journey for a day, looking for him among their relatives and acquaintances. Not finding him, they returned to *Jerusalem* in search of him. On the third day, they came upon him in the temple sitting in the midst of the teachers, listening to them and asking them questions. All who heard him were amazed at his intelligence and his answers. When his parents saw him, they were astonished, and his mother said to him: "Son, why have you done this to us? You see that your father, and I have been searching for you in sorrow." He said to them: "Why did you search for me? Did you not know I had to be in my Father's house?" But they did not grasp what he said to them. He went down with them then and came to *Nazareth* and was obedient to them. His mother meanwhile kept all these things in memory. *Jesus* for his part progressed steadily in wisdom and age and grace before *God* and men.

Jesus became a carpenter (today, more likely an independent contractor). He lived with *Mary* and *Joseph* until *Joseph's* death and departed from home about age thirty. From infancy, he had continued to study and learn his *scripture* and came to be aware of his calling to live, die, and be resurrected. His learnings likely included that he was to be the paschal lamb (Ex 12), the suffering servant who gives himself up for humanity (Is 3), and he is to die and fulfill *God's new covenant* (Jer 31). He learned his *New Testament* death, makes beneficiaries and heirs of every human being created to be imperfect, now to be perfected by his death and be *one* with *God* in *God's* eternal kingdom. When he left home, he went to his cousin *John* who was baptizing people at the *River Jordan*. *John* announced *Jesus's* appearance as the *"Lamb of God"* and, to conform to *Old Testament* scripture, baptized *Jesus*. At that time, they heard a voice from *Heaven* announcing to *Jesus*: "You are my beloved Son. On you my favor rests." Thereafter, *Jesus* retreated to the *desert* and empowered by the *Spirit* returned to begin his teaching in *Galilee* at the *Nazareth* synagogue. When the *Book of Isaiah* was presented to him, he read from the scroll and announced that he presently fulfills the anointed person therein referred to as bringing glad tidings. But because he added he was not to cure anyone there, as in *Capernaum*, the audience expelled him. *Jesus* continued curing and teaching elsewhere and called disciples to follow him as he performed miracles and cured people on his roundabout journey to *Jerusalem*. His teachings included the *Lord's Prayer*, praying "thy kingdom come" meaning the kingdom of the *New Covenant* that would come with his life, death, and resurrection. Both teachings and miracles *Jesus* did in public and there exist records of their numerous observations and hearsays to credit *Jesus* as being *God's* authorized agent. Since *The Gospel According to Luke* records them, I refer you there, rather than plagiarize *Luke* excessively. By the time *Jesus* entered *Jerusalem* to face his ordeal, *Jesus* had gathered quite a following that disturbed the leaders of the *temple*, especially since he criticized them in his teachings and, to make matters worse, disturbed their peace violently in the *temple's* business area. The leaders made plans to pacify him, and their plans came to fruition on the weekend that *Jesus* and his apostles were welcomed into *Jerusalem* for their last Passover meal together. At supper, which is called today the *Last Supper, Jesus* shared words with *Judas*, his betrayer, and when *Judas* left to sell him out, *Jesus* cautioned the others to love and serve each other, meaning everyone created. At supper *Jesus* also voiced the "interdependent" words explaining his death, words that more plainly tells us today, with our hindsight, more of the mystery of *Jesus's* sacrifice and resurrection. As mentioned, the *Cross* appears foolish to us reasonable people; but as an exercise of faith and trust in *God* and *God's Jesus Christ,* we accept it and struggle to reverence them both in the *passover* like suppers we share in their memory. Little children can believe the mystery and events better than we wise guys, and we should similarly accept their truth lovingly and trustingly.

The apparent foolishness of the *Cross* requires the story of *Jesus* in his passion to be reflected upon in detail for *God* to define for us his death and resurrection. No greater sign will be given to us of the *mystery* in this age except the message of *love* in *Jesus's* death and resurrection. Consider *Jesus* believing he is the *Savior* of humankind, which truth he began learning at his mother's knee, and learned he is to be like *Moses* (see Dt 18:15-29) who must take *God's people* from life to passover to everlasting life, by his death and resurrection. To accomplish this, *Jesus* foresees the experiences he must suffer and tells his followers, at times, of them in ways not understandable to them, until after it happens. They believe more by hindsight and faith afterward, enough to die in martyrdom (but for *John*) for their beliefs, while evangelizing their faith. *Jesus* disciplined himself to die for us and persevered, throughout his prolonged ordeal based on trust in *God's* love, to offer his death into *God's* hands for the expiation of our evildoing.

Think of *Jesus Christ* and him crucified rather than any persuasion in human hearsay, opinion, or argument. "As a consequence, your faith rests not on wisdom of men but on the power of *God*." (1 Cor 2:5). Recall, after supper, *Jesus* enters the garden with his apostles and sweats out his wanting to be relieved of the task, "his sweat became like drops of blood falling to the ground," from worry about his ability to perform. *Jesus* finally resigns himself to trust *God* and continues into the shameful agony of "dying on a tree." He perseveres through the penetrating flogging, from soldiers who may have poured it on because his follower mutilated the ear of one of whom they consider their own, and they may have heard that *Pilate* might release *Jesus.* So they half-killed him in their scourging, the evidence of which appears later in weakness from bleeding and the internal bleeding exposed in his chest cavity, after death when he was speared. When the soldiers had finished flogging him and mocking him, they led him in a tortuous and prolonged way, carrying his wood, to crucify him. The beating was so bad that, although he was used to laboring in his work, *Jesus* fell at times under the mere weight of the wood, aggravating his wounds and adding to his bleeding, externally and internally. Arriving finally at the site of crucifixion, he is forcefully stripped of his garments and left naked to be exposed to both public view and the cold. He is forced down onto the cross beams and brutally nailed with spikes, first one wrist and then the other, and also both feet to the post. “Excruciating” is the descriptive word for pains of crucifixion. The spikes are hammered home to torturously tear through his flesh, the sound of which is easily heard over his shocking silence. Then *Jesus's* is lifted up, his body only supported by the spikes penetrating his acutely wounded flesh, and Jesus is violently posted upright. Later he uses the spikes as supports, through his mutilated flesh, to breathe and provides us precious words. He even comforts others than himself at the price of pain and loss of breath. Nailed to the cross, he begins an increasing cycle of pain and trauma, to breathe or rest, to survive each moment. As he hangs on his wounds, he feels asphyxiation, the drowning sensation because he cannot breath, which must continually be relieved by strenuously pressing momentarily on the spikes, those which penetrate the wounded limbs. He gains momentary relief and, in agony, catches a few breaths, before settling back into painful suffocation, and, again to need precious air and force the temporary lifesaving cycle. He feels his hold on life weakening and, with increased drowning sensations, feels panic over the pain. Instinctively, he must raise himself with great effort to strain, suffering the excruciating pain, to gasp for air while well aware that the fear of the unknown with death is looming and avoided as long as he stays conscious. Death will relieve him of the vicious ordeal he suffers, but his diminished consciousness increases his baser instinct to keep alive. He may be aware some crucified hang alive for days, while he persists in fighting futilely for life. *Jesus* as *God* can decide "enough" but as human he persists. *Jesus* as man, probably, perseveres, out of love, to do *God's* will and save us all. As *God* he would prove nothing; but as man doing a *God*-like thing, *God* glorifies him to be *one* with *God* forever as *Jesus Christ The Lord.*

When he speaks "Forgive them for they know not what they do," earlier in his crucifixion, he expends needed air to speak on our behalf, and he may be pleading with *His Father* to perform *God's covenant* pledge to forgive all humanity and not just the *Jews* and *Romans* nearby. His ever weakening effort, as his energy is progressively bleeding away, awakens his baser instincts to survive and to think more of himself. He has a basic conflict of interest, to survive or to die and save us, that he progressively fights. Likely unappreciated is that his loss of blood is causing his acute thirst. He hears and suffers the cruel mocking of those watching, succeeding in hurting his feelings, and yet *Jesus* accepts the increased agony to express gratitude by assuring the other crucified victim words that he will be with *Jesus* in *paradise* (Lk 23:43, abode of soul's waiting the Messiah in limbo). Later the "thirst" cry likely wrenched from his less conscious state, forgets his statement not to drink, and *Jesus* welcomes the offer of vinegar wine only to be fooled by the unquenchable. His cry "I thirst," confusion and feeling abandoned may indicate symptoms to *Luke*, the physician, of *Jesus's* loss of body fluids hastening his death. We hear *Jesus* cry "My God, My God, why have you abandoned me . . ." the opening words of the Ps 22 he memorized, that also pleads for *God* to return hastily to rescue him, a plea that is cut short. Finally, he realizes he is to die and cries out, "it is finished," ("it is fulfilled" in *Greek*) and utters trustingly, "Father, into your hands I commend my spirit," and breathes no more. He is later speared near the heart and blood with water pour out of his chest cavity, indicating the effect of prior internal injuries and trauma suffered throughout his body that killed him before the other two crucified were deliberately killed.

Luke reports of the *Resurrection* that first *Easter Sunday* from hearsay of *Jesus's* followers who also witnessed his return appearance on earth. He wrote that *Jesus* opened some minds to the understanding of pertinent *scriptures* but none apparently mentioned his *new covenant* performance. They recall *Jesus* said *penance* for the remission of sins is to be preached to all nations. A definition of *penance*—calls for us to devote ourselves to others in repentance. *Jesus* added a blessing: "I send down upon you the promise of my Father." That promise may be the *covenant* relationship, defined when *Jesus* was taken up on the *Cross* or from death. I suspect the *penance* is in loving others, which is hard for us to do but is known by heart as the teaching and law of *God*. But *penance* may be *Christ's* teaching of service to be performed for others as constant redemption until the world's end, for we who need it, to improve us as a loving gift to be given to *God. Penance* may also be the word of the witnesses and not spoken by the *risen Christ* who is aware of the fact *God's Covenant* pardoned everyone's sin and has secured *God's law* of love forever, without *penance*.

After *Jesus* died, resurrected, and ascended, he appears to have an afterthought. He selects and taught a thirteenth apostle, *Paul (Saul)* from *heaven* to tell everyone created of salvation and to share *Holy Communion* with *Jews* and *Gentiles* all over. *Luke's* conversion to *Christianity* was as a disciple of *Saint Paul*. They traveled together until *Luke* began his own ministry, which included his *Gospel* and his supplemental writings. Much earlier *our Lord Jesus Christ* converted *Saul of Tarsus*. No longer "emptied of divinity", *and now* fully cognizant of the *New and Eternal Covenant* in *God's* further relationship with *God's* human creatures, *Jesus Christ* selects this learned Pharisee and Helenist scholar, to carry *God's gospel* to the world of *Jews* and *Gentiles*. He may have given his new apostle a "crash course" or graced him with the learning we read in his letters (*Epistles*) but specially instructed him in those words, he used at the *Last Supper* that were "interdependent" for meaning in his death. *Jesus Christ* handed on to *Paul (Saul)* what *Paul* handed on to all he contacted, that *Jesus* took bread, gave thanks, broke it, and said, "This is my body which is for you. Do this in remembrance of me." In the same way, after supper, *Jesus* took the cup, saying, "This is the *new covenant* in my blood. Do this whenever you drink it, in remembrance of me." *Paul* did as he was instructed, thus proclaiming *Jesus's* death in context of the *New Covenant* and instructs us to do the same until *our Lord Jesus Christ* returns or comes.

Luke continued to supplement his *Gospel* by writing of those being converted by all the *Christians* to share the *Eucharist* as instructed and to live their life in the *penance* that they thought *our Lord* preached. *Luke* quoted the risen Christ, at *His* departure to welcome his *Spirit*, who would baptize them in *Spirit* and empower them to be witnesses to the end of the earth. Some followers devoted themselves to a communal life (*The Acts of the Apostles*, Chapter 4, version 35 to 37), and *Luke* describes a part he witnessed, as follows:

> "*Life of the Christians.* The community of believers was of one heart and one mind. None of them ever claimed anything as his own; rather, everything was held in common. With power the apostles bore witness to the resurrection of the Lord Jesus, and great respect was paid to them all, nor was there

> anyone needy among them, for all who owned property or houses sold them and donated the proceeds. They used to lay them at the feet of the apostles to be distributed to everyone according to his need.
>
> There was a certain Levite from Cyprus named Joseph, to whom the apostles gave the name Barnabas (meaning 'son of encouragement'). He sold a farm that he owned and made a donation of the money, laying it at the apostles' feet."

Americans would suggest *The Wealth of Nations* by *Adam Smith* should be read by everyone before they venture to sell their properties and commune. Humans were not created by *God* to be so naturally good, and a social benefit was made by *Smith* in pointing out the capital of all the *People of God* is enhanced when individuals pursue their own wealth. Unbridled capitalism, he warned, however, causes the rich to become richer and to engage in "a conspiracy against the public." *United States'* capitalism has become the most wide-spread economic theory in history, but it still wants *Christian* morality to restrain human greed. Jesus told the story of the *rich man and Lazarus* (Lk 16:19ff.) that warns of chastisement or torment for the rich who carelessly ignore the poor. *Jesus* is likely telling his story as a *Jewish* person because of his traditional thinking, but he serves a moral lesson for those addicted to capital riches. The *Chinese* communists and the *Soviet Union's* ex-communists will appreciate that *Christian* standards of fair play in capitalist markets are best over time to temper free marketing as the students of *China* already concluded after their twenty year study, and ventures in free marketing have proved to *China's* benefit.

I have struggled in life to know, love, and serve *God* and accept *Jesus* as *God*; but it is in serving mankind that I see my failing. I am told and believe *God* is *love*. Still I must trust *God* to persuade me to love, outside of loving myself, as I should attempt to love *God*, *Jesus*, and other people. My first experience of love that I recall was my mother's love for me. I recall thinking moreso of what she meant to me once when *Eddie Gatlin's* mother died in or about our fourth grade. He had come home from school and found her dead on the kitchen floor. Afterward, I was on my way home, on a winter evening from school, and the traumatic thought came to me. "What if I found *Mama* dead on the kitchen floor?" I began reflecting on the loss to me, of my mother, and especially the loss of her love for me and realized my trust in her love. I was at an insecure age and dependent on my mother's love for me, being aware of little to love in me, but I treasured *Mama's* love for me. I since have learned from *God* to trust in *God's* love for me as I recall *Mama's* love. I try to make me love others, not as she loved me, but as an exercise of will to love others because *God* wants me to do this unappealing thing. Today, reflecting on our unknowable, invisible, and mysterious *God,* I struggle to love *God* as *God* and *Mama* loves me, but it is beyond me. However, I am at peace trusting *God* loves me even if I cannot love enough. I believe *God* is active in atoms in space, everywhere, in *God's* divine providence, because I am informed *God* is active there, and manifestations of *God's* love, too, are perceptible to me in the multiple ways *God* is in creation, to easily persuade me toward trusting *God's* caring for all creation in its largest and tiniest things. I equate *God* with the laws and forces of nature in the universe and then try to love *God* as *God* wants me to do, hoping it becomes an acceptance more than an effort. I am convinced and acknowledge that the love *Jesus* demonstrated to fulfill *God's Covenant* may be the love I should aim for or try to do. Through *Jesus* efforts *God* persuades me to trust *God* is "love" and that *God* loves me, no matter what I do. *God's* love is more than the memory of love *Mama* left me. I am told it is unimaginatively more, and my best experience of *God's* love is yet to come. Today, it is enough to trust *God* loves me and to meet *God* in *Holy Communion*. *God* chose not to imprint in me *Mama's* type of love for *God* so that love would be naturally effortless; but, *God* appreciates, instead, what I try to do in copying *Jesus's* efforts to love others and his *Father*, my *God* of *Love*, by depending on *God's* help.

My more *Christ*-like human love appears in exercising my will to do something for another, which is distasteful or contrary to my own willful interests.

While I love *Pope Benedict XVI*, it is by an act of will, which I suspect *Jesus* also willingly exercised throughout his passion and death on the *cross*, to love people like *Pope Benedict* and myself. Neither of us is naturally loveable, and because *Jesus* was not acquainted with us, he may have also felt we *Gentiles* were "dogs," but in conforming to *God's* law of love, he willed to love us to his death. Thus, *Jesus* fulfilled the will of his *Father*—by saving everyone for everlasting life, *Jesus* succeeded in performing, but by great human effort, *God's New Covenant* that saves all human creation. He also makes up for my failings in love, carrying them away in his death.

As I try to reciprocate in love I have to ask *God* for help again and again to love *God* and others as I should. Unlike my *Pope Benedict* and myself, *God* is loveable by people because we tend to love our mothers. *God's* motherly love wants us to be free, never chooses to have dominion over us, and loves us as evildoing as we are. *God* is content with whatever love we try to return on an individual or group basis. Still, I am told by *God* to ask to receive *God's* help to not only love but also to pray and to write these thoughts. *God* knows best what we need and even brings good out of our taking *God* for granted. *God* may instill in us motivations, in addition to imprinting *God's* law in our hearts as promised in the *New Covenant,* and see to *Christ's* fulfillment of it but generally leaves us to live and love *God* freely. So I must try often to ask *God* to intervene because I suspect *God* is content with us whether or not we pay attention to *God. God* favors us no matter what we do to be happy and wants us to be happy and at peace about the future. By mysteriously and *scripturally* informing us of *God* and *God's* law pardoning and forgetting our sins, through *Jesus Christ, God* wants peace to be within us in life. It is what *God's* angels heralded as *God* favors all of us impartially and not just "people of good will" as traditionalists insist our creed reads. And *God* favors everyone equally, even the "holy" ones of us, such as *Pope Benedict XVI.* In the deal *God* unilaterally makes with us all, each and every one of us is favored by our *God*, and we, all, are the *People of God* evolving to be like *God. God* teaches us all we need to know about *God* even us who needlessly study about *God* and *God's* law. To obey *God's* law, we need only do what comes naturally and try not to harm anyone, which I suppose is acting natural to *God's* law as *God* creates us to be lovers. *God* imprints in our hearts and minds this law to be conscientiously performed while our animal instincts tell us to act selfishly and evilly to be life successes. Recently, I read of *Shin Dong-hyuk* in *Escape from Camp 14* that questions the last sentence. Ignorance of *God* and *God's law* in *Shin* is made up by *Jesus* who carried *Shin's* sins and ignorance onto the cross to be forgiven and forgotten by *God*; but *Shin* never had a clue of *God* or love until he escaped.

Our ideal shepherd, *Pope John XXIII*, now being venerated as everybody's ideal pope, was *God's* blessing to *the People of God,* meaning everyone. He called the *Second Vatican Council* and opened it to free thinking, placed restraints on the inner bureaucracy of the *Vatican* and allowed the worldwide bishops and theologians to hear silenced *Teilhardists*, liberation theologians, and others with different views on *Christology*, democracy, and the sciences to be heard in open discussion. The *Spirit of God* graced *Pope John,* the gathered bishops and experts, to bring up to date our understanding of the *mystery of Jesus* fulfilling *God's* unilateral *New Covenant* in a modern setting and a global *Church of Christ. Jesus Christ* is the prevailing light to all *God's* created people who have naturally evolved to be a civilized *People of God. Pope John* and his council of bishops were subject, perhaps unknowingly, to the *New Covenant* relationship of the *Spirit of God* as evidenced by the *council's* one global *Church of Christ,* the membership of which are all *the People of God,* as defined above, means everyone created. The *council* stated, "this *church* constituted and organized in the world as a society, subsists in the *Catholic church*," but only when the latter conducts itself true to the fundamental *Christian* virtue of loving every person impartially and equally as *Jesus* demonstrated during that first *Easter* weekend. This ideal church community, society, state, or government, described by the *council* as the *Church of Christ* is what *God* always has in mind for the *New Covenant* relationship. This *kingdom of God's* coming, when *God* alone is our king, is what we pray for in the *Lord's Prayer.* We acknowledge the global *church* and Kingdom in *Eucharist Prayer II* as "spread throughout the world" to be brought to its fullness by charity. *God* foresees its human realization and acceptance to be enjoyed here on earth as *God* plans, fully realized perhaps with *Christ's* return, to finally perfect the evolution from *Alpha* to *Omega* according to *Teilardists'* follow-up on *Darwin.*

I mailed over three hundred letters seeking fatherly advice from *Pope Benedict* on the subject matter concerning an open *Eucharist,* and an ignored *New Covenant* that *God* made and performed with the *Blood of Jesus Christ*, to reveal that every human being created is already saved and cared for by *God.* I hoped my *bishop in Rome* would agree that in reciprocation of *God's gifts,* we should lovingly live now and forever, together, as *one* community or *church.* The only response I received from the *Holy Father* was oppressive silence to my letters mailed over the years, even though I have a constitutional right in No 37 (*Lumen Gentium*) to the *Pope's* "fatherly consideration" of the suggestions proposed by me. He is supposed to respectively enlighten us *(Lumen Gentium)* not be silent to concerns in this earthly city and advise me. *Scripture* reports that *Jesus* said if your brother . . . ignores you . . . "refer it to the church." So I hereby refer the matter to the members of the global *Church of Christ,* to the *People of God,* to all humanity who share the right to *God's* gift of light and *Eucharist.* Rights of *Eucharist* vest on *Jesus's* invitation alone: "Take this all of you, and eat . . . and drink." Also, I refer it to every human being, as rightful heir and beneficiary of the *New Covenant* or, in other words, of *Jesus's* last *will* and *testament.* Please accept the fact that *God* imprints in us knowledge of our *God* of love and of *God's* law of loving each other, as *Jesus* demonstrated and died to reveal. Additionally, I repeat, *God* told *St. Paul* from *heaven*, in effect, that everyone inherits the *new covenant* relationship and rights of *Eucharist* free of charge, with no conditions of faith, works, or strings attached. *Jesus Christ* orders only that we take, "take this all of you" and consume *Holy Communion* together in thanksgiving of *God's* gifts to each of us.

Pope John XXIII's intent was to modernize the *Church of Christ,* and his experts discussed and decided that we are a priestly people united in *Christ*, and at *Mass* we have universal sacrificing and are supposed to have universal *Eucharist.* As a priestly people, I suppose, we could designate one among us to preside to ask for blessing of the *Holy Spirit* over our gifts of bread and wine already consecrated by the *sacrifice of Christ* in order to share *Eucharist.* Notable is *Pope Benedict's* homily this *Holy* Thursday of 2012, the news of which I received from the *Associated Press* after I wrote up to this point. *Pope Benedict* denounced over three hundred *Austrian* priests and supporters for calling parishes to celebrate *Eucharistic* services without priests. But the *Pope* conceded their disobedience was a way to bring the *church* up to date because of the "slow pace" of the *church* to answer their concerns for the good of the *church.* The *Pope* says he hopes to open dialogue with *Austrian* bishops because the priests are expressing the opinion of the people at the base of the *church*; so threatening schism apparently got the *Pope's* attention. It made me feel good to know some in the clergy are awake to *God's* will to speak up bravely and enlighten us that it is *God,* not *church,* we worship.

Jesus said to the chief priests and the elders of his hierarchy that "the *Kingdom of God* will be taken away from you and given to all people that will produce its fruits. Since the fruit of charity is primary, I have hope, maybe wishful thinking, that the likes of *Bishop Thomas Gumbleton* would rally the bishops of the *United States* to pick up the mission of the *kingdom of the New Covenant* to more charitably fulfill its calling for the life of the *people of God* because of *Pope Benedict XVI's* "slow pace." During *Pope Benedict XVI's* reign, we are uncharitably being deluded by the *Roman Catholic Church.* The bishops each have this calling from *Jesus Christ's Last Supper* words instituting the *Eucharist*, which is being misappropriated, to serve a few. At *Vatican II*, the bishops' representatives showed the *church* that the founding principles of the *United States* were more *Christian* than the traditions of *Catholicism* upon which the *Documents of Vatican II* are miscalled the "light to the world." But *our bishop* in *Rome* is having justice delayed because delusively he is following "human caprice" and not following true obedience to *God's* will. Bishop *Gumbleton* has been sent to *Marmato, Columbia*, for its seven hundred inhabitants' care who are sitting on a deposit of ten billion dollars' worth of gold. *Bishop Gumbleton* is there to mediate a compromise and save the community while others will be extricating the gold for a *Canadian* mining interest who wants to move the town. *Gumbleton* is at risk as was the predecessor of the town's pastor who was assassinated, prompting the presence of the *bishop.* Among my hopes for the *bishop* from *Detroit* was that he would read this book and volunteer an *Imprimatur.* I contend *Imprimaturs* are an uncharitable imposition, but sheepish *Catholics,* my sister for one, obey them. I am worried that the bishop, like *David's Uriah*, sent to the front may suffer a fatality as happens to good priests down there. *Fr. Ferdinand Azevedo, S. J.,* a local native of our *Sacramento Valley* was murdered in *Brazil.* He was involved in liberal efforts for women's rights and was killed; his neck was fractured, by unknown assailants (see unanswered letter of 1/3/11, attached). *Fr. Federico Lombardi, S. J.,* at the *Pope's* front desk, did not respond either even though the inquiry was about a member of his *society.* (A society by the way founded and missioned by *Basques.*) It is enough to make a sinner like me lose heart to the ways of my brothers in *Rome,* when they will not lift a finger for a likely martyr's family, seeking the cause of death in a foreign land.

The brilliance of *God's New Covenant* is the greatest mission statement ever experienced. *God* makes it through the agency of two prophets, *Jeremiah* and *Jesus,* both of whom are killed by their countrymen but one for bearing the message. *Jesus* was a dedicated traditionalist who learned from past generations' *scripture* that he was meant by *God* to sacrifice himself in expiation for the sins of humankind. *Jesus's* followers were also traditionalists, and those deluded by *scripture* teachings feel their traditions needed to negate *God's* will and rationalized *God's Covenant* away. *God's new* deal was brilliant, allowing humans to make new laws for each evolving generation to come. One generation's laws on a succeeding generation may be an act of force, not a right, because the earth belongs to the living. Thus, *God's* idea to solely perform the *New and Eternal Covenant* unilaterally was brilliant, but its light was blinding to human beings who trusted more traditional and earthy ideas to be acceptable. The foolishness of the *Cross,* combined with trusting *God's* performance of the *New Covenant,* was brought to earth by the wisdom of men who wrote their own gospel statements. So we have the traditionalists negating the evidence of *God's* statement in the "Gospel before the Gospel" that everyone is solely saved in the *Blood of Christ.* But the global *Church of Christ* can be our *Lumen Gentium* relighted to renew us to what *God* always intends and allow all of us to proclaim that the will of *God* unilaterally saves us for everlasting love to be shared together liberally.

This book is my last book. I am convinced that I am too limited by age and abilities to persuade my *spiritual* siblings. *Pope Benedict XVI* is eighty-five, five years older than I am, and in my dotage I have lost my hopes in his ever responding to *my* message of love in *Covenant* or *Eucharist.* He did not answer my request for an *Imprimatur* or my request for help to investigate *Fr. Freddie Azevedo's* covered-up death. He plainly disdained to stoop this low, or, in his delusion decided not to respond, to an obvious sinner less holy, concededly, than he. I now offer the obligation to express these concerns. I think we are competent to write about, to my siblings in *Christ* and ask them to express their concerns and dialogue with all other human beings in the world, by all media means available. Some might succeed and cure these concerns for the good of the *Church of God.* Many have access to the amoral and secular world of online *Internet* in order to competently communicate these concerns from the knowledge *God* imprints in each of us. The knowledge, which you already know by heart, might awaken every human being to their gifts of *Eucharist* and the *New Covenant* relationship in the global *Church of God.* An incentive to you might be the thought that a proclamation of your own expressed to the whole *Church of God* will be participating as a voice of *Christ* in the mission of *Christ.* You may more effectively fulfill *Jesus Christ's* mission to alleviate the lives and faiths of all created humanity on earth than all churchmen have ever done. Each of us is favored authority by *God* to try this. Whatever good you do or good you try to make, it will last as a memory forever between you and *God* of an exercise of your free will, something you lovingly give to *God,* which *God* would not possess otherwise. It is an actual *gift to God,* free of any exchange for merit or in gratitude for the multiple *gifts God* gives to each of us. It is a jewel that you give *God,* to treasure for the eternity we are to be together, as it keeps on giving when you are unable to give freely because you will be melted into *God's* love.

God Almighty created us with free will to do good or evil and does not intervene in life but respects our autonomy to awaken to *God's law* imprinted within us as activated by others, like mothers, who show us first that *God* exists and teach us to practice the *Golden Rule* of loving. *Jesus* tried by stories to tell us of *God's* plan in our lives, particularly, about the rich and poor we always have with us. He taught us that (1) the rich will be tormented forever in ignoring the plight of *Lazarus,* (2) the rich addicted to possession risk perfection because of his greed while (3) *Zacchaeus* succeeded in doing *penance* on earth for cheating and got everlasting relief from memory of how he was enriched. *God* does not intervene in the world to avoid evils even in nature; for example, we see the love of *God* and a mother ignoring the struggles of a chick (see 3/25/11 letter attached) and read of both loves in the light of *Camp 14* where *Shin Dong-Hink* was born to die, not knowing *God* or a mother's love (see *Escape from Camp 14* by B. Harden). *Love* is mysteriously of *God's* realm to use lovingly as *God* knows best.

Saint Paul may teach an answer to what humankind might do in *penance* to avoid speculated *eternal* memories of harming the *Lazarus* in our lives: "Awake, O sleeper, and arise from the dead, and Christ will give you light," (Eph 5:8-14). "Brothers and sisters: 'You were once darkness, but now you are light in the Lord, Live as children of light, for light produces every kind of goodness and righteousness and truth. Try to learn what is pleasing to the Lord. Take no part in the fruitless work of darkness rather expose them, for it is shameful even to mention the things done by them in secret; but everything exposed by the light becomes visible, for everything that becomes visible is light.'" It won't hurt to try and follow your conscience *Paul's* way.

Jesus Christ, as *God Almighty,* gives us light to show the way we should live. Awakened, you are free to do nothing, free to continue your way of life as you choose and free to do what you feel you ought to do for others that come to light in your ever-widening view of sisters and brothers in the world. This light might reveal truths we rather not know and lead us where we cannot imagine to go. Whether or not you volunteer, *God* has made you a member of the global *Church of God* and gives you a conscience to love others whose needs you ought to perceive in your ever-widening awareness of life. No matter what you do, *Jesus Christ* has secured for you a heaven in the hereafter where all your wants will be satisfied. Trusting the pledge of *God* that your evildoings are forgiven and your sins forgotten, *God* assures you are loved fully for eternity, and you are at peace except, perhaps, for a *Lazarus* that bothers you. Can you forget the evil done especially when persisting harm was caused? Eternal life in the *real presence of God* may have us carrying this troubling guilt forever if we do nothing to satisfy it when we have free will to pay like *Zacchaeus.* We must ask *God* with our "daily bread," to furnish us the will of *God,* to correct what may be instilling guilt in our conscience, enlighten us to what we need do to accomplish the good and grace us to do it during our lifetime to be at peace, knowing *God* makes good of it all anyway.

Therefore, all of you "awaken," especially you *Pope Benedict,* and stop looking backward more so than forward, trusting *God* is with us on the course *God* has set as we forever improve to be more loving like *God* who loves us *Godlike.* My present concern is with *Pope Benedict XVI* involving *US* bishops in politics that he is neither competent nor entitled to delve into but for his delusions of grandeur. I write of his January 19, 2012, address to the *US* bishops about his concern for our intrinsically evil practices, including those of birth control and tendency to reduce religious freedom to mere freedom of worship without guarantees of respect for freedom of *Catholics* not having to finance laws that furnish means of birth control. He involved his bishops to have them persuade the millions of *Catholics* to vote against financing our *President Obama's* Health Act that our poor so badly need and the absence of which is a shame to this nation. In our country of equal freedom for all, conscientious objectors may exempt themselves from wars, but they cannot escape paying taxes that support our policing. By the same freedoms, *Catholics* can choose not to use contraceptives, but, as citizens, they must pay for others' health needs that include abortion benefits. *God* is likely content with leaving *US* citizens free to sin or not as a matter of choice of their individual freedom of conscience. *God* at the beginning furnished us the *New Covenant* relationship with *God's* guarantees of teaching us to know *God* and *God's* law of love as a standard of conduct imprinted in everyone's conscience. *God* frees us to sin or love *God*, and cannot help loving us and forgiving and forgetting our evildoing. We know *God because God* imprints this knowledge in our minds and hearts.

The Good News According to Tradionalists

Jeremiah, like *Jesus,* lived when his nation was subjected to *Gentile* rule. *Jerusalem's* temple was destroyed in both of their generations. The words of the *New Covenant* (Jer 31:31-34) were uttered about the time *Jerusalem* was previously destroyed, and the prophet was forced into *Egypt* where traditionalists had him murdered by his countrymen. *Jeremiah's* influence, however, succeeded in having "The Gospel before the Gospel" included as a sublime teaching in the *Old Testament* published about then. *Jesus,* in studies, learned of this landmark of the *Old Testament* and was moved to passionately sacrifice his life to fulfill it for *God,* his *Father.* Thereby *God* reveals all sinful humans are baptized in the *Blood of Christ* to be perfected *one* with *God* in community as human creation is meant forever to be, meant by *God* from creations beginning.

However, mankind uncharitably misinterpreted *God's* messages from their beginning, for example, commentaries of the *Old Testament* written in *Egypt* by *Jewish* survivors of the *Babylon* invasion, record *Exodus* reports *Moses,* in giving the people the *Ten Commandments*, quoted *God* saying: "I am a jealous *God,* inflicting punishment for their fathers' wickedness on the children of those who hated me, down to the third and fourth generation." *Jeremiah* and *Jesus,* however, showed us a loving *God* in prophesizing and fulfilling *God's New Covenant,* "the Gospel before the Gospel" (Jer 31:31-34). The days *God* foretold in it were fulfilled by the *Blood of the Lamb* extending *God's New Covenant* from the *Jews* to benefit all human creation as represented by *Jesus* at the *Last Supper* (Lk 22:20, Mk 14:24, and Mt 26:28) and from *heaven* (1 Cor 11:23-26). *Jesus* taught us that the *God* feared by *Moses's* people is really *our God of Love* who unilaterally saves us all. Traditionalists, like *John,* the evangelist, the *Bishop of Hippo* and his disciple *Pope Benedict XVI* overlooked the *New Covenant* to cling to human traditions. They burden us today with man-made dogma, for example, *The Gospel According to John*, *Original Sin*, and the *Catechism of the Catholic church*. A knowledgeable *Jewish Rabbi* wisely said that to love *God* and love neighbors as one loves oneself defines our *Bible,* all the rest is commentary. More than commentary, however, are the following combined *Scripture passages* of the *New Covenant* (Jer 31:31-34) and the *Last Supper* words of *Jesus* referring to the *New Covenant* in the context of the mystery of his death and resurrection (1 Cor 11:23-26, Mt 26:28, Mk 14:24, and Lk 22:20). All the rest of religious writings fall into the traditional category, in contrast to these teachings of *God,* as commentary to salvation in *Jesus Christ.*

The earliest records in the *New Testament* are letters of *Saint Paul*; also, he writes *Jesus's* words at the *Last Supper,* incorporating the *New Covenant* to benefit all humans, as voiced by the *risen Christ* from heaven. *Jesus,* soon after being glorified by *God* to be *one* with *God,* repeats the *Last Supper* words, incorporating by context the fulfillment of *God's New Covenant;* while assigning to *Paul* his mission to share the *Covenant,* the *Cross,* and, the *Eucharist* news with all *Jews* and *Gentiles,* as follows:

> "This cup is the *new covenant* in my blood. Do this whenever you drink it, in remembrance of me." (Emphasis mine.)

Those words were "interdependent" with the death and resurrection of *Jesus,* meaning without them the death was a mere execution, and the death, in turn, redeems all humanity while giving universal definition for the *Eucharist* to be shared with each and every human being without preconditions attached. By executing *God's* pledges of forgiving everyone's iniquity, defined as forgiving everyone's evildoing, all individuals are worthy to receive *Eucharist* and all are eternally saved. *Paul,* unfortunately, missed the *New Covenant* effect and added his traditional-based comments of examining consciences before *Communion* and warning that he who eats the bread or drinks the cup "unworthily" brings a judgment upon himself. The truth is *God* solely cleanses us in the

Blood of the Covenant, and no one can possibly consume the *Eucharist* "unworthily" or be denied salvation for sins absolved by God.

Traditionalists established that the earth was flat with four corners, and *Bishop Ireneaus* felt that only four gospels could make up the *Canon.* He, thus, trashed the viewpoints of the other apostles, including the feminine one of *Mary Magdalene.* The bishop made sainthood for his martyrdom, but I submit he was unauthorized to destroy our good news from these other saints. *Saint Paul,* missing a *New Covenant* effect, was corrected in the *Gospel According to Thomas* who acknowledged the divine light *Jesus* brought to the world *(Lumen Gentium)*, a light of interiorly knowing *God* and *God's* law of love, which is shared by humanity, since we are all made "in the image of *God*" and imprinted in conscience with that knowledge, pledged by *God* in the *New and Eternal Covenant.* This is the central theme used by *Christian* mysticism that *Thomas* expresses according to *Protestant Elaine Pagel* in her book *Beyond Belief.* Sadly, one of these trashed books reported the apostles' eyewitness news of observing *Jesus* kissing the *Magdalene* on the lips, and such intimacy might have given us feminine insight into *Jesus* at the time. But *Irenaeus* had his heart set on the traditional *John,* who believed *Jesus* alone brings divine light to the world and buried the *Magdalene's* views with the contrary writings.

Saint Ambrose, however, appreciated the *Covenant.* He was not *Church* baptized when he admitted receipt of *Eucharist* often because he sinned often, deferring baptism to his deathbed. As a lawyer, he ably saw the *New Covenant* as unilaterally performed by *God* alone, needing no reconciling by us or *Church* baptizing, to forgive our sins. *Jesus,* too, probably appreciated the good news of *God's Covenant,* made to the *Jews* centuries earlier because he learned his *Old Testament* well and incorporated it in his death at the *Last Supper.* Soon after meeting *John the Baptist*, he told his disciples that *John* was one of the greatest born of the *Old Testament* but that the least born into *God's New Covenant* relationship, the *New Testament* "kingdom of *God,*" was greater than *John. Jesus* traditionally read *scripture* it appears, but I would say a more charitable reading would have *God* immaculately conceiving every human created in the *blood of the Covenant* for everlasting life. Likely those who died before *Jesus* died were re-created in *Christ* so that *John* too was redeemed by the *Blood of the Lamb. Jesus* successfully shed blood for all humanity ever created. After his death, *Jesus* visits *John* and the dead in *paradise* to tell them the good news that *God,* out of goodness and love, solely created all humans and recreated them in *Christ's blood* to share eternal life with *God* as *God* always means to do.

Christian writings, however, followed tradition and entirely overlooked *God's* unilateral performance of the *New Covenant* in the death and resurrection of *Jesus.* The most erroneous report and translation of *Christology* should be credited to this cult that came out of *Ephesus.* These *Christians* wrote the *Gospel According to John* and other writings, including *Revelation* attributed to *John.* Someone quipped that *Revelation* was written by one of *John's* disciples while on "acid." No one knows who should personally be accepting author credits for the *Fourth Gospel* of the *Canon*. However, *Irenaeus, Bishop of Lyons, France,* was a student of *Policarp, Bishop of Smyrna in Asia Minor,* who claimed that *John* the *Son of Zebedee* converted him; so biased *Irenaeus* gives credit to that *John* and added his *Gospel* to the *Canon*. There are other claimants, such as *John* the most beloved disciple, and multiple writers of the cult who used the name *John.* I sensed they tried to replace *Peter* with *John,* until the change shown in their *Appendix. The Gospel According to John* traditionally became the standard *Christian* view of human salvation through the death and resurrection of *Jesus.* It promises "eternal life" to "whomever believeth in *Jesus Christ.*" *Roman Catholics* accept the truth of this traditional gospel and make its traditions law in their *Dogmatic Constitution on the Church (Lumen Gentium)* Chapter II "On the People of *God,*" No. 9. *Pope Paul VI's* hierarchy fraudulently invented their own forged version of the *new covenant* and misrepresented that *Christ* instituted—"this" *New Covenant* (Jer 31:31-34) in his *Blood* (cf. Cor 11:25) to form the new *People of*

God. These hypocrites promise salvation based on *John's Gospel*, "For those who believe in Christ who are reborn . . . from water and the Holy Spirit (cf. Jn 3:5-6) . . . are now the People of God." The *church,* as promulgated in law by *Pope Paul VI,* becomes more anti-*God* than the *Fourth Gospel's* version of blasphemy denying that *God* does it all. We are now left with this "small flock" of a "messianic people" to do what *God* already does in *Christ.* Shame on us *Roman Catholics* sheepishly replacing God's Covenant! (See copy attached to Letter of 2/7/11.)

The Gospel According to Mathew, I distrust because the ex-tax collector made up stories from the beginning, for example, on the three kings, the murder of the infants by *Herod,* and the trip to *Egypt* to report that the family came out of *Egypt* like *Moses,* which fabrications are disproved by *Mary's* history of the infant *Jesus.* However, the author makes a point at Footnote Mathew 12:31ff, the footnote in *The New American Bible* I own. Those who negate *God's* saving us, by *God* solely performing the *New Covenant,* and insist on our contribution of faith or good works, teach an evil principle. Their negations are *anti-God* and a blasphemy against *God's Spirit* because it negates the evidence of *God's* unilateral saving action in history. Obviously, the author of this footnote overlooks the fact that *God* has already forgiven the blasphemy as *God* forgives everyone's evildoings in *Jesus's* death, fulfilling *God's* pledged *covenant* for salvation. I do not know what authority, if any, to give to the footnote. We have clearer and more convincing evidence for charging the author *John* for completely negating the *Last Supper's* key words, by failing to mention the words of *God*, indicating that *Jesus's* death was in context of fulfilling the *New Covenant* and in the rest of *John's* good news negating that *Jesus* expressly refers to the *Covenant's* guarantee for our salvation (Lk 22:26 and Jer 31:31ff.). In incorporating the *Covenant* by reference, the words are "interdependent" in giving meaning to *Jesus's* death, and the death, in turn, giving universal meaning to the words instituting the *Eucharist.* Words and death are mutual acts of universal application. Thus, "take this all of you" are sounded throughout *Christ's* sacrifice. Not reporting the most important event in human history and the evidence of *God's* sole participation in salvation should qualify *John's Gospel* for the *Pope's Index of Forbidden Books*. Our *Dogmatic Constitution* makes my *Roman Catholic Church Antichrist* and *anti-God* in consort with those who publish and proclaim the blasphemy of the *Fourth Gospel.* Plainly speaking, my *Pope Benedict XVI* and his *Vatican* are *Antichrist, anti-God,* in condoning the law, and at best, delusively so as *Albert Einstein* would say, for negating *God's New Covenant* message.

Jesus, lamented the betrayal of *Judas* at the *Last Supper,* and said "It was better for him that he was never born." By implying *Judas* should have been aborted, *Jesus* is overlooking *God's* words of the *New Covenant*, which soon pardons *Judas'* sin in the *blood of the Covenant. Judas* becomes *one* with *Jesus Christ* after their deaths. Our *God of Love* foresees *Judas'* evildoing from the beginning of creation, creates *Judas* in love, and is in love with him forever. It is *Jesus* thinking, man-wise quoted above, but *God* solved the problem, by forgiving *Judas* as *God* does all human creatures in the sacrifice of the *Cross,* from their beginning in *God's* mind.

Traditions have always been a part of human nature because we want mothers or someone else to do the thinking for us. *Jews, Christians*, and people of the *Book*, from the beginning, were stuck on following customs, such as circumcision and baptisms, to assist in pacifying a fearful *God.* Every human creature is baptized into the paschal mystery of *Christ's* death and resurrection, whether they are aware of it or not, for the fulfillment of *God's new Covenant* love relationship. We are baptized in *Christ's* blood thoroughly, and all *church* baptism does is symbolize it, if that. *Christ* also consecrates the *Eucharist* on the *cross*. The sacrifice of the *Cross* is continuously made present at every *Mass*, to make congregations remember *Christ's* loving deed to urge them to give love, thanks, and to praise *our Lord.* The action of two or more human beings meeting in memory of the sacrifice of the *Cross* may make *God,* in *Jesus Christ*, consecrated in the paschal mystery of *Christ's* death actually present on the *Cross* in their *Holy Communion.* However, we humans have traditionally looked to priests to celebrate sacrifices and ignored *our Lord's* priestly actions. *Vatican II* suggested an expansion of the priestly people to include us all, but ordained priests were traditionally retained for our services because it is the way we always did it in the *church*. The *spirit* of *Vatican II* is still with many of *God's* created people, but its spiritual light on humanity has been dimmed by the *church.* The *Catholic church* is trying to stay traditional, but the *spirit* refuses to cooperate, and *God* remains teaching. The *Second Vatican Council* spoke publicly to learned people in world affairs. They listened and will not forget since the *Spirit* remains. Traditionalists, however, feel the formulas of past ages should be binding, and *church* authority should enforce them. An example is the new *English* translation of the *Roman Missal*, so awkward in parts because it is not of *God,* or of us but of one pope's whim. The *Pope's* words "incarnate" or "consubstantial" are rebutting his colleagues' *Christology* arguments. *Hans Küng* questioned *Jesus* preexisting to become incarnate, as did *Karl Rahner*, but the *Pope's* ego gets the last word in argument. He discards the *council's* formula for truth discovery, the pope in dialogue with the college of bishops, and rules by his own caprice. Bishops must answer to *Jesus Christ,* for silently condoning this and surrendering their own independent thinking. They each also owe *God* and their people their own proclaiming of the *New Covenant.* Theologian *Joseph Ratzinger* wrote in 1964: "For many people today the church has become the main obstacle to belief. They can no longer see in it anything but the human struggle for power, the petty spectacle of those who with their claim to administer official Christianity, seem to stand most in the way of the true spirit of Christianity." (see *NCR* 3/16-19/12, page 12.) We hear, thus, my thoughts on the human contribution from a healthy *Ratzinger* before his breakdown or reversal of convictions.

Later writings than *Paul's Epistles*, such as the *Gospel According to John* and *The Didache,* are surviving *Christian* literature that compound our human errors and are kept alive by *traditionalists*, such as *Pope Benedict* cites them. Both *John's* and *The Didache's* writings negated the point of *God's* saving action in the *New Covenant's* performance benefitting all human creation. They reject evidence of the *New Covenant* pledges of *God,* which were so dearly executed by the passion and death of *Jesus* on the *Cross,* to project their own opinions and interests. In fact, by negating the evidence of the *New Covenant,* in failing to completely and accurately report the words of *Jesus,* maybe words he was instructed by *God* to say (see Jn 12:49, 50), the author(s) of the *Fourth Gospel*, its publishers, and those supporting it are all in willful denial of *God's* plan for creation. They are attributing salvation to be dependent on human actions and not solely the accomplishment of *God*, out of *God's* love and goodness as *God* repeatedly reveals. *God* revealed dearly the good news of the *New and Eternal Covenant*, in the passion and death of *Jesus,* and repeated it daily so it cannot be ignored. My ignorance was because my *Roman Catholic Church's* hierarchy kept me ignorant of what was being announced in *Eucharistic Prayers*; to wit, *God's New and Eternal Covenant* constantly redeems us. *God* and *God's* law of love are known by heart, subjectively from natural life, and **God** added *Scripture* and *Jesus's* performance to reveal: "For I will forgive their evildoing and remember their sin no more" (Jer 31:31-34). *Jesus Christ* fulfills the performance of *God's* pledges universally by bleeding to death on the *cross,* in remembering *God's* motherly love for all *Jews* and *Gentiles* and, at *Christ's* memorial suppers, making *God* present, actually, for everyone's nourishment. We all are ordered by *Jesus* "to take" and consume the consecrated bread and wine of the *Eucharist.* You *Jews,* you *Moslems,* and all you people created by *God* should take *Eucharist*, consume it, and let *God* communicate with you as *God* wishes from your gut, mind, and heart. *Anti-God* and *Antichrist* are those who cling to their traditions and refuse to acknowledge the truth that *God* alone constantly renews in every natural human being their *baptism in the Blood* of *Christ.*

All should accept that *God* competently cleansed everyone to be "worthy" to receive the *Eucharist,* and everyone should know each individual is *God's* love creature forever saved with the *People of God*. Our *God* of love has done enough, even if we deny what

God does or are made ignorant of love and *God* as was *Shin* until his teens because we are all saved by *God*. Critical thinking *Einstein* says *God* does not play tricks, and it is proved in his quantum studies. The mystery or the foolishness of the *Cross* remains a problem to skeptical people, and they persist in trying to improve on *Christ's* assumed ineptness to save them. Thus, they do human acts of faith and good works, in distrust of *God's* word, and fearfully grasp for human ways of salvation. That is not to say that faith in *Jesus Christ* and acts of loving one's neighbor are not what *Christ* instructed *Christians* to do; but they have no significance in our salvation as *God,* in *Christ's* sacrifice, completely accomplished everyone's salvation. *Christians* in this sense mean everyone created by *God,* and all are members of the *Body of Christ. Luther's* "faith alone" also misunderstood *God's New Covenant* salvation but like *Pelagius* was closer to the truth than the *Catholic church's* "faith and works." Besides, any human contribution that *God* needs is supplied by *Christ* for us. *God* will lift our veils of ignorance; but we must await death, to see. Until then we trust *God's* words, to likely be at peace while alive in knowing *God* is love and secures our salvation.

Jesus, as man, obviously wanted us to be perfect for his *Father* and to present us as such to *God Almighty* on our *Judgment* day, but we will always be what *God* wants us to be. Perfection is for *God,* and Risen *Jesus*, alone to possess and give. *Jews* may continue wearing their phylacteries, *Moslems* their praying toward *Mecca*, and *Catholic* clergy practice celibacy if they wish, but such are not needed. *God* seems content to let us live and love and maybe appreciates these efforts toward perfecting ourselves, whether or not deludedly we try to gain salvation by them. *God* needs nothing, possesses everything, but appreciates our self-disciplinary efforts, if out of love, to please *God.* Our spontaneous deeds of love, not to gain merit or show gratitude to *God,* are things *God* foresees from the beginning and may have been persuasive in *God's* troubling with creating us in the first place. *God* alone knows why we are created in *Christ's* blood and now to be everlasting like *God* with *God. God's* love makes us like *God,* and *God's* love in us makes us more *God* like. Mystics visualize us as becoming a melted cauldron of iron in the fire of *God's* love forever.

A symptom of our *Pope's* problem is seen in *Cardinal Joseph Ratzinger's* claim that *The Didache* is equal authority to *scripture* in his argument against the post-*Vatican II New Testament* scholars' criticism of the *church's* exclusive *Eucharist.* The *church's* exclusive *Eucharist* and the *New Testament* scholars clashed at *Vatican II*. Their contention is that *Christ* meant for an open *Eucharist,* wherein no one was barred from sharing because of denomination or unworthiness. They were opposed by *Cardinal Ratzinger* in 1988, not the *Ratzinger* of 1964 *Vatican II*, but he who uncharitably argued that the traditional

Fourth Gospel and *The Didache* could rebut the scholars. (See *God is Near Us*, pp. 59-60, by *Cardinal* Ratzinger.) *Cardinal Ratzinger* who wrote against an open *Eucharist* in his *Catechism on The Church* (1994) cites as authority *The Didache* on the *Eucharist,* which also states: "give not that which is holy to the dogs." A more enlightened *Jesus* ordered, "*all* to take and drink" of the cup when he took the cup and said, "take this and divide it among you" and repeated the order from *Heaven* as *God* when *Jesus* exists *one* with *God* and launches *Saint Paul* on mission.

When *Pope Benedict XVI* attained the *Papacy*, by an unprecedented campaigning and votes of cardinals he appointed, instead of ruling in rebuttal to the *New Testament* scholars contentions, he released his hypocritically entitled letter "Sacrament of Love" (*Sacramentum Caritatis*) in 2007. It misrepresents that "Final judgment on these matters belong to the diocesan bishops," which assertion proved in execution untrue. Instead of passing-the-buck as the letter represents, it was a work of artful deceit. The *Bishops in Synod* received a secret document from the *Vatican* that directed them not to allow non-*Catholics* reception of the *Eucharist*. Here in my *Sacramento Diocese,* our servile *Bishop Wiegand* had already posted a statute, conforming exactly to the *pre-Council* tradition of excluding *non-Catholics* and others from our *Eucharist*, the summer before *Sacramentum Caritatis* was released. *Jesus Christ* forewarned us, and *Isaiah* prophesied accurately that our hierarchies would cling to human traditions and precepts to violate *God's* commandment of loving your neighbor. *Jesus*, himself, charged "hypocrites" would make "a fine art of setting aside *God's* commandment in the interest of keeping your traditions!" (Mk 7:6-10). Cowed bishops, thus, obediently squeezed out these uncharitable laws and exclusive communions. I doubt if any diocesan bishop dare do otherwise and lose his job. But the *Pope's* letter literally authorizes courageous bishops to obey *Jesus,* ignoring the *Vatican's* artful hypocrisy, and adjudge that the *Eucharist* is open to all humanity in their diocese. Our bishops ought to love us and *God* more than their security or ambitions and make the effort to obey *God's* will as true *Christians* are called to do. I doubt if many bishops exist whose allegiance is more to *Christ* than to *Rome* and will pick up the gauntlet dropped for them here.

The *Second Vatican Council* was called by *Pope John XXIII* to bring *Christianity* up to date with the modern world. He invited worldwide bishops and competent experts in *Christology* to enlighten the world (*Lumen Gentium*). In attendance were leading theologians, including *Joseph Ratzinger,* who wrote a book during the session enthusiastically praising the *Church's* openness. *Bishops* from the *United States* presented the basic principles of our *Democratic Republic* that taught many at council our far more charitable principles, more in conformity with what

Christ had in mind, of incontestable *God*-given rights than many in attendance had ever heard. As a contributing result, the *Council* submitted the ideal *Church of Christ*, considered to extend throughout the world, awaiting to be defined and brought to fullness by experiencing *God's* law of charity, to share it with all humanity. As a result, a fruit of this openness was to be the release of the long misappropriated *Eucharist* that *God* gave, with no strings attached, free to everybody. To be manifested was the *New and Eternal Covenant* making everyone in the world "worthy" to receive the *Real Presence* in *Holy Communion*, but *Pope John XXXIII* died, and these principles were soon betrayed by *Pope John's* successors and the free reigning *Curia* of the *Roman Church*. However, Chapter 8 of the *Dogmatic Constitution of the Church* (Lumen Gentium) submits the global *Church of Christ* to be of record, although now awaiting future definition by generations to come, as follows;

> "This *Church* constituted and organized in the world as a society, subsists in the *Catholic Church*, which is governed by the successor of Peter and by the bishops in communion with him, although many elements of sanctification and of truth are found outside of its visible structure. These elements, as gifts belonging to the *Church of Christ*, are forces impelling toward catholic unity." (Emphasis mine.)

"The Catholic church, which is governed by the successor of Peter and by the bishops in communion with him" has again overruled the direction of *Jesus Christ* that they are not to rule but to serve (see Lk 22:25*f*). I was appalled to read that our *US Bishops* are raising a cry for "religious freedom" to prevent financing President *Obama's* badly needed health insurance coverage law because it provides contraception benefits for employees. The bishops hypocritically couched their attack as a battle for "religious freedom" to foist *Humanae Vitae* on our citizenry, while knowing that the vast majority of *Roman Catholics* practically rejected *Pope Paul VI's* traditional dogma. The citizens of the *United States* are now harmed by these bishops crusading for the *Papacy. The bishops* rallying cry to *Roman Catholics* whose rights to freedom of conscience or religion to use contraception if they choose is being violated in the guise of obedience to *church* teachings. My hopes for the bishops to represent us in forming the *Church of Christ* have been shattered because they obey *Rome* and rule not serve the *people of God* in their purported working for *Christ.*

At *Tübingen, Professors Joseph Ratzinger* and *Hans Küng* agreed that *Jesus* did not intend to found a particular *church*. After *Vatican II*, *Ratzinger* taught in 1968/69 that the *Eucharist* and the *church* to serve it were instituted among the words of the *Last Supper.* The *Eucharist* gained meanings from the *New Covenant* words which benefited *God's* "people," words which were "interdependent" with *Jesus's Cross. God,* in *covenant*, pledges to teach us all we need know and forgives us our evildoing. Plainly speaking, *churches* are not "needed" to teach or rule but to serve, and clergymen, especially the *Curia*, are paranoid by this translation. I see only the consecration of the *Eucharist* to be concerned about; but even that may be by *God* and a *Priestly People,* for all I know. *Jesus* said, amongst the two or more meeting in his name, he will be present. *Jesus*, now being the *Real Presence of God*, with any two priestly people who meet, presided over by *Jesus Christ,* can have the two do what *Jesus* said to do simply "take" of the *Real Presence*. Ordained priests or a *church* to serve may impliedly not be needed, to "consecrate" Jesus' body and blood. Needless reconciling of recipients by priests, also, are dismissed "for" we are forgiven according to *scripture* passages (Jer 31:31-34, Mk 14:24, Mt 26:26, Lk 22:26, and 1 Cor 11:23-26). *Jesus* makes the words of *God* significant, and all other teachings are commentary on the cited words of *God*. Today, we may not look to our *Roman Catholic* spiritual leaders to govern us as *Lumen Gentium* says, unless they lead us by service lovingly and by obeying *Christ*. We, the laity in the *Catholic church*, must grow up and use our own *God*-given abilities to charitably translate the new relationship we have as beneficiaries of *God's New and Eternal Covenant.* We must acknowledge the original *Gospel of God,* "The Gospel before the

Gospel," and proclaim it to every human being. We are the common priesthood of *God* and should use the ministerial servants of our churches or societies to serve us in *God's* calling. This, I feel, is the choked off message *of Vatican II*, to exchange the monarchy in *Rome* and make it a world servant like *Christ* or build our own society or *Church of Christ* and invite all humanity to serve with us as *God* means, from the beginning of creation, with *our Lord Jesus Christ* only to guide and rule us.

Joseph Ratzinger's mentor is *Saint Augustine*. He wrote his doctoral dissertation on the *Bishop of Hippo's* confrontation with *Donatism* in *North Africa* and agreed with *Augustine* that the *Donatists* were not true *church* because they excluded others from their *sacraments*. The exclusion proved their lack of the fundamental virtue of *Christianity*—charity. *God's* law of loving others equally, in equity, is the defining characteristic of the *church of Christ* and is *God's* law imprinted in every human heart, a truism, better heard from the United States' founding fathers. *Professor Ratzinger* taught at *Tübingen* in 1968/69, and a seminary student taught by *Ratzinger* became Professor of Theology *Ronald Modras at St. Louis University. Modras* wrote, with transcripts of *Ratzinger's* lectures to aid him, an article on what *Ratzinger* had taught. He reported that *Ratzinger* taught that *Jesus* linked the *new covenant* (Jer 31:31) with the "for many" (Mk 14:24) words of the *Last Supper,* and, the "for many" words meant all people were beneficiaries of Christ. The *Last Supper* words prevent any *Christian Church* from becoming a select community of the righteous and condemning the rest of humanity to perdition (*Commonweal* 4/21/06). At *Tübingen, Ratzinger* still apparently supported *Dominican* theologian *Yves Congar* who felt "Vatican II acknowledges, in sum, that non-*Catholic Christians* are members of the mystical body." *Ratzinger* had published a book enthusiastically in support of this new openness; but, *Ratzinger* in 1969 exchanged his enthusiasm and faith convictions to seek fame or to cling to traditional compulsions, which may have possessed self-righteous churchmen inability to see that all humans are *Christians* in the *Blood of the Covenant.*

Pope Benedict XVI recently met with his colleague from *Tübingen, Hans Küng. Küng* personally witnessed the *Pope* to say, "I have to keep the tradition" of the *Church. Professor Küng* witnessed the *Pope's* compulsive behavior from, his bizarre change of convictions after 1968/69 at, *Tübingen.* Circumstances may have triggered some psychological breakdown, rather than the willful seeking of ambition or the deluded following of "human caprice," by *Ratzinger.* As *Professor Joseph Ratzinger, Küng* describes him as a humble liberal, until he claimed to be traumatized by rebellious students in the chaos of the 1960s and changed markedly. The later 1960s had theologians and students freely arguing about *Vatican II* changes. *Ratzinger* did not win many arguments, I suspect, with *Hans Küng* and the other more competent theologians. *Ratzinger* abruptly packed up and moved camp, disturbed, when the students also disagreed with him. He attached himself to the rising star *Karol Wojtyla*, later *Pope John Paul II*, and rode up into *church* heights with him. They worked together to counter the openness and charitable principles of the *Council of Pope John XXIII.* However, these *Council* ideals were released to public awareness and remain as popular residuals of *Vatican II. Pope Paul VI* and his *Curia* had in 1964 promulgated the *Dogmatic Constitution*, which tried to negate the *new covenant* brilliant principles, betrayed the spirit of *Pope John's* council, and substituted their own caprice, seemingly in *Antichrist* response to the heady openness of the global *Church of Christ*, to bury us in past traditions and obliterating *Vatican II* with the New Covenant into oblivion.

Our *US Constitution* was formed also to strengthen those in power from, in part, the *Whiskey Rebels* who did not want to be taxed and against the idea of freedom for each age to make their own laws. The *Dogmatic Constitution* primarily was meant to preserve our "holy" clergies' status quo. The *Papacy* and *Curia* betrayed the open ideals of the earlier members of the *Council* and even used a forgery of the *New and Eternal Covenant* (Jer 31:31-34). They added the fraudulent claim that *Christ* instituted "this" forged *covenant* in his *Blood*, making "those who believe in Christ," and who are baptized "from water and the Holy Spirit (Jn 3:5-6)," the only *people of God.* I realize that I may be repeating myself; but it bears repeating that these churchmen we trust to make our laws negate *God's* plan and deceive us. The *Curia* scribes wrote that the few saved are established by *Christ* as the hope for salvation of the whole human race. The provisions of this document plainly negate the *Covenant* principle that *God* solely saves all of us. The *Roman Church* is thus, to use this "small flock," in lieu of *God's Covenant in Christ* for the redemption of all humanity, negating *God's* salvation principle. At *Tübingen, Ratzinger* lectured that the words of *Last Supper*: "This is my blood, the blood of the covenant to be poured on behalf of many" . . . prevents the *Church* from becoming simply a select community of the righteous, a community that condemns "all others to perdition." Yet that is exactly what blasphemy the *Curia* scribes have drafted, and the *Dogmatic Constitution* promulgated by *Pope Paul VI* states law.

To secure their role and comforts in the *Roman Church's Vatican*, the *Curia* deviously forged away *God's* pledge and *Jesus's* testaments. They only bring judgment upon themselves since *God* brings good out of all of our evildoings. Those whom *Saint Francis Xavier, S. J.*, described as "brutes," feel now entrenched again in the comforts of the *Vatican* to enjoy life until another *Pope John XXIII* threatens. I read that *Pope Benedict* intimidates the *Curia* with his smarts and captains these pirates who tried to appropriate our *church* for their "small flock," and I question his ability to correct them. *Pope Benedict* unchecked, I think is delusively leading the *church* far astray, within his megalomania—or egomania-like compulsions, focused on the past. A point, in proof, I return to is his using the word "chalice" in the *mass* liturgy, even though our vernacular "cup" was consistent with *Jesus's* use of the word "cup" and *Jesus Christ*, as *God*, from heaven called it a "cup" (1 Cor 11:25). But corrupted by illusions of infallibility, and the *Curia's* bias belief in the *Pope's* perfection, our pope dictates to use "chalice" and no one dare use the word *God* uses. *Ambrose* used "*Calix*" in his *Latin mass,* and *Ambrose* was the teacher of *Augustine* whom *Pope Benedict* admires as much as using *Latin*. In our parish, we have an *Augustinian* parish priest, *Father Arlon Vergara, OSA.* On our first meeting, I accosted him with his being our first *Basque* priest. I told him *Nick Osa* was my close *Basque* friend, and here we finally had an *Osa* as our minister. *Father Arlon* interrupted me: "No, *Fred*, it is *O-S-A* of the *Order of Saint Augustine.*" Father is not going to be happy, now, with what I am about to write, but it should be said to reveal a basis and bias of our pope's delusions.

Constantine the emperor of the *Roman Empire* became a *Christian* (d. 337) likely for political circumstances. He ruled to make the religion dominant and unite his people for easier control and peace. United under his rule, the spiritual and practical were balanced in a militant church discipline that spread *Christianity* globally under its human rule. *Moslems, Catholics, Mormons,* and so on, followed the same discipline, and *L. Ron Hubbard* submits it as the pattern to follow to form a church. But *Jesus* cautioned we are not to rule as the *Gentiles* but to love each other as equal human servants. *Augustine* the *Bishop of Hippo*, in 395, was converted and taught by *Saint Ambrose*; but, in his learning, he was misinformed by a translation of *St. Paul's* letter to the *Romans*, which left him believing we inherited *Adam's* sin. So when the *Bishop of Hippo* argued with the *Irish* monk *Pelagius* about the innocence of man, *Augustine* insisted that mankind was guilty in inheriting original sin of *Adam,* and only *church* baptisms in water (Jn 3:5-6) could save men from *hell* (women were not mentioned as *Augustine* did not believe they were created in the image of *God*). Poor *Pelagius* who was likely of the *Church of Christ*, which then questionably subsisted in the *Roman Catholic Church*, was probably treated as a lesser *Catholic*. *Augustine* rallied the nearby bishops, who were in *Council in Carthage,* to excommunicate *Pelagius* for his "heresy" and run him out of town. *Pelagius* fled to the east where he was conveniently murdered. Meanwhile, *Augustine,* who was big on *Plato's* writings helped add to the militant *church* of *Emperor Constantine* further order and discipline with elites to govern the *church*. The *Greek* philosopher, *Plato,* influenced *Augustine* to reject democracy for the *church*. Since democratic jurors condemned *Socrates* to death, *Augustine* distrusted placing judgments in less than the elite of the *church*. So we have the presumably more holy and competent *Curia* with *Popes, Cardinals,* and *Bishops* to rule us as *Gentiles* ruled. *Jesus* said not to rule thus but to serve each other, in his parting words to his followers. *Creeds* that *Constantine* used to discipline his army were added to control the laity, and *Augustine's* student *Pope Benedict XVI* is having wonderful times adding his caprice to *Creed* changes in our *Missal*. *Hans Küng* and *Karl Rahner* who bested *Ratzinger* previously now hear *Pope Benedict* empowered by his *Papacy* getting the final word using "human caprice" to make dogma of human precepts.

The *new covenant* relationship, or in other words, the *Kingdom of God*, that *Jesus* left us that first *Easter* weekend, should have had everyone nearer peace today; but the spirit of *Pope John XXIII's* openness may revive *God's* idea. The global *Church of Christ* may in the future succeed to reveal that we all are saved for everlasting life, based on grass roots opinions added to the natural knowledge *God* imprints in us. *Muhammad's* call, like *Paul's* apparition on the road to *Damascus*, testifies to the universal character of religious experience that we have had with *God* and *God's new covenant* relationship recreating humanity. But the *Roman Catholic Church* shut its doors to many *people of God* having communion, including *Muhammad*, and he justifiably felt rejected by *Jews* and *Christians*. He respected the prophet *Jesus*, whom *Moses* prophesized about, and *Jesus* who *Muhammad* believed was the son of the virgin. *Muhammad* felt called to form his own worship of our mutual *God of Abraham*. *Muhammad* acknowledged *Jesus* and on faith could assimilate *God's* sacrifice of *Jesus* with *Abraham's* sacrifice at *Moriah*, to share in the sacrifice at *Eucharist.* Within generations of the *Bishop of Hippo's* reign, *Augustine's* diocese was overcome by the *Muhammad's Arabs,* and to this day, the militant *church* of *Islam* rules the diocese area as children of *God* but may be open to membership invitation by *God* in the global *Church of Christ,* as equal members to serve with *Judaism* and *Christian* people, by right of heirship in the *People of God*.

So, too, because of a difference of opinion as to the wordings of *Creeds* that *Constantine* insisted upon, a split occurred between the *west* and the *east* in *Christendom*, which likely would not have occurred with the *New Covenant* provision against further teaching than *God's*. Ignoring the words of the *New Covenant* in the death and resurrection of *Jesus,* and clinging to the traditions like the *Gospel According to John*, both *churches* continue to err on *Christianity* and *Christology. God* is defined by tradition into a *Trinity of Divine Persons—Father, Son, and Holy* Spirit, and the third linkage to the second, all figments of tradition, is dividing us; although I suspect the power struggle that exists is more due to crusaders harming *Constantinople*. So what really separate us

Catholics are the traditional delusions *Einstein* speaks of unlovingly dividing our spiritual leaders who are incapable of overcoming delusions by acts of *Christian* charity. The *Church of Christ* is left open to include all *Gentiles* and *Jews* if they choose to be in *God's New Covenant* relationship of *Jesus Christ*, where we can dialogue within *God's New Covenant* relationship and settle the human differences to be *one. Jews* and *Moslems* believe *Jesus* at best is a prophet and born of a virgin according to *Islam*, to discuss his agency with *God* qualifications. *Jesus's* saying "I Am" may disturb some; but *Jesus* speaking to reporters of being *God,* in life, has questionable meaning or opinion for the reporters. Besides, thinking of *Jesus* as knowing he is *God* on the *Cross* dehumanizes and diminishes the glory of *Jesus* of *Nazareth* trying to love me not as *God* loves everyone impartially without trying. *God,* being *God,* is fully in *Jesus* as *God* whenever *God* wishes. *Jesus's* real awareness is not until *God* received *Jesus's* commended spirit, and that to me is the most charitable interpretation of *scripture,* introducing his glorification. But, better yet, it is what the *Jews* and all *Gentiles* can rationally in our common knowledge believe. Should Jesus's awareness be needed, which I doubt need be, it helps bring us together in one *Church of Christ* on *Earth* to talk out the differences. Parenthetically, a classmate of mine explained to me why he left his *Mormon Church (The Church of Christ of the Latter Day Saints).* He said it was because they did not believe in the *Trinity.* Assuming *Mormon's* so believe this *American*-born *church* can accept *Christ's church* of the *New and Eternal Covenant* and share in its open *Eucharist* (avoid the drinking of the wine as our children do) while differently believing in the *Mystery of God.* Accepting the mystery of the *Eucharist* as everyone's *Holy Communion* should be acceptable to everyone on *God's* invitation because it is a free bit of bread and free wine, regardless of what others make of it. We can all unite in the global *Church of Christ* and respect each other's faith convictions, as equals under one *Shepherd*, if we but open our hearts and minds to *God's* saving action in *Jesus Christ.*

The loving *God* that is obvious to me in *God's New Covenant* relationship would not care if I was ignorant or agnostic about *Jesus's* status as prophet, *Christ*, or *God* on earth, so long as I am aware how *God* in *Jesus* reveals that *God* is *love.* We all should be able to concede *Jesus* was the agent *God* used during *Jesus's* lifetime to give us the good news of the "Gospel before the Gospel." I actually think of *Jesus* as an ordinary guy who did marvelous things for us at the expense of his suffering and death to obey *God*. Those who view *Jesus* as *God* during his agony diminish the grandness of what *Jesus* did; to *God,* it would be an effortless "cakewalk." But *Jesus,* thus, made lovable, acted out of human love for even strangers, *God* like. The *Eucharist*, as the celebration of the sacrifice of *Jesus* made present, is the best way to praise *God* and thank *God* for creation, the glory of *God's* salvation, and to experience the love of *God* and *Jesus,* in order to reciprocate love. *Jesus* as an ordinary guy, emptied of divinity say, is performing the phenomenal act of love while we are present at *mass,* at the foot of the *Cross,* to love him for dying so for us. *Jesus* is here at *Eucharist* on the *cross,* as though time and space are arrested by *God.* He is like *God* and I, made in *God's* image, and not the superman *Acquinas* conjectured. *God* experiences us in *Jesus Christ* crucified to show *God's* love for us from the spikes supporting *Jesus. God* hopes that we too will love *God* for loving us so, in *Jesus's* humanly imperfect efforts to love each and all of us. *God* loves us all perfectly because we are *God's* creation, just as *Mama* effortlessly loved me. We fortunately know that *God* loves us also, in *Jesus* strenuously trying to love *God*, and all of us sinners whom *Jesus* was trying to love and redeem. That's why *God* made *Jesus* so ordinary, in order for *God* to experience excruciating pain, shame, and helplessness and hopefully to show us we should return love, like that of *Jesus,* to *God.* The *God* I was taught about in the *Bible* could threaten to have us love *God* or else face everlasting torment in *hell* while *God* watched. *Aristotle's Pure Act* or traditionalists' *Jealous God* could be that *God* and not a *God* of love. But *God* is not in any way other than our *God* of love and, in the *New and Eternal Covenant,* the *God* whom *Jesus* so demonstrably died to reveal, and we experience *God* solely saving us out of the goodness of *God's* love. When we die, each and every one of us will be compelled to love *God* because we will not be able to do otherwise as *God* is too lovable. We become *one* like *God* in community of the *Godhead.* Consequently, while we are now free to love or not to love *God,* it means more to come to meet *God* in *Eucharist* and do something to freely love *God* by choice. *God* may not want your celibacy or worship sacrifices outside of the *Eucharist* celebrations and in *community* loving others. Listen to the *Spirit of Jesus Christ* and hear *God's* invitation to come to *God*, and if you don't hear, come anyway to experience *God* in *Eucharist*, thanksgiving, on earth before you are absorbed forever in *God's* love.

Back to our crisis of *Pope Benedict XVI's* delusions which are due to his clinging to what is human tradition as seen in his duties of *Grand Inquisitor. Cardinal Ratzinger* in 1984 was wearing the mantle of *Pope John Paul II* in his last years and was reputed to be an enforcer and, commonly, the pope's *Rottweiler.* However, he surprisingly selected biblical scholars representing silenced "liberation theology," *Teilhardists* and colleagues to a *Pontifical Biblical Commission* in 1984. He had silenced *Leonardo Boff* of the liberation theologist movement in *Brazil*, purportedly for the movement's appearance to be like *Marxist* communists, and they risked worship to do good works, which struck the biases of both the *Polish Pope* and the *German Ratzinger.* Theologians from *Vatican II* as well as the 1984 *Pontifical Biblical*

Commission, however, gave "liberation theology" legitimacy in answering a call to discuss how *Christ* is related to our atonement. The movement's social structuring against oppression and for liberation of the poor is in keeping with modern *Christology,* certainly a main concern of *Christ,* in the world today. *Jesus* came to herald the "Kingdom of *God*" by means of the *New Covenant*, and he wants us loving others, especially the poor. *Christ* is *God's* solution on earth to share the struggles of the world, for greater freedom and justice by *the People of God.* The risk involved in "Liberation Theology," that the movement may sacrifice worship for works, is a concern of the *Church* but not of *God. God* does not want our sacrifices at the expense of our works of loving others. *Jesus* prophesied our hierarchies would disregard *God's* commandment of loving neighbors, deem them unworthy to attend the *Lord's Supper* and instead cling to human tradition keeping the *church* as it is. After 1984, the *Vatican* relapsed into its traditional stance without apparent challenge from the *Pontifical Biblical Commission.*

In an article "Reading Ratzinger" (1984), *Anthony Grafton* suggested, while professionally reporting, that *Cardinal Ratzinger* could wield proofs of texts in his malleable and powerful hands as an ideologically partisan jurist to preserve his austere purity of beliefs. He gave us an example of translating the *Vatican II* text *Ratzinger* read in different ways from 1964 to 1984, to justify his silencing of *Leonardo Boff.* The text resulted in the explanation that the true *church* "subsists" in the

Catholic church, which is governed by the successor of *Peter* and by the bishops in communion with him. "Nevertheless many elements of sanctification and of truth are found outside its visible confines." *Boff* argued his "Liberation Theology" movement fit among the "elements" mentioned. *Ratzinger* argued, socratically in rebuttal, that one must bear in mind a theologically weighty noun—*substantia*—closely related to *subsistit,* the verb that he claimed the fathers had used. *Substantia,* meaning *"*substance,*"* refers to the essence of a thing (as in "transubstantiation"). According to *Ratzinger* when the *Council* fathers used the verb "subsist" it stated in the strongest terms that the true *church* "both is and can only be *fully* present" in the *Roman Church*, with all its hierarchies. *Grafton* was not "snowed" by *Ratzinger's* verbiage or his play with *Latin* words and *Thomistic* metaphysics; so he simply rechecked the historical contents of the text and found it all to be a *Ratzinger* misrepresentation (see reporter *Anthony Grafton's* eyewitness statement in *The New Yorker* 7/25/05). *Commission* secretary, *Msgr. Gerald Philip,* told *Hans Küng* that "subsist in" replaced "is" because "we want to keep the matter open" thus also discrediting *Ratzinger's* claim. Still *Leonardo Boff's* movement of "Liberation Theology" was silenced in *Brazil*. The enlightening part of this is that the global *Church of Christ* is "open" to further defining and awakening to *God's New Covenant* relationship. Its *Communion* calls all human beings created to evolve to be *one* with *God* on earth. The light of this portion of *Lumen Gentium* is with us, while all humanity is perfecting itself toward *God* individually and as a civilization in a natural way *God* designs.

Our *Pope's* delusion also appeared when *Australian Bishop William Morris* was demoted for asking for ordination of women priests to help his diocese's desperate need for priests. *Pope Benedict* misrepresented, in his letter denying the request or demoting the bishop that a prior letter of *Pope John Paul II* stated "infallibly" that the *Pope* was unable to ordain women to the priesthood. A mere comparison of the letters, both of which were likely drafted by *Ratzinger,* shows that in *Pope John Paul's* signed letter, the writer took pains to indicate that it was written expressly, to state that "this judgment is to be definitively held by all of the *church's* faithful" a phase used to avoid it being "infallibly" characterized as Benedict claimed in the austere purity of his ideological partisanship. I take *Pope Benedict's* bizarre conduct not to be deliberate but a symptom of his delusion and attribute it to the austere purity of his bigotry. It is *Jesus* who consecrates and makes present *God* in *Eucharist* for women too to serve us *Holy Communion.*

When *Pope Benedict* was *Cardinal Ratzinger* and at the *Congregation for the Doctrine of the Faith,* he wrote a letter and enjoined the episcopate to secrecy in handling the clergies' child abuse claims in 2001. His *church* was being attacked and, in his delusion, he did evil to protect the *Roman Catholic Church's* image. He is secure as sovereign of the *Papal States* and subject to answering to no civil courts for his actions if he confesses his fault. *Hans Küng,* up to then in free exchange with his colleague, pleaded personally for *Pope Benedict* to publicly confess his involvement to relieve the bishops from carrying all the blame in a scandalized world. *Küng* thought it was symptomatic of the *Pope's* condition, from being corrupted by power, that *Pope Benedict* is placing the *church* in crisis with his bishops' cover-up of criminal child abuse. That is why *Küng* in 2010 suggested a peaceful way of removing our absolutist leadership short of a *French*-like revolution. *Pope Benedict* refuses to admit any wrongdoing to this day and cut off communications with *Küng* who, up to then, was exchanging views as at *Tübingen. Küng* recalls it was at the time when the *Pope* lifted the excommunication of the schismatic *Lefebvrist* bishop who continued to deny that the *Holocaust* occurred. When the world complained, the *Pope,* instead of admitting fault, blamed the excommunication error on his *Curia,* symptomatically consistent with his illness. *Küng* thinks *Benedict* is also a throwback to the dark-age *church* in the eleventh century, and "[h]e is an antimodernist in the deepest sense of the word." Obviously, *Benedict* feels popes know everything, and nothing new is to be known while he refuses to acknowledge *God's New Covenant* and the teaching *God* imprinted. He feels *Catholics* need only carry out the *Pope's* orders as though he is the *Trinity's* fourth member, and be "obedient in faith" to *Church* teachings. Professor *Küng* was asked by me to help me with *Pope Benedict XVI,* but the Professor wrote me that he is under doctor's orders and cannot be involved. What I know of *Hans Küng's* honesty is that he merits his "straight arrow" reputation, which is far more credible than *Benedict's. Pope Benedict* is being devious to protect his ego or his delusions. Thus, I must defer to *Küng's* opinion that *Benedict* has been corrupted by fame and power, and his condition is not due to a breakdown. Our pope refuses to see *God's* will in the *New Covenant* that *Jesus Christ* died fulfilling. He sees instead, the will of *God* in human traditions and precepts going back past the medieval ages of his militant church into the *Old Testament*. He is keeping the *New Covenant* relationship from us like a *German Shepherd* guarding a "small flock" of *Roman Catholic* believers in *Christ*.

Our *New Testament* scholars, inspired by the *Second Vatican Council's* global *Church of Christ*, presumably to be peopled by all humanity, criticized the *Catholic church's* exclusive *Eucharist,* and contended *God's* gift was meant to benefit everybody (see *God Is Near Us*, p. 59, by *Cardinal Ratzinger*). Their contention was consistent with *Ratzinger's* doctoral dissertation's conclusion that the true *church* could not be found on the uncharitable exclusion of others from its sacrament. But *Ratzinger* changed his mind or heart to oppose the principles of *Vatican*

II and the openness of the *Catholic Communion.* He welcomed being enthroned as *Pope*, whereby this controversy is concealed in the confines of the *Catholic church.* Now, with the *Internet,* it should be aired by our bishops, or if they are cowed, by any of the *People of God*, as equal members of the *Church of Christ* or their community within *God's* corporate *Spirit.*

A *protestant* minister here in the *United States, Rob Bell,* wrote an enlightening book *Love Wins*. He accepted that *God* is *love* and love will win out in the end. He could not accept his *church's* traditionalist's view that *Mohandas Gandhi* is in hell. *Bell's* book has people rethinking *Christology.* The standard *Christian* view of salvation through the death and resurrection of *Jesus,* he accepts, was summed up in the *Gospel According to John*, which promises "eternal life to whoever believeth in him" (see Time, 4/25/11). Traditionally, *Christians* acknowledge *Jesus* is the *Son of God*, and the Evangelical *Christian* pastor was taught that either you accept this or go to hell. *Bell* begs to differ with his teaching and suggests that *Jesus* redeemed "every person who ever lived." *Bell*, unfortunately, does not expressly attribute this truth to the *New Covenant's* "Gospel before the Gospel" stating *God's* words. His book ignited a new holy war in his *Christian* circle and beyond. The word of *Love Wins* reached the *Internet,* and conservatives in *Bell's church* tried to evict him from the community. The president of the *Southern Baptist Theological*

Seminary correctly concluded that the book is "theologically disastrous" to them. Another young pastor, a father of four youngsters endorsed the book and is now unemployed in depressing times to be fired. But that may be the *penance* being asked of us by the *risen Christ* according to the evangelist *Luke*. Caveat, *Catholic* bishops in the *United States*, who are not responsible for wives or families, *you* should copy this example and proclaim *God's New Covenant* relationship that *Jesus* died so excruciatingly to proclaim in passion and death. The *Fourth Gospel's* theme is merely traditional to *Rob Bell's church*, but it is recorded (although forged) in our *Dogmatic Constitution On the Catholic Church*, to be law. The law, however, was written before the *Internet* opened up to reveal it to the world and face repeal by the *People of God.*

Popular evangelist *Billy Graham's Crusade for Christ* is testing *Internet* evangelism translating their traditions to an *Internet* environment. But old people on *Internet* look at only what they want to see. Success is sought in younger people who are more attuned to videos than the text on a computer. Experience shows that focus on the younger generation should be by live conversation versus creative presentation. Still the challenge remains on how many who participated have changed their lives on the videos loosely tied to John 3:16. Unfortunately, it is the same traditions of *Rob Bell's church* negating the principles of the *New Covenant* and is *Antichrist*. *Billy Graham's*

Associates expect new *Christians* will result from their program, and discipleship courses following the video will encourage many to join local churches that are cooperating with the *Graham Crusades* project. I mention *Billy Graham's Associates' Internet* to show its utility for any global *church* or *Community of God* to return or revive *people of God* to the *New Covenant* relationship that *God* initiated in *Christ*. We see *God's* deal has been negated by human traditions, but it is salvageable by *God* and our social media, apparently if we only accept the world *God* furnishes us.

I began writing hundreds of letters of concern, never irreverently I hope, to *Pope Benedict XVI*, copied to my spiritual leaders, in obedience to a duty first placed on me by our *Dogmatic Constitution on The Church* (*Lumen Gentium*). Rights and duties appear in Chapter IV for "The Laity," and No. 37 thereof "obliged" some of us having knowledge and competence to express our opinions on those things, which concern the good of the *church* in fulfilling its mission for the life of the world. The *Roman Catholic Church* when it acts charitably conforming to the whole *Church of Christ* can claim being "true" *church*. On reading my constitutional duty, I felt called to express my opinions, and I began to mail and hand deliver them by the organs available to me, expecting the fatherly response that the *Constitution* represented my spiritual shepherds would lovingly furnish me, a vested right belonging to "everyone in the earthly city" (see p. 66). Oppressive silence, instead, was my response, thus, keeping me in darkness. I began writing in criticism of the exclusive *Eucharist,* even before made aware of a statute, which my diocesan bishop had posted in compliance with *Vatican* directions at bishop synods, to return *Catholics* to prior *Vatican* II traditions. Meanwhile, the *Pope* was performing an artful setting aside of *Gods'* commandment of love, with his *Sacramentum Caritatis* letter, to cling to *church's* traditions of exclusiveness. While corresponding, I wrote more and more argumentatively, in hopes I would receive a response from my spiritual leader at the *Vatican.* The constitutional right vested in me by Part No. 37 was violated by both *Pope* and bishop. I came to suspect, in my efforts, that the *Catholic church*, in negating "The Gospel before the Gospel" and *God's* unilaterally performed *New and Eternal Covenant* (Jer 31:31-34), consciously violated *God's* law. I began implying that concern in my letters to no avail. Additionally, I broadened my concern to *Vatican II's* global *Church of Christ* which body is that of *God's People,* everyone created, but they do not yet exist as a body. I am defeated by traditions' powers, and the *People of God* stay ignorant, by design of the *Catholic church.*

Human traditions are untrustworthy to follow; yet, we have a *Spiritual Shepherd* who leads us as if he is bound to them. I once had a neurosurgeon or neurologist who was treating me for a mild stroke, and he told me about a papal tradition that the

Catholic church practices. Popes use three or two finger blessings, traditionally restricted by our clergy for their use alone. My doctor said that paintings back through the ages prove that one pope started the cupped fingered blessing and popes afterwards followed making the same gesture. *Catholics,* who are aware, never question the practice. My *Neuro* told me that among those of his discipline, the consensus of opinion is that a dysfunction of the nerves from the elbow to the fingers can cause the sign in the hand similar to the *Pope's* blessing. It is symptomatic for the diagnosis of syphilis. I wish I had heard this when my pastor *Father Joe Bishop* was alive. We had great exchanges, when traditions were humorously discussed. He thought *"transubstantiation"* was *Aquinas's* futile reasoning to explain *divine* mystery with logic. Later another pastor told me that *Catholic* seminarians are taught that *Jesus* really sweated blood when physician *Luke* reports, "his sweat became like drops of blood falling" in the *Garden.* The later absurdity is sensitive to me as I was terminated from teaching *Bible* studies to the homeless at a *Southern Baptist* mission for refusing to say it was blood, not "like blood," that *Jesus* sweated. Our seminarians are taught to make *Jesus* appear more like a freak than an ordinary guy and are being "dumbed down" by "human caprice." *Aquinas* wrote, obedient to the *church's* traditions, but conceded before he died, that his works were wrong. *Father Bishop* is amused today as is *our Lord* with our naïveté, I suspect, but

I recall *Bishop's* distress when people held hands during the *Lord's Prayer* because it detracted from the *Sign of Peace.* I wonder how he would feel today with *Pope Benedict's* insistence on using "chalice" (*calix*) at *Mass.* Chalices are used by priests, but cups are commonly used. In his egotism, *Pope Benedict* appears to be correcting *Jesus* use of "cup" as *God* from Heaven. Then again, *Joe Bishop* was a good priest too and likely had priestly disciplines that we laity are not subject to which would make him comply with the *Vatican's* traditions. I would think, he would be reasoning that *God* could not care less if chalice for cup of wine is used, so long as its contents end up within every human creature who drinks of it. "I will be their *God,* and they shall be my people" (Jer 31:33). *God* simply wants to be intimately with us to teach, forgive, and transform each and every one of us to be more *God*-like because *God* always cares for all of us *God's* creatures, simply because *God loves us* constantly from that initial instance *God* thought to create us to evolve to be more *God-like* in life. We are created imperfect to become more in *God's, image* and become *one* in *God's* love forever. You likely considered the title of this book *God Loves Everyone* and, on reflection, might wish to try and reciprocate by loving everyone as *God* teaches you in conscience and as *Jesus Christ* demonstrated in passion.

The Good News According to Modernists

Subjectively, I believe there is a *oneness* to us all, and we all have a common knowledge and goodness caused by *God.* These things in us are subject to improve as we mature to gain perfection and be more like *God.* We should relax since we all are predestined to be *one* with *God* and each other forever. Besides, *God* oversees us for good or bad as *God* wants us to be free to love. As a whole, we have gained a common awareness that *God* is with us in our evolution and in our charitable growth advancing civilization together out of *Africa* to the world's limits where we are today looking ever onward.

Watching television, I became aware of the common conscience we have in *Shin,* a brother born in a concentration camp, raised brutally, so that in his early teens he betrayed his mother and brother to their execution he witnessed proudly. He later escaped the camp and the darkness of *North Korea* to learn to love others by witnessing love's exercise among civilized people. The awareness of *God* and *God's* law of loving others, imprinted by *God* in his conscience, was activated and are now being awakened. Unlike most of us, *Shin* never had motherly love or heard of *God.* His mother to him was a competitor for the food that was his most important love. He heard of grilled meat on the streets of *China*, and it was his incentive to escape. (*Escape From Camp 14* by *Blaine Harden*). *God's* pledge to imprint the knowledge of *God* and of *God's* law of love may need to be socially awakened in us by experiencing love, for example, by *Jesus's* sacrifice or *God's* motherly love in nature. Otherwise God and love may not be known until our death like some *Shin* left behind to die never knowing *God* or *God's law* of love of others, loving only themselves.

Modernists might realize by reading this far that the *new covenant,* given *Jeremiah* and fulfilled for all humanity by *Jesus* sacrifice, is of *God's* doing and man's undoing. It is "The Gospel before the Gospel." We should acknowledge it as *God's* perfect gospel before we human beings added our precepts to obscure it or conditions in life to negate it. *God* is Love and made us in *God's* image for eternity and solely pardoned every one's evildoing so we know by heart that *God* cannot have created anyone for a future of torment. *God's* love permits lives of torment but, in *God's* time, brings good out of the evil.

The basis for my modernist faith conclusions are mainly what *God* in *Jesus Christ* tells me. *God* says it in this book as I quoted (at pages one and two) and *Jesus Christ* fulfills in his blood as he says in his *Last Supper* words (at page three) and emphasizes from heaven (at page six) that *God* redeems everyone created. The mystery and sacrifice of the *cross* are made clearer to me from the many morning

Masses I attended, when I paid attention and heard repeatedly *Christ's* sacrifice proclaimed. They recall his struggles to love me, experienced mysterially, in the consumption of the *bread of life* and *Chalice* of *Salvation,* served at *Communion.*

Fortunately, in my lifetime, I was enlightened by the *Spirit of God* in action at the *Second Vatican Council.* Human attempts were conscientiously begun by participants to modernize the *Roman Catholic Church* and open it to be the *Church of Christ* spread throughout the world and aided to its fullness of charity by an open and all-inclusive *Eucharist. God's Eucharist,* without any preconditions or denominational restraints, simply on *Christ's* invitation for all to take and actually consume our *God,* is how our *Council's* principles were idealized. But traditionalists betrayed the *Council* leaving it up to *God* again to fulfill *God's* planned kingdom to exist (see Ps 127:1 and *God Is Near Us*, p. 59, by *Cardinal Ratzinger*).

I want individual readers to think about their knowledge of *God* and of *God's* law imprinted in their individual conscience, even though they disbelieve in my ideas, to accept by heart that we should love others as we do ourselves. Having read my book to this point, you might distrust what you have read and that's good. I want you to think on your own what *God* teaches you and trust that you know the lesson by heart. Even though you deny reasonably the evidence of my *God,* consider any human teachings you have received contradicting my claims, as the cause of your distrust. Accept that you have been influenced by the unneeded teachings *God* mentions in the *New Covenant.* These human teachings have already handicapped you to reject the love that *God* imprinted in your mind and hearts to be true. However, with a mind open to be enlightened come to take and consume the *real presence of God* in the bread and wine *Jesus* gives you freely to enlighten us.

René Descartes (1596-1650) was another lawyer taught by the *Jesuits.* He had a *Catholic* religious faith and claimed to his death to be a devout *Roman Catholic.* His works were placed by the *Pope* on the *Index of Prohibited Books*, but he was in good company since *Galileo* was condemned in his lifetime. As a scientist he was deemed to be the "Father of Modern Philosophy" and his influence is felt among Western thinkers to this day. To his credit, he bridged algebra and geometry* and fathered analytical geometry and the analysis of infinitesimal geometry. He was called a "Scientific Revolutionist." He is best known for his Cartesian statement, "I think, therefore I am." He thought all truths are linked and his using logic would open his knowledge to them. He learned by subjectively thinking and knowing truth must come from his *God-given* essence. He trusted only in his subjective knowledge that he was thinking and found things from the external world to be objective and material but based upon trust that *God* would not deceive him as to the transmitted ideas. *God* gave him, thus, trust and belief in *God* and *God's* law within him, but unlike *Shin,* of North Korea, he had teachers who awakened him to the laws of love he trusts.

Sir Isaac Newton was also a scientist, decades later, and was theologically influenced by the mysticism of the *scriptures. Newton* revolutionized physics, mathematics, and astronomy but was more into *scripture.* He said *scripture* furnished a "code" to the natural world. To him science and faith were all part of the same world of thought. But he overlooked the *New Covenant* "code" that was buried by human gospels in *scripture* to trust it. He, too, learned to love through human teachers.

Albert Einstein, known in my lifetime, is one of our *US* immigrant experts. Infamous for the atomic bomb, but his learned thoughts (quoted in my letter 7/24/06 to *Pope Benedict XVI*) included the following:

> A human being is a part of the whole called the 'universe,' a part limited in time and space. He experiences himself, his thoughts and feelings, as something separated from the rest, a kind of optical delusion of . . . consciousness. This delusion is a kind of prison for us, restricting us to our personal desires and to affection for a few persons nearest to us. Our task must be to free ourselves from this prison by widening our circle of compassion to embrace all living creatures and the whole of nature in all its beauty. Nobody is able to achieve this completely, but the striving for such

achievement is in itself part of the liberation and a foundation for inner security. (extracted from *Everyday Grace* by M. Williamson)

Pope Benedict XVI may suffer a delusion similar to what *Einstein* talks about by narrowing his compassion and refusing to embrace all humanity as the *People of God* in his fantasy world, in his uncharitable acts of mass excommunication, and in his exclusive *Roman Catholic Church. Pope Benedict,* in his delusion and artful clinging to an exclusive *Holy Communion,* disregards *God's* law and covenant and does not see the *Body of Christ* is everyone. He and *Einstein* miss that *God* is needed to overcome our intellectual conceit and human delusions, but *God* made it so we too learn of *God* and love, if human love furnishes lessons as *Shin* proves.

Scripture furnishes us with codes, such as the *New Covenant* (Jer 31:31ff., and 1 Cor 11:23-26), to apply with scientific information we are receiving from society, to add to that gained from *our Lord God Almighty. God,* in *Christ,* solely saves humanity for eternal life, which "code" we know from *God* and *Christ* revealing it at his moment of glory described in *scriptures.* With the exception of those like *Shin* who are born and die ignorant in *Camp No. 14,* even the least of us essentially know by heart what *God* imprints in all of us—the knowledge of *God* and the knowledge of the law of *God*—so we need no further teaching "for I will forgive their evildoing and remember their sin no more" says *God* in *Covenant* (Jer 31:34) to all humanity through *Jesus Christ* (1 Cor 11:23-26). I quote the ending of the *New Covenant* as it appears in my *Bible* "*The New American Bible*," because "for" reads as a cause and effect word to accept the mystery of *God's* teaching, forgiving, and forgetting benefits saving every human created. The *New Covenant's* promise occurs several centuries before *Jesus,* who expressly dies to execute *God's* pledges and, thus, fulfills them for us all. We trust this to be true because *Jesus* laid down his life to reveal the *New Covenant* and because *God* shows it in the foolishness of the *Cross,* which we believe by trusting *God* and *Christ* not to deceive us. We trust we are being told the truth because *Jesus* trustingly laid down his life to prove it, and we proclaim our own beliefs authentically with *God's* authority, simply because *God,* in *Jesus,* tells us so!

The general rule in interpreting the ambiguities of *scripture* is to translate it according to the standard of *God's* law of love. For example, "take this all of you" charitably means everyone is to share the *Eucharist. Pope Benedict XVI* preaches this standard of translation but does not practice it when he excludes almost everyone from our *Eucharist.* For instance, *the People of God* is referred to when *God* says, "I will be their *God* and they shall be my people," means everybody created because to exclude anyone from any *New Covenant* benefit is plainly uncharitable, unjust, and un-*God* like. The

Blood of the Covenant shed by *Jesus* baptizes all *Jews* and *Gentiles* charitably, and *Christ's* charitable bequests in *Covenant* or *Testament* can only include every human being created and exclude no one. Thus, everyone created is included in the *Church of God* and its *Eucharist.* Our deluded *Pope Benedict,* however, excludes most people from both because we *Catholics* have traditionally done so. *God* and *God's* law experienced by each one of us in our individual ways tells us our *Founding Father's* ideal in the *United States*, of everyone created equal, is more *Christ*-like. *God* imprints in each human being this uncontestable truth that we are to love each other impartially. Our *Catholic* clergy delusively obscures this truth, as has all *Christianity,* from the beginning. We experience *God* in mysterious and varied ways, but the mystery of *God's* love is more revealed in children, whose innocent minds and trusting ways have not yet been deluded to prevent them from believing *God* loves all equally, evidenced by *Jesus Christ,* to be *one. Descartes, Newton*, and *Einstein* give adults confidence to freely think about gospel traditions, to discard *John* and keep most of the *synoptic.* The least of us unconsciously trust *God's* imprinted common knowledge of *God's* law of love, discern delusions of human limits, and trustingly accept the universal value of the global *Church of God.* Once we accept *God's* brilliant idea, as we charitably should for the good of *the People of God* throughout the whole world, we can love everyone trusting the love of *God.* If we judge that our spiritual leaders will not change their ways, which seems to be the case after millenniums of division, we all should try to construct the united *Church of God,* with its inclusive *Eucharist,* to accomplish the mission of *Christ* to make us *one* incorporated *community.* We should decide together, bypassing the leaders of our separate churches, on how we are to do *God's* will and spread *Christ Jesus's* love among us. Essentially we must share *Eucharist* with every human creature because *God* says so! *God's* words "take this all of you" are spoken by *Christ* at *Supper* and, in effect, to all humankind from the *Cross* and in person continuously at daily *Mass*, around the world. We should leave the *Vatican* to contend with its *Roman Catholic Church's* "small flock." There is little hope for *Pope Benedict* and his *Curia* to help us, unless *God* intervenes. And if *Jesus* found no particular church, as *Ratzinger* taught at *Tübingen*, we are free to bypass his church to unite in one *Eucharist* and within one global *Church of God,* allowing all the separate churches to remain as satellites, including *Catholicism's* "small flock," if they wish.

Father Raymond Brown, the acknowledged expert on *scriptures* at the time stated in the *St. Anthony's Messenger,* May 1971, pp. 47-48, in part, the following: "I do not believe the demons inhabit desert places or the upper air, as Jesus and Paul thought . . . I see no way to get about the difficulty except by saying that Jesus and Paul were wrong on this point. They accepted the beliefs of their times about demons, but those beliefs were superstitious." Think of *Jesus,* fully human being here today and possessing our "hind sight," seeing the mess we have made with our uncharitable interpretations, he assuredly would support the global *Church of God* idea and repeat his order for all to take the *Eucharist,* in accordance with *God's* instructions. We should unite as one people and be assisted to love each other by *God's* gift of *Jesus Christ*, now *one* with *God,* as divinely taught by *scripture.*

Jesus purportedly said in his ministry "things that come from within are what defile . . . From within the man, from his heart, come evil thoughts . . . folly and they defile" (Mk 7:14-23). Later, after admittedly instructed by *God*, *Jesus* incorporates by reference the *New Covenant* in his blood sacrifice of performing the *Covenant* (Mk 14:24) and ordered "all of you take" of *Eucharist* correcting *Jesus* previous "dog" prejudice. *Jesus's* culture traditionally taught him from the *Old Testament* that *God* was to be feared and inflicted punishment to the thousandth generation on some ignoramus who hated *God* (Ex 29:1ff.). Still, *Jesus* warned us some things we hear or read may be latrine destined. So might be all of the *Old Testament* except for the *New Covenant* passage and the *Golden Rule* he died to proclaim. Indelicately as *Jesus* described, what I write too should not cause any children of *God* to lose faith or be upset. Use your own common abilities to think, refer to your own conscience, and trust *God's real presence* to continue teaching you to love each other. Trust *God's* law of love. All the rest is untrustworthy human commentary, hearsay, and opinions that may close your heart and mind.

I represent, in writing to you and to my spiritual shepherds, that I sincerely claim some knowledge, competence, or ability to express the opinions I spell out here, but they are based on my readings and my limited judgments. I feel confident to express opinions on these subject matters to my spiritual shepherds who could correct me, so I pray *our Lord* that my words do not harm anyone whose naïveté may risk their faith. My competence to write, I submit, is based, in part, on life prejudices. Racially, I am *Basque American*, of a first generation of immigrants, born in the *United States* and possess the common knowledge *God* imprints in all human creatures. Historically, *Basques* were not a literate people and being volatile their exploits were downplayed by *France* and *Spain*. I was graced to learn from reading books and learned scholars in a land of literacy their scant history of my roots. My teachers accompanied my freedom to learn the whole story of *God's* relationship with us in *Eucharist*. *God's New Covenant* and its fulfillment in *Jesus* were learned much later in life, in fact, since *Vatican II*. I was always taught that *Jesus Christ* bled to death on the *cross* to save me for everlasting life but taught that I need to do more, to improve my chances, by works. I was to have faith and do good works too in order to be saved. I was taught and directed to be "obedient in faith" unquestionably to the teachings of the *Roman Catholic Church*, with the threat to obey or else face torment hereafter. I was to believe *Jesus* was *Christ*, the *Jewish* Messiah, or *God* in order to be saved. I was indoctrinated from the top down about the divine rights and holiness of the *Pope*, who spoke infallibly, to believe and obey him. I have come to believe all humans are like *God*, and the truth is more in all of us than in one of us. Recently, in faith I am thinking that *God* made me like *Jesus*, an ordinary guy, but by his death and resurrection, *God* glorified *Jesus*, and at my death, I am to be *one* with *God* and *Jesus* not because of my works but the works of *Christ*. Consequently, I can say "*I am*" like *Descartes* and will be whatever *God* makes me to be. *Jesus* saying "*I Am*" or "*I am*" may contemplate his incorporation into the *community of God* as all humans are and will be. I feel graced by *God*, to experience the *new covenant* relationship, as fulfilled by *God* in *Christ*. I wonder how to share the peace, being *one* with *God* and everyone else in *community*, and communicate with everyone effectively about this subject matter. Being *Basque*, historically self-ruled from the earth up, and an avid reader, I thought I might path-find humankind, as my forbears had, to explore the mysteries of our relationship with *God* in the pressing reality of our ever diminishing world. The task requires ever expanding tolerance and cooperation of differing religious and political convictions in the minds of *God's* people living like *Basques* on earth.

Teilhardist's (Pierre Teilhard de Chardin, S. J.) seem to describe the *oneness* of us all evolving from *Alpha* to *Omega* and being *one* with *God*. The *new covenant* promise and performance by *God* alone, in *Jesus Christ's* death and resurrection, occurs constantly from our conception to death perfecting us. Many people might become aware of *God's* relationship with us continuing constantly in gaining knowledge as we live. I never heard of the *New Covenant* until I was old, about two decades ago, even though it was being voiced in my *Eucharistic prayers*, in *English*, since *Vatican II*, but its extent has yet to be known because few competent write of it. *God* imprints essential knowledge in me, to translate what I receive, but my ignorance is not to be overcome fully until I die and *God* lifts my veil of ignorance.

The *Catholic church* is silent on my concerns in its hierarchy's interest or in vincible ignorance and has kept me dumbed down. I was conditioned to believe *God* loved me only if I was good, but I have overcome that delusion. I trust now that *God* always loves me. I was taught nothing by the *Catholic church* about the *New Covenant* or the *scripture* story of *Jesus* voluntarily bleeding to death to fulfill all humanity's *new covenant* relationship with *God*. I pray with more emphasis "thy kingdom come" to overcome the ignorance caused in me by men negating that *Jesus's* self-sacrifice causes *God's Covenant* relationship.

I later learned *God* forgives our evildoing no matter what we do, solely out of *God's* goodness, and our conduct is irrelevant toward our salvation. *God's* love of me, a sinner, cleanses me thoroughly in *Christ's blood* for everlasting life with *God*. I am saved from birth, regardless of my ignorance or evildoing, because of the love of *God* and *Christ*. *God* is always aware of me throughout my ignorance and while I was sinning, and now that I am at peace, knowing I escaped the hell I was told I faced, simply because *God* loves me and has forgotten my sins. *God* perfected me while my *church* was predicting torment in purgatory or even hell to get me to perfect myself by being more perfect than *God* makes me. I was being deluded into believing I was destined for heaven only if I disciplined myself to obey the *church* and its laws. As one of *God's Roman Catholics* I learned from the *church* that with my record I was destined, at best, for *purgatory*. At funerals I would hear "chastised a little" (*Wisdom*, 3:5) and feel relieved for a more hopeful predestination. Today, I am truly at peace, regardless of the past teaching, conditions, and delusions. I no longer need to blindly follow the *Catholic church*, and I want to share my good news. *The New Covenant* news reveals *Catholicism's* errors in faith, and it evidences, especially to an attorney, that we have got it made. On later reflections, it dawned on me that the unanswered suggestive letters from me to *Pope Benedict XVI*, in law, are implied admissions of the concerns suggested. My understanding was firmed up when *Pope Benedict XVI* delusively continued his clinging to traditions so uncharitably. He refuses to consider the truth if it comes from the likes of me. At least the three hundred *Austrian* priests who tried to bring the *church* up to date were heard last week and, though denounced in homily, may yet dialogue of sorts with the *Pope*. I was being deliberately deprived of my *Dogmatic Constitution* rights, but now I see that being deprived of those rights is likely due to a deluded *Pope Benedict* who hasn't a clue of what harm he causes humanity in misappropriating *God's* gifts to everyone. Most all of us are ignorant of being the *People of God's New Covenant* and heirs of *Christ's New Testament* benefits. We are supposed to be equally sharing in *Jesus's* mysterious death and resurrection as a new creation far greater than *John the Baptist*, *Jesus* once said. We have been "dumbed down" by delusions, like those *Pope Benedict* suffers from in his intellectual conceit resulting from our *Roman Catholic Church's* traditional treatment of popes. In my case I was told, once, by my diocesan bishop that I was in need of faith and obedience to my *church's* teachings. It is true, I no longer have that faith because of my reliance on *God* and conscience, but I certainly am not in need of the blind obedience suggested. I see now that "obedience in faith" to the *church* teachings, which *Bishop Wiegand* wrote is what I needed, misleads many deluded spiritual leaders. I write now to try and enlighten the world to the truth, if I can, and, to have ordinary people analyze *church* disciple's blindness to *God* and *Christ's* teachings. We all are subject to our own religions' respective delusions, and most dare not think on their own. *God* forgives us all and brings us to good by simply forgiving and forgetting everyone's sins of disobedience and vincible ignorance. A recent case in point of the bishops' blind obedience is their cry for "religious freedom" in the *United States*. Even though they know *Catholic Americans*, the vast majority of them disagree with *church's* teachings on birth control, that is, *Humanae Vitae*. *Popes* place contraception on par with murder, and the bishops insist on calling on the nation's sixty-seven million *Catholic* faithful to campaign against *Obama's* health finance law that furnishes contraception coverage among its provisions for citizens. *Jesus* gave each apostle directions to serve, not rule, as *He* in our midst serves us (Lk 22:26-27). But the *US* bishops show that their allegiance is to the *Roman Church* and not to represent the free choice of lay citizens who need health coverage and can choose its birth control or not according to individual consciences.

The *Vatican* spokesman, *Jesuit Fr. Federico Lombardi*, said that the "*Eucharist* wording lay at the heart of the church," and there is no doubt that *Jesus* died so "everyone" might be saved. (*NCR*, 5/7/12). *Cardinal Ratzinger* said much the same when he wrote that the words of the *Last Supper* and the death of *Jesus* were "interdependent" giving universal application to redemption and to *Eucharist* (*God Is*

Near Us, p. 29). But *Pope Benedict* violates his own rule of charitable translation of *Bible* ambiguities when he chooses the traditional words "for many" rather than *Luke's* more charitable "you" for every human creature (Lk 22:19-21). His new *mass* words ambiguously support the forged version of the *New Covenant* saving only a "small flock" of *Catholics* (see *No. 9* of *Lumen Gentium*). The changes, and *Humanae Vitae*, are fundamentally about power: the pope possesses it, and the bishops stupidly obey it. The *US Bishops*, under the guise of "Freedom of Religion," are foisting the *Catholic* ban on contraception on the *American* citizenry, rather than allowing contraception be a matter of choice, and interfering in financing of *Obama's* Health law. The baby will be tossed out with the bath water by political power from the noncitizen in *Rome*. Obviously, *God's* law of loving everyone equally may be corrupted by *church* interests deeming contraception as comparable to murdering.

Ann Cruz Ithurburn, my wife, has her own *Catholic* faith convictions that do not agree with mine. She also has a newsworthy heritage and background that binds her to the *church*. For example, her first *American* ancestor *Peter Joseph Cruz* entered the country with the *Trappist Monks* centuries ago and settled in *Kentucky*. He was an orphan, about twelve years of age, and, while sailing over from *France*, experienced the ship being boarded by pirates. The monks gave the youngster their gold to hide, and he hid the gold in a soap bucket that was used to maintain the ship's ropes or riggings. With the wealth saved, the monks invested in the building of *Gethsemanae, Kentucky*. (Later *Thomas Merton's* famous monastery.) Nearby lives *Ann's* sister a retired Provincial Superior of the *Sisters of Charity of Nazareth* in *Kentucky*, whose nuns serve worldwide *the People of God*, with Mother Houses from the *Americas* to *India* that I have reason to believe are bringing charity to fulfill the *church* spread out in the world.

I proposed marriage to *Ann* when she was a *navy* nurse and outranked me. For over one-half century, she lovingly managed our home, and I rarely got to command our household. *Ann* and I raised eight children in *California*, two of whom, in effect are "excommunicated" by the *church* for marriages outside the *Roman Catholic Church*. One excommunicated son sensibly continues receiving the *Eucharist*, but the other one is waiting for the *church* to invite him to return, while he considers sharing other *church's* versions of the *Eucharist* since they invite him to share their supper. He once asked me to define the difference in *Communions,* and I was unable to do so. *Jesus* ordered: "Take this, all of you" without offering distinctions if you are excommunicated by a church.

We local *Basque-Americans* put on an annual *Mass* followed by a lamb barbeque with wine to share in a sheep range memorial celebration. Over the years, I have been responsible to bring the *Basque* priest, and this year, I negligently failed to have any priest so, we did not have the *Mass* before we broke the bread, drank the wine, and enjoyed the festivities. I was tempted to address the crowd by microphone and invite them to consider that we should proclaim the words of *God*, *Jesus* talked and walked, in the paschal mystery to assume that *God's Spirit* blesses our bread and wine. After blessing we can take the bread and wine we had, which *Jesus* already consecrated at *Supper* and on the *Cross*, and serve *Eucharist* to everyone. It would be up to *God* if we had *Holy Communion*. But lacking faith in my convictions and fearful of scandalizing the traditionalists among us, I took the prudent way out and used the loudspeaker to apologize for my failings, to bring the priest. Yet I write you all consider doing what I "chickened-out" doing if your conscience allows. A priest, later suggested that I, as an extraordinary *Eucharist Minister*, should take the *Austrian* priests' advice, and serve consecrated *Eucharist*, but I assume he and the *Austrians* meant hosts from the tabernacle. Still you will scandalize many self-righteous traditionalists from community or church. Next year, I will arrange for the priest and publish this book for others with courage in their conviction, to venture where I dared not go, should the priest not show.

I had the advantages of being surrounded by many family members who, by good works, cause me to remain in our *Communion*. I had a maternal uncle, a *Benedictine* priest, *Fr. Charles Jean Espelet* who set up a mission parish pre WWII for the poorest of the poor *Hispanics* in *"Simons Brickyard"* located in *East Los Angeles*. He formed a *Basque Club* both to support the parish and to preserve the cultural songs and dances of *Basques*. His annual *Basque* festivals caught on and spread throughout the *West*. Also, I have a nephew, my sister's eldest son and my *godson* who serves the poor and challenged *African-Americans* in *Chicago* (*Cabrini Green* was part of his parish). *Jim* was given a silver cassock for protection in nighttime gang shootouts and survives. I also have a niece, my brother's younger daughter, who manages a hospice adjacent to *U. C. Davis Hospital* and a summer camp at *Eagle Lake* for needy families and damaged youngsters. These closer relatives silently exemplify *Jesus* serving others and so I always have good models urging me to try to do good works as a *Catholic*. Less demonstrably, I am taught silently by my immediate family, for example, our eldest son has partnered with me as a lawyer for decades as was a younger daughter (now deceased), and all our children have occupations that serve the needs of others. I am proud enough of them to brag here, although their good works are more to my wife's credit than mine.

Shamefully, I sin a lot and enjoy *Eucharist* often, but I have a past pertinent evildoing to share with my pope: I did wrong as an officer in the *US Marine Corps*, out of an excess of bias similar to what I think *Pope Benedict XVI* is deluded into doing, to preserve an institution's longtime traditions. I had the pride of position as a rifle platoon leader in *Dog Company,*

2nd Battalion, 7th Marine Regiment of the 1st Marine Division. I was with them a few years after the unit was wiped out west of *Chosen Reservoir, Korea*, by the *Chinese* who overran its position. The M-1 rife had held the enemy at bay when all other hand weapons froze in the cold, but a snow blizzard cut the *Marine's* vision down to remove their advantage. My wrongdoing was while still *Semper Fi* deluded, and the *Marines* assigned me a different mission. I was transferred to the *Marine Corp Recruit Depot* when *Congress* was investigating our training program, which caused the deaths of over a half-dozen marines in the swamps of *Perris Island*. I was made investigating officer for the western *US* and found our position indefensible. I simply buried my report, believing I would only get a letter of reprimand when I left active duty to an inactive reserve status. I "bit the bullet" because of my faith delusions to cling to the traditional training of the *corps*. I delusively believed the *Marine Corps*, clinging to its traditional ways, was good for the *Corps*, and I overcame my duties to tell the truth to higher authorities. In time, things changed and so did the *Marine Corp* from training mainly to kill others. So, too, with the *Roman Catholic Church*, regardless of *Pope Benedict* clinging excessively to tradition to retain *status quo* for the *church*, it must improve to love everyone and not favor *Catholics*. First, the church *must* repent for not using *God's* original plan. *God* has in mind, from the beginning of creation, spreading the *Church of Christ* to the fullness of charity worldwide, to include everyone, in a universal *church* or *community* with an open *Eucharist*. People are to live *God's New Covenant* relationship, serving and not ruling from top down, which has been denied humanity since the birth of *Christianity*, by human caprice and traditions.

Occupation wise, I became an active plaintiff's personal injury trial lawyer and tried cases for decades on the principle that every person had equal standing before juries. I focused on trying causes of victims harmed, by established corporate or government interests, to jury verdicts—a constitutional right we in the *United States* have as citizens. My number of defense verdicts are too numerous to remember since I may have tried more than anyone, losing two of three cases tried. It proved to be nonlucrative as adversaries, money supported, wore me out by attrition. After years of waged conflict, I discovered my client's civil rights were being progressively denied by status quo judges denying them jury verdicts. Meanwhile, I became aware my *Catholic church* was victimizing people, also by denying their rights, *God*-given, to the *Eucharist*, a wrong that directed my advocacy to recover these divine rights which pursuit is ongoing. We have no court for *God*-given rights denied by *church* injustices, so I instead try to reveal what is being misappropriated, of people's *God*-given rights, by my *church*. I have yet to be successful in my efforts, but once I enlighten the minds of ordinary people, their reaction, as individuals harmed, may result in self-help remedying the greatest of injustices. *Catholics* are reluctant to accept criticism of their *church* and tend to deny its shortcomings; so I offer to disclose hereby to all human beings baptized in the *Blood of the Covenant* the facts of their *God*-given rights being misappropriated. I think this might be a definite service that *God* calls me to try, a case I happily am trying to pursue with human assistance of the *People of God*. *God* likely needs no lawyer to advocate the law of love we owe each other as imprinted by *God* in our hearts, but because of the wrongs of *church* teachings, in ignorance of the *New Covenant*, I invite all humanity to wake up and act. I think we initially should pierce the illusion of *churches'* bubble of holiness, to serve *God* upward from our roots. We should rethink the truth of our *oneness* in *God's* relationship with us in the *New Covenant* and the global *Church of Christ*. I am reporting the good news to you *People of God*, to help *Jesus our Lord* build *God Almighty's* world *church*, or society, to include all humanity as equal members and build it spiritually from the ground up on the foundation of *Christ*. Retired *Australian Bishop J. Robinson* says *Catholics* need now to attack the profoundly unhealthy elements in the *Catholic church* that have cost the credibility of the pope and bishops, leaving an alternative restoration to the *People of God* as a choice (see *NCR* 4/13/12) and be helpmates to our *God* of *Love's* goals for humanity from its inception.

The *Jesuits* taught me, in about 1953, of *Saint Thomas Aquinas's* ideas of *God* based on *Aristotelian* philosophy. I recall being taught metaphysics that *God* is *pure act,* and everything else is subject to change (*potency*). As disciplined Papal soldiers *Ignatius* and Xavier founded the Jesuits to teach Catholic truths; but they were both raised *Basques*—a name given them by *Argentineans.* My French cousin calls us *Basc.* Population wise they are a minute fraction of humanity. They are called *Eskualdunak*—speakers of *Euskara*—at home. The *Basque* language is unique, not even *Indo-European*, and though I understand my parent's tongue, I am less *Basque* literally for inability to speak it. *Basques* have been located in their economically poor environment at least since they left their caves, in or about the *Pyrenees* Mountains. They left pre-historic drawings when all were illiterate people. When the ice age warmed these lone survivors from the cold, they spread their DNA throughout *Europe*, leaving its remnants today along the outer borders of *Europe*, while other people migrated into *Europe*. *The Oldest Europeans* by *J. F. Del Giorgio* takes liberties with the mysterious history of *Basques*, as I do, to write his story. He writes of the *Basque* involvement in the same culture of *Greek* legends and includes *Homer's Iliad* reports of the religious war to overcome the pagan religion, symbolized by *Helen*, with its nondiscrimination of women. The earlier culture extended to the *UR*, *Abraham's* birthplace, when *Basques* worshiped a pagan *Goddess Mari* (pronounce *Mahdí*), and respected women consistent with *Del Giorgio's* speculations on ancient Greeks. Genetics establish we humans came out of *Africa*, improved in civilizations about the *Fertile Crescent*, and some went to *Europe* becoming our *Basque* ancestors. *Basques* were not converted to *Christianity* until well after other *Europeans* converted. When *Rome* took over *Basque* lands, before the time of *Christ*, they stayed for over a millennium (naming *Pamplona* after *Pompei*), while *Basques* lived untouched by Roman influence in the security of their homes. Ever resourceful, they contracted out services to *Rome* as mercenaries. Throughout the centuries, they retained their language and culture. Women were respected as equals unlike *Christianity* and the *Eastern* societies *Basques* experienced with the *Moors*. Many homes today are customarily ruled by the lady in the kitchen, in compliment to a charitable enlightenment. Relatively, the *Basques* isolated themselves, especially by retaining their unique language, in their autonomous household democracies. *Cervantes* had *Don Quixote* sneer at a *Basque* speaking *Spanish*, but the typical *Basque* speaking *Spanish* likely was not concerned with conversing formally with non-*Basques*. *Basques* are so politically volatile *France* and *Spain* records of them downplay their accomplishments, and records of them are biased. *Basques* were never defeated as a people but remain intact as a democracy without a country to the present day. On a rare occasion, they fought united when pagan *Basques* in *Navarra* caused the *Christian Emperor Charlemagne* to suffer his greatest defeat. *Basques* wiped out the *Christian* army's rear guard and killed the legendary *Roland*, in 778, at *Orreaga* (tree area). *Explorer S. Vizcaino* (*The Basque*) named our *State of Oregon* from this site famous to us *Basques*. *Christianity* came late to the *Basques*, a strongly stubborn people, who tend to tolerate and ignore their would-be invaders, suffer poorly rule by governments, and avoid foreign influences. They prefer peaceful homestead democracies. The *kingdom of Navarra*, in their midst, lasted several centuries but fell because of being mutually ignored. *Kingdoms* and *churches* fail when divided from their people a lesson for *Pope Benedict* to learn. The pagan *Basques* converted after *Rome* left and whenever *Catholicism* came to appeal to them. The nobles of the *kingdom of Navarra* later became *protestant,* and they further divided from the people. The *Navarra Basques*, however, were untouched in the change of faith by the nobility becoming *Calvinists* or *Methodists* and remained *Catholic*. They always claimed self-sustaining democratic equality of their own to match claims to nobility. I submit that the global *Church of Christ*, with membership separate but equal, combined as a democratic and capitalistic community, would appeal to *Basques* who never had a country of their own.

A cousin in *Biarritz* made me a family tree that extended my awareness of my ancestor's lineage into the no longer existing *kingdom of Navarra*. To me, it serves as another example of evolving change in the world *God* maintains for us. Also, it cautions *Pope Benedict*, that what the *church* binds on earth, binds not the consciences of the *people of God* on earth. My cousin, *Maïté*, included the following identities of my distant relatives who, at my age, may be closer than distant relatives: *Inigo Arista* (851) the first king of *Basque Navarra*; *Princess Semana* (1025) who married *Viscount Garcia* (*Hartza* in *Basque* means bear) and moved to live in *Echaux* (their household castle) to continue my maternal lineage to our homestead *Hasqueta* in *Aldudes, France*. *Semana's* siblings continued living in *Pamplona,* and in time, produced *Princess Berenguela* (about 1200), who was born into the "*Camelot*" of the *Kingdom*. She married *Richard the Lionhearted* and a sister became *Denmark's* queen. They spoke *Basque*, having learned it from the servants, as did her brother *King Sancho VII le Forte*. He crusaded with *Richard* to the *Holy Land* and returned to extend the kingdom to the *Bay of Biscay*. Soon after this spurt of growth, the *Kingdom's* nobility became *Protestant* and faded away. Similarly, I experience with the *US Basques* in diaspora that we are melting away into our country's stew pot, as did the era of *Basque* sheepherders fade into history, in my lifetime. I personally herded sheep with a donkey packing (*astopaketan*) my camp and left carvings on aspens which too faded away in time.

The converted *Basques* were nonconformist in their *Catholic* faith practices as a maternal relative of mine shows in his conflict during an *inquisition*. A descendant from *Princess Semana*, *Catholic Bishop Beltran de Echaux*, was born in the castle home in *Baigori, France,* which stands today. *Basque* homes are their castles. He became newsworthy when he terminated the *inquisition's* execution of *Basque* priests, after forty were torched, for witchcraft. Witches tales were told by custom in the rural homes and the pagan traditions seeped, by song and dance, into the *church* after the *Basques* relatively recent conversion to *Catholicism*. *Basques* became, however, loyal *Roman Catholics* continuing to give the *church*, as in the past, sons like *Ignatius Loyola, S. J.*, and *St. Francis Xavier* (French census version of, *exe berri*) whose family home (*eche or exe*) was located nearby my father's home in *Nevarre*. The *Black Pope Arburua, S. J.*, a more recent headliner was replaced by the present regime because he was too much a free thinker for the *Papacy*. *Basques*, by nature, today continue to insist on freedom of thought, religion, economy, and democracy. Disturbing are the invasions into their homes in modern times of the secular media, interfering with the youth retaining the rural *Basque* language and changing *Basque* traditions to conform with those of the world.

When the *Kingdom in Pamplona* was on its last legs, the *Basques* proved their potential for exploring new ideas by making history in sea ventures, from whaling, ship building, and deep sea fishing. They had ventured to the shores of *New Foundland*, after the *Norsemen* discovered it, where they found cod fishing so lucrative that they kept the site secret for generations, while they enjoyed a market monopoly in *Catholic Europe*, especially on days of abstinence, for cod, and its bacalau dish. Not until *Cartiér or Cabot* discovered their fishing site was the *Basques'* secret revealed. The *Basques* enterprisingly built the ships for ocean travel—supplied two of those *Columbus* used and even furnished crewmen, for his "discovery" of *America*. Later, *Basques* escorted *Magellan*, when he "circumnavigated" the world, although only *Basques* returned home with *Juan Elcano* captaining the surviving ship. *Basques* were mostly sojourners during the *Spanish, Portuguese,* and *French* settling in *America*. Settlers from *Mexico* named our *State of Arizona* after another *Basque* tree area (*Global Vascona* by *W. A. Douglas*). The *Basques* naming *Oregon* and *Arizona* "bookended" many *Basque Californians*, for example, *Palo Alto (6'8," P. Altube)*. Other *Europeans*, who tended to settle the discovered lands, included *Protestant Knox's* people of *Scotland* who were taught to read the *Bible* and had an advantage with literacy and language over the *Basques* in *North America*. In *Latin America,* fairer opportunities invited *Basques* to become landed gentry from the beginning. However, the advantages of the *United States* have leveled the playing field, and *Basque* offspring enjoy equal opportunities with all *Amerikanuak* (*Basque Americans).*

My father *Bertrand Ithurburn* was born in *Ascarat, France* (*Basse Navarre*), and as a teenager, he entered this country, in 1909. He suffered at *Ellis Island*, the substitution of an "n" for the "u" in the family name *Ithurburu* (fountain head). He became a sheepherder and, shortly afterwards, a conservative Westerner with success as a sheep owner from before World War I for the next half-century. In my father's time, *Basques* came to this country to serve the need for herders, and there were no quotas on *Basques.* They were the last generation of this trend, as the resourceful *Basque* will no longer suffer the lonely life of herders but instead succeed with families in lives of urban services. I recall it was all family, with our herders being treated equally in sharing my mother, *Catherine Espelet Ithurburn*. Herders were exploited elsewhere, I suppose from what I read, a few rich oppressing the poor. Activities in our extended family in *South America*, rich and poor alike from long ago, are more newsworthy in *Basques* more so being oppressed. They became newsworthy in gaining and defending human freedoms and services for the oppressed and poor against dictatorial regimes and exploitive employments. *Evita (Ibarguren) Peron* exemplifies a rich one who artfully climbed out of her poverty. We, *Ithurburus*, with other variations in the name, made news among *Latin Americans*, rich and poor. They include the poet laureate of *Spain's* civil war *Caetano Ithurburu* (sic), from *Argentina,* who fought against *Franco* (and the *Church*) with the *International Lincoln Brigade*. His daughter *"Negrita"* was the "puppy love" of the revolutionist "*Che*" *Guevara. Che's* favorite aunt was *Carmen Ithurburu*. He was a physician, often depicted as the communist rebel, with a *Basque* beret. History should credit him, against his killings in *Cuba* and *Africa*, with contributing to the end of colonial rule in the world like his hero, another *Basque*, *Simon Bolivar* in *South America*. Recently, in *Argentina's* "dirty war" at least nineteen of these *Ithurburus* (sic) disappeared, likely were exterminated, for their service in freedom-seeking civil rights for people. They died for ends similar to those sought by "Liberation Theology" enthusiasts, a peaceful movement based on claimed principles of *Vatican II*, a type of *Christology* and arguably an element of the global *Church of Christ*. They are ordinary people attempting to improve conditions for *Christians* which would herein means humanity. The *Christians* I refer to are all people baptized in the *Blood of the Covenant*, or, in other words, every human created by *God*. The poorer *Latin Christians* are meant to benefit from these basic autonomous communities as were the earliest *Christian* communes that *Luke* wrote about, but in a modern setting on earth. As part of the global *Church of Christ,* they fit outside of the "visible structure" of the *church* (see No. 8 of *Lumen Gentium*) in one human viewpoint but are full members and not constrained by the word *church* or commune, or whatever we are to call ourselves later.

Jesus and *Pope Benedict* seemingly agree in claiming a *oneness* with the *Divine*. At the beginning, *God* existed only and creation conceivably is made of the substance of *God*, in the greatest and smallest "transubstantiations" of creatures because nothing exists outside of *God*. Our being created in the *image of God*, like *God*, allows *Jesus* to say "I Am" and truly be *one* with *God* in *Eucharist* and in *community* as *God* wants us all to be here on earth and forever. Modern ideological thinking has me concerned over the delusions *Pope Benedict XVI* is having in selectively focusing on the past. He is disregarding *God's* unilaterally performed *New Covenant*, which intends to benefit all the *People of God*, as though this *God*-made relationship does not exist. He believes he is "infallible" in holding this disputable view and, as *Pope*, bound to maintain his *church* like a monarch ruling *God's Kingdom*. Actually, *God's* distrustful people wanted a monarchy as evidenced before *Saul's* appointment in *Old Testament* times. Again, contrary to *God's* wishes (Hos 8:4), in the face of *Christ's* orders, to not rule as Gentiles do, the *Roman Catholic Church* maintains itself as a monarchy with the *Pope* claiming rule by divine rights. The *Pope* rules actually by personal choice, which rule can be changed in peaceful ways, says *Hans Küng*.

The *Imprimatur*, which all *Catholics* are taught to obey by *church* teachings, is a sensitive subject for me at the moment. *Catholics* are not to read any book or writing not imprinted with the *Imprimatur*. This censors effectively many *Catholics* from reading my books, expressing a layman's concerns, on matters which affect the good of the *church* in fulfilling its mission for the life of the world. My freedom to express concerns for the *New Covenant*, its call for *Eucharist* in context of the *church's* mission, is denied me and everyone else. It plainly denies us freedoms of expression, press, and conscience in respect to the book you are reading. Since I am "obliged" by our *Dogmatic Constitution* to competently and correctly express my concerns to my Spiritual Leader, when he refuses to respond to them or my request for my books' *Imprimatur*, *Pope Benedict XVI* has effectively denied me freedom of speech and press. Also my *constitutional* right, No. 37, of *Lumen Gentium* is being violated illegitimately. Over three hundred letters, many of which are those attached to this book, were mailed or hand-delivered to *Pope Benedict XVI* over the years while he denied me my civil rights. He "illegitimately" (his words to the *UN*) denied me *God*-given or *Dogmatic Constitutional* civil rights by disdaining to do his charitable duty. Ignored by the *church* I publicly referred the letters, by attachment of copies to published books, *God's Gift To You* and *God's Gift To You: A Sequel*. The books are *online* and lodged in the *Library of Congress*. However, due to the oppressive silence and deliberate refusal of the *Imprimatur* by *Pope Benedict XVI,* our *Pope* censored them to keep dumb down *Catholics* from being enlightened by my books. The *People of God*, meaning everyone created by *God* and members of the global *Church of Christ*, are all victimized by censorship of this book by our *church's* leaders. These denials of freedoms of press, speech, and conscience should be challenged by all *people of God*, especially in the *United States*, because it is an illegitimate exercise of power that *Christ* cautioned against and a violation of basic civil rights, incontestable rights in the *United States*, and of charity. The worse of it prevents fraternal correction because dumbed down *Church* leaders will continue to ignore *Jesus's* words that we are to love each other, serve each other, and lord over no one because the *Kingdom* acknowledges *God's* reign alone according to the *New Covenant*. Notable is the ability of users of *Internet* to avoid *Imprimatur* censorship and exercise rights to speech, press, and religion, a capability *God* may be waiting for us to use.

This *Holy Thursday* of 2012, *Pope Benedict XVI* denounced a group of three hundred *Austrian* priests for calling parishes to celebrate *Eucharist* services without priests and for publicly criticizing celibacy and speaking up for female and married priests. In homily, the *Pope* argued "*Jesus* followed true obedience to *God's* will not 'human caprice.'" We have a saying of "the pot calling the kettle black." Obviously, disobedience and threatening schism are measures to get the *Vatican's* attention. I beg the *US Bishops* and the *people of God* to obey *God's* will and not "traditions' human caprice," or the *Pope's* delusion. Instead, be obedient *Christ*-like in an *American* way. The *Internet* is a *Godsent*, to avoid the *Catholic church's* censorship, and proclaim God's gospel by those computer literate with modern methods.

America, the idea of it, was ably taught *Vatican II* in the teaching of *US Catholic Bishops*, who educated the members of the *Second Vatican Council* with the unique thinking of our *Founding Fathers* and contributed to the openness of the members, suggesting the global *Church of Christ*. The *council* was impressed with our principles of equality and freedom, but the entrenched *Curia* and succeeding *Popes* were not. I submit that the *United States* bishops today can be more *Christ-like* than those in *Rome* who misrule us, ignoring *Vatican II*. Unfortunately, our bishops are selected by and subjected to *Rome's* rulers to be distrusted. *Roman Catholics* support today a militant church monarchy out of misguided obedience to a hierarchy possessed of paranoia to the *Pope John XXIII* ideal. *Catholicism*, obscured by the *Gospel According to John*, listened to the likes of *Constantine* and *Augustine*, to maintain the wrong church up to *Vatican II* and reverted to it on *Pope John's* death. *United States'* citizenry, *Catholics* included, ought to follow our revolutionist founders, avoiding fanaticism, self-alienation, and human degradation in churches' actions, to confront *Antichrist* principles based on *church* militancy that our founders experienced in

Europe. Religious liberty became our first freedom and First Amendment right to freedom of conscience. *Democratic* principles assigned in *Christ's* last words, based on the *New Covenant* and *Golden Rule,* have been delayed, for two millenniums, but *Democracy* constantly reawakens them. Our democracy spread to *Europe*, where *France's Revolution* for civil rights ran amok. Later, monarchists of *Russia* and also *Europe* restrained democracy so harshly that *Marxism* and *Fascism* appeared attractive. The *Catholic* hierarchy remained traditionally, monarchist, and it sided with fascists shamefully. After *WWII America* became the world's accepted power supporting democracy, capitalism, and modernism. Its success in the world market place prompted students in *China* to study the reason why, and they concluded that the *Christian* element of fair play was enriching the West's capitalist democracies. Modern media had *English* become the language of business, and those like the *Beatles* utilized the media to flood world societies with our culture. *Vatican II's* global *Church of Christ* was a timely suggested idea to open to its membership, every human baptized in the *Blood of the Covenant*, with an inclusive *Eucharist*, and a *God* to human relationship timely staged for our human evolution. Modern *Christology* appears dormant in the hearts and minds of our *US Bishops,* but social media calls them to do the duty *Australian Bishop's* show and suggests. *The light of the people* should have kept them awake to see *God's* brilliance evidenced in

God's Covenant plan, in *Jesus* fulfilling the *new and eternal covenant* and make them the *Second Vatican Council's* ideal of one *global Church of Christ*. *God's* brilliant plan has always been negated by fearful men who felt it was too unreal for their comfort. The *United States'* founding father *Thomas Jefferson's* idea that each generation was to be free of past made laws met with similar lack of faith and so *James Madison* brought us down to earth with a *constitution* of laws. However, in *God's* plan *God*, and not law, is constantly with us in *Eucharist* and conscience to maintain the *New Covenant* to benefit everyone without needing traditional constitutions, laws, or kings to rule us. *Americans* may prove to be more *Christian* than *Christian Churches* and be called to apply *God's Covenant* in a global *Church* or society conforming to both *God's* way and an *American* way of freedom while still being ruled by *God's* law.

Building a *Church of Christ* establishment is problematical; for example, the *Roman Catholic Church* monarchy is sitting as a dog in the manger, not distributing *Eucharist* or teaching *God's New Covenant*. The shining promise of *America* as the democracy to copy may be handicapped by our monarchial *Church* and an influencing "plutocracy" weakening democracy. "Plutocracy" is a political phenomenon that the *Roman Catholic Church* is well experienced in dealing with in world matters. The largest donors of money to the *Vatican* are the *Bishops* of *America* and *Germany*. *America* donates its alms with no strings attached, but the *Germans* have insisted on having a say in the use of their donations. It has been said that the *German* influence on the motherland from *Latin America* has persuaded the *German Bishops* to pull strings in the *Vatican* and allow them greater representation than other *Catholics* in the *Papacy*. Also, in the *United States* money interests, and *Catholic Bishops* lobby to disadvantage the ordinary citizen's influence. The "Liberation Theology" movement silencing of *Leonardo Boff* is relevant evidence of how *Cardinal Joseph Ratzinger* delivered favor to *Germany*, not because *Boff's* "Liberation Theology" was a threat to *Catholicism*, nor because of its *Marxist* communist appearance, but because it was seen by those in power in *Latin America's* conservative governments to be a threat to their wellbeing. The *Church of God* must not rule, separate from *God*, certainly not like the *Gentiles* in *Jesus's* time. It will be endangered and susceptible to money interests or "plutocracy" regimes, which pay and have an unfair say to risk any democracy or representative society. *Germany's* success economically and politically today concern others in the world who see power ruling our societies and threatening our democratic free markets and civil rights. We see *Germany* threatening *Greece*, *Spain*, and so on, in *Europe's* free market because money power speaks, and *Germany* rules to gain an unfair say in who is free to market. Thus, we see might in action evidencing power corrupts democratic communities.

Adam Smith's book *The Wealth of Nations* was a work of art by an economist, but he was also a moral philosophist, and he warned us of the successful capitalists. We are aware of the *United States'* economic and democratic vulnerability in history and know of ups and downs in our past. However, we as a nation proclaim "In God we trust" because *God* pledges to free us to live with freedom to act, while we evolve from *Alpha* to *Omega*, until we are all *one* with *God* forever. *God* decides we humans are to be forever with *God*, even while we sin until then, because *God* made us to so be. *God* loves creation, just as *God* observes us struggling toward *God* every day, and leaves us to live trustingly.

Anthropologist *William A. Douglas of the University of Nevada Basque Studies* (and far more competent to write of *Basques* than I) wrote of the problem for *Basques* in their *American* diaspora retaining their ethnicity in an ever evolving humanity that likely will plunge these *Basques* into historical oblivion in a matter of generations. He contemplates, with the age of the *Internet* and further technological advances a day in which each individual may be taught by a personal computer in his own residence and, from there, have access to the world's store of knowledge. The anthropologist *Douglas* suggests that each *Basque-American* construct his or her own desired "information superhighway" to preserve their way of life that unfortunately for *Basque Americans* is destined to end. Based on some of his thoughts, I think it is now possible to speculate that each human may use the same methodology to hasten becoming *one* people of the *Church of God* (heretofore called *Church of Christ*). Being computer illiterate, I defer to *Professor Douglas* on visiting neighbors on laptops. Since it makes no record, each age can renew the *church* to fit more *God's* will as we evolve to be more *God-like* and correct traditions or laws that oppressively impose on our evolution. The *people of God* can use the professor's advice to reintroduce and reinforce their faith in *God's New and Eternal Covenant* by modern means, of dialogue, be secured with *God's* actual presence in *Eucharist* but subject to renewal with *God* alone as our benevolent ruler in each more advanced generation. To fulfill the entire construct, I would suggest we consider sharing *Holy Communion* often in a global *Church of God* that gathers on air in *Spirit*. Thus, we share *God's real presence* intimately in *Eucharist* without intimidation from cathedrals, synagogues, churches, mosques, or temples. With only *God's Spirit* presiding, we may better be realizing and appreciating *God* is definitely with us. All of this attempted, however, without the essential ingredient of charity may not assure *God*, or "the force," as *Professor Douglas* would say, will be with us. We should do it *God's* way in *Christ*, as *God* blueprinted for us millenniums ago, a universal *Eucharist* practice that we have never tried yet, trusting that *God* knows what is best. The permanence of the *Church's* rule by law is oppressive to "many" *Christ* freed. We now have a *Pope* who feels he can do no wrong and, though deluded, expects to be obeyed by his people, views the past to see the will of *God*, and is convinced that *Christians* are and can only be "fully" present in the *Roman Catholic Church*. Instead, let us try the relationship of *God's covenant* and *Christ's* democracy, in the *Church of God* as *God* and *Jesus Christ* suggested by committing ourselves to serve *God* (not church) and humankind like *Jesus* demonstrated in the sacrifice of the *Cross* at *Mass*.

Social media is having a major influential impact throughout the world, and it should be here used to reveal *God's* wishes for all humanity in *God's Covenant* relationship established by *Christ's Cross*. It has become the communications technology of choice and a strategic means for revolutions against oppressive powers. Proclaiming the "Gospel before the Gospel" appears to be an immediate mission we are called to perform, assuming the established faiths have obviously failed in their mission, and with *God,* we can remedy the wrongdoing. It is a means to instantly move the feelings of large numbers of people on earth, in ways never possible before. It can lead to a worldwide coordination of The *People of God*, meaning everyone created, causing movement toward a global united democracy, no longer church and government separated except by the law of charity that would avoid established interests or religious controls. Social media can take advantage of the circumstances today to allow the common *people of God*, a global voice, to challenge established traditional religions, and return the *Church of God* to *God* and its roots. *God's New Covenant kingdom* or *community* serving and ruling benevolently all people created under one king, *God Almighty*, should also be everyone's democracy.

It is very difficult to influence the world, and that's always been the case because of our free wills and our self-interests. *God* wisely created the world, using gradual evolution to improve our lot, as we learned from *Darwin* only yesterday. The best of *God's* ingenuity in human politics is the democracy of *Athens*, of the *Basques,* and of the *United States of America* showing that *God's* law of love imprinted in common people proves that equality with fraternity work in a *God*-trusting and loving people. *America* is what the world looks to today for order on *Earth* and certainly not the *Roman Church's* monarchy. Democratic forces in *Europe* are working, but autocratic leaders like *Fascist* and *Marxian Communist* exist too. All civilized people have something to offer—our right to love and serve each other. Since *WWII* the *United States* became the leader of the world largely because it respects other autonomies. *God's* people listen to others outside of their societies and make demands we see when genocides and crimes against human dignity erupt about. Unfortunately, police powers seem needed to help save people from places like *Camp 14*. I suggest the knowledge of *God's* law imprinted in everyone's hearts, activated by our loving each other virtually, is what is calling out to us in the *United States*. I assume the civilized world must self-discipline itself to cure the delusions that result in genocides and concentration camps. *American* individuals hear *God's* callings to unite the world in *God's Commandment* of loving our neighbor, and we contribute a united peace force to remedy conditions such as the one that harmed *Shin*. *Democracies* have declined in *Russia* thanks to the likes of *Putin,* but the influence of the *United States* and *Russians* experiencing freedom makes all people convertible as *People of God*. Like *Shin* their love, imprinted by *God*, will grow from experiencing love. Recently, *Robert Kazan* wrote *The World America Made* and disputes statements that the *US* influence is in decline. He argues, in essay form, how unique our democracy and philosophy are that helps make capitalism the most widespread economic theory in history. He may be right. Since we owe *China* trillions of dollars in debt, we continue open trade with *China* because *China* trusts our stability and fairness to be willing to deal with us monetarily. *Chinese* scholars' extensively studied years ago the success of the *United States* in world markets and attributed it to the fairness of *Christianity* in the market place. *America* helps *China* today because it is to our and the worlds interest to continue to cooperate toward unity in the future that we gamble on to be profitable. *China* still has a problem with exploiting its people and is concerned with the might of the *United States'* police powers especially its nuclear capabilities, but the *United States* keeps *China's* neighbors comfortable so long as the *United States* holds power and keeps watch. *Germany* had a similar discomfort with neighbors before *WWII* and went to war for relief, but *China* knows that history and so far respects it. Today is a good time for social media to enlighten *China* with advantages of *Christianity* and democracy. *Communist China* is living with both and will conform but in a *Chinese* way. It will be difficult to influence the world as *God* knows well, but we have the means, the message, and *God* is with us, or, to atheists, the force is with us to fulfill the *Kingdom of God* on earth, together, in democratic ways and *Christ*-like relationships, someday in our future on earth.

Human attitudes about particular relationships with *God* and with humankind differ, but we are to be *one* in *God's Image*, in a global *community* on earth and perfectly so later in *Heaven* from where we all began. The thought *of Christ* in his passion, death, and resurrection should be constantly with us until then. People ought for *Christ*, even with the foolishness of the *Cross*, because the foolishness of the *Cross* reveals the essence of loving as *Jesus*, the ordinary human demonstrated, in a way we can appreciate. The *Sign* for this evil age is the love shown by this man in the paschal mystery of his *Cross* and resurrection, and the peace *Jesus* depicts that we are *God's people*, struggling to be better yet. When *Jesus our Lord* exists interiorly within me at *Eucharist*,

I sometimes want to share with everyone his *love* to the extent that *God* will help me communicate it. Rest assured that *God* pledges that each of us are to be happy with *God* forever, and while we suffer life, we should trust that *God's* love is with us and is bringing us to good, to *God*, no matter what we experience. Experience often *God's Eucharist*: To secure our trust, *God* gave us *Jesus Christ* to publicly sacrifice himself for us and expressly authenticate the *New Covenant* as true, by demonstrably incorporating it for us daily in *Jesus's* bleeding death on the *Cross*. He secures *God's Covenant* by being the blood sacrifice as was the ram in *Abraham's* sacrifice and the *Lamb of God* bearing our imperfections. *God*, being our *God of love*, has sacrificed *Jesus* so excruciatingly, however, as to grab our attention and persuade us to love *God* and each other because of *Jesus's* love, a language understandable to us. So at *Mass,* you should appreciate the "Sacrrifice of the *Cross*" being continuously present and ask *God* to awaken you to *Christ's* love. With the *Eucharist* we consume, pray detached from seeking comprehension of *God* within you, and focus on *Jesus's* passion and *cross*. I think *Jesus* loving us and having *God* within us, awakening us to this love, urges us to love others. It may cause me to write as I do more because of what *Jesus* did and does than to make me feel good. To best communicate what I experience, I invite each and every one of you to try *Communion* and consume *God's real presence* by simply taking and eating the bit of bread or sipping of the cup of wine in a *Roman Catholic Church's Eucharist*, or if you rather share *Holy Communion* elsewhere, do it to experience *God* within you. In all likelihood, you will perceive nothing. *Mother Teresa's* claim comes to mind. She said her nuns could not labor as they did in the slums of *Calcutta* without having received *God's real presence* in *Eucharist* each morning. *Pope Benedict XVI* concedes (*NCR*, 5/10/12) it is precisely the *Eucharist* that impels *Catholics* to service the poor and the needy. These experts' opinions persuade me to write, even though I accept them on faith, to help me when writing to trust that I cause no harm. They free me to infer what *Christ* demonstrated on the *cross* on how we are to love *God* and human beings created by *God*. We are all brothers and sisters in *Christ*, baptized in the blood of the paschal mystery of his crucifixion and resurrection. Thereby *Jesus* fulfilled *God's* performance of the *New Covenant* and saved every one of us for everlasting life and love with *God*. Interrelated with his death, *Jesus* instituted the *Eucharist* to have the Sacrifice of the *Cross* continuously remind us of him and teach us that *God* makes *God's Real Presence* to be within us to nourish us and transform us to love each other. *Jesus*, thus, is a model for us to obey God's law of love, imprinted in us, to love and serve *God* and everyone living on earth.

Today the *United States* seemingly takes the advice of *Jesus* and is an "empire of influence" in exercising its police powers in cooperation with the *United Nations*. Still the *Second Vatican Council's* suggestion of a global *Church of Christ* is impliedly built on the *Kingdom of God* ruled by *God* alone and according to *God's* law of love. *God's New Covenant* deal had *Jesus* establish, a democratic relationship wherein *God* gives everyone daily nourishment to fuel their minds and hearts. What *God* intended, however, was never tried by mankind. *Cardinal John Henry Newman* converted to the *Roman Catholic Church* and thought there was nothing on earth as beautiful and as ugly as the *Catholic church*. He probably suffered the meanness of our nondemocratic institution toward any who did not fully agree with its law. I suffered the traditional ugliness in the oppressive silence to my correspondence. However, I too love the beauty in my *Roman Catholic Church,* which I became habituated to accept on faith most of my life. Some injustices are ugly, but they need not be if *Pope Benedict* would change his mind and heart to return to the ways he saw wrong in 1968 and conform the institution to the essence of the *Church of Christ*. It is going to take a jolt like *Christ* dealt *Saul*, I think, but, then again, it may be too late, and *God* may want other people better instilled with knowledge of *God's* law of love, to try to do what *Jesus* suggested as "penance" for *God's People* to serve. To date, we have accomplished little affirmative in the way *Jesus* advised to reciprocate for what *God* did for us. In enjoying the peace of awareness that *God* loves us and always will, we are free to serve *God* and others lovingly as we make our *Church of God* a sign of unity and an instrument of peace among all people. *Jesus* did his part, when he persevered and died seemingly accomplishing little. But when he gave up his spirit "Father into your hands," *Jesus* did all he could do before he breathed his last. At that instance, *God* glorified *Jesus*, and, as *God* planned from the beginning of creation, the human creatures *God* made with free will and self-interests to soil themselves, *God* perfected and pardoned in the *Blood of the Covenant*.

I began writing *Pope Benedict XVI* when I became aware that he was the prime resistor to *Vatican II's New Testament* scholars and theologians' criticism of our exclusive *Eucharist* and contentions that *God* meant for an inclusive one. While in that one-way correspondence, I was awakened to our anti-*God* inattention to the *New and Eternal Covenant* by every *Christian*, *Jew*, *Moslem,* and human being *God* simply out of goodness solely saves to be one with *God* forever. *God* implies people need no further teaching than what *God* furnishes, and the teachers plainly include the likes of me because: "No longer will they have need to teach . . . all from the least to greatest shall know me, says the LORD for I will forgive their evildoing and remember their sin no more."

LETTERS TO POPE BENEDICT

January 3, 2011

Dear Holy Father,

My diocese promulgated in 2006 our Diocesan Statutes of the Third Diocesan Synod, which artfully established, obedience to Vatican working documents an exclusive Eucharist, a dogma of mere human precepts excluding non-Catholics from our Lord's Supper. The Third Diocesan Synod was likely a Synod of pre-stacked and selected bishops to whom the Vatican working documents trustfully dictated not to invite non-Catholics to share the Eucharist. Likely, our Bishop William Wiegand was in attendance and obediently agreed to cling to the church's exclusive Eucharist without analyzing God's wishes. The Vatican did his thinking, and he obeyed without questioning its fallibility.

Once this gnat of a law was squeezed out to control everyone in our dioceses, you released the uncharitable exhortation *Sacramentum Caritatis* in 2007, as "The Sacrament of Charity." A misnomer of a title, to say the least, it disregards God's commandment of loving others impartially to excommunicate most everybody. Jesus prophesied, "You have made a fine art of setting aside God's commandment in the interests of keeping your traditions." (Mk 7:1-13.)

Copies of your letters are sent to my spiritual shepherd in the Diocese of Sacramento with the hope my diocese's bishop, his predecessors, and the theologians might dialogue the matter of the Eucharist. I personally handed Diocesan Bishop Jaime Soto my business card, and he led me to hope that I would receive from his office an appointment to discuss my concerns. His predecessor had written me in August 2007 that I was simply incorrect in analysis and was in need of "obedience of faith" to the teaching of the church. I do not see where my analysis is incorrect, although I do concede my obedience to my informed conscience and the teachings of *our Lord* on the subject matter overrules the church's teachings. Even your own teachings and preachings, the incorrect analysis of which, should be discussed openly so "the whole Church . . . may more effectively fulfill its mission for the life of the world" (see No. 37 of *Dogmatic Constitution on the Church*). Rather than a blind faith to "obedience in faith" in accepting the church's traditional Eucharist, the laity are expressly obligated to express concerns and vest each of us the right to be heard, a "constitutional" right to be heard, and considered with fatherly advice.

At minimum, do you not agree I should discuss with my diocesan bishops, Most Reverend Soto, or he and his predecessors Most Reverends Wiegand and Quinn, the specifics of how my analysis on the subject is incorrect?

Sincerely,

January 4, 2011

Dear Holy Father,

My letters' monologue started at the beginning of 2006 expressing concerns of the church's exclusive Eucharist. My opinions on the subject were addressed mainly to you because much of my informed opinions were based on your expressed teachings. I sought to confirm my analysis by your fatherly analysis but never succeeded to receive an answer from you. So my analysis suffers.

I have conjectured what you might have said occasionally in response to my writings. You previously acknowledged that the Vatican II's ideals global church and Eucharist implies that Holy Communion cannot be conditional on anything and must be open to everybody according to our New Testament scholars' "tempting" opinions. Although your scriptural translation differed you did not declare dogma as Pope Benedict XVI to oppose their precepts. Instead, you declared the "final judgment on these matters belongs to diocesan bishops" (see *Sacramentum Caritatis*). Yet, you still teach that it is our own conscience that must be obeyed before any ecclesial authority rules. What God has imprinted in every human's heart and mind is God's law of love for which God's covenant cautions we are to listen to no other teacher.

You taught me that Jesus Christ's death is linked to God's new covenant. Also I learned from you that the words instituting the Eucharist are "interdependent" with Christ's universal death, redeeming all human beings and all who are in covenant relationship with Christ as Paul was told from Heaven to be the fact (1 Cor 11:23-26). The death's universality gives meaning to the Eucharist that is universal. This is our God-given truth and but for misguided Christians who listen to other righteous men, rather than God, our Communion would include everyone and not only Catholics or only Christians.

I have come to appreciate your dilemma. Since Jesus did not found the Catholic church, you believe it is a creation of the Holy Spirit built on Christ's earthly works. You give great credit to the Church's tradition on maintaining its exclusive Eucharist as exclusive for those reconciled to traditional rules because of the Spirit's influence. Although God left man to the freedom of conscience, God's law of love, and the only order made by God, through Jesus, was to consume Eucharist, the only exchange God insists upon is that we take and eat but not all because some are worthier than others. However, if God unilaterally performs the new covenant relationship with us God alone teaches and forgives us all in Christ, to save every human created. But the Eucharist required the exchange on our part only to consume to perfect our spirits made more God like in shared Communion, all as God's doing.

We who continue evildoing to the end of life are saved by the blood of the covenant as are those who do not obey Christ's Eucharist order are saved for the hereafter, and, then, judged for excuse or justification to mitigate chastising delays of our eternity to be with God.

Sincerely,

January 7, 2011

Dear Holy Father,

I find myself shying from attending bible studies where I will likely express my opinions against your exclusive Eucharist or your disregard of the new covenant relationship that God meant for everyone's enjoyment. I fear a millstone may await me for causing the loss of faith of any of my fellow students. Since *our Lord* has allowed the church's traditional Eucharist to exclude so many for so long, except for those moments of the Second Vatican Council, who am I to criticize the way faith of others accept religion. Besides, suppose I was successful and convinced the world, other than Pope Benedict XVI, that all peoples must be invited to the LORD's supper—Who would I have to prepare or serve Eucharist if not his Catholic priests?

Presently, *our Lord* has many Catholics faithful to their church receiving the Eucharist. But, in two millenniums, Catholicism's practice of self-absorbed evangelizing has made little progress in extending Christ to the world. God intends that all the world's many people receive Jesus Christ's Eucharist and be transformed thereby. Thus, God offers a new covenant relationship with Eucharist to perfect everyone's conscience to possess God's law of love and share Communion. God purifies everyone's soul in the blood of the covenant regardless of the Eucharist but perfects us in love thereby, sharing Eucharist, to carry the Gospel message of Communion to everyone.

To perfect all people, God's inclusive Eucharist remains as God's preferred formal way of worship and God's means to teach and transform us all. It is in communion of the Catholic rank-and-file believers that we experience in the *United States* improvement in our lives causing us to keep coming back for replenishment as distinguished from the dysfunctional "Church" of Vatican, Bishops, and its uncharitable dogmas of human precepts. (See *United States Today*, 1/3/2011.) Roughly 60 percent of Catholics have left the church—en masse, and, it is suggested to stem the flow the Vatican should conform to the democratic values it espouses to serve and not lord over others as Christ cautioned. The church will always have something unique to offer—the real presence, unless it continues to uncharitably appropriate it for good Catholics only.

Yours in Christ,

January 10, 2011

Dear Holy Father,

Another attorney, later known as St. Ambrose, gave us the form of the Eucharist we have today, except that Vatican II dropped the Latin. He was graced in stating the Eucharist's origin "of the new and everlasting covenant." Of course, he quotes Jesus referral to God's covenant of *Jeremiah* 31:31ff. (see *Lumen Gentium*, No. 9) wherein God forgives all our evildoing and redeems all humans (1 Cor 11:23-26). Consequently, Ambrose often received Holy Communion because he admittedly sinned often. Also, Ambrose was not baptized until he was appointed Milan's Bishop and until then still received Communion.

The New Testament scholars after Vatican II informed the world, in effect, that Ambrose's form of Eucharist conformed to the design of Christ's unconditional open Eucharist.

Your mentor, St. Augustine, however, contradicted both Christ and Ambrose, perhaps fueled by the heat of argument with the Irish monk, Pelagius. Augustine disregarded God's new covenant and concocted original sin as his scripture translation. As a result, he uncharitably excommunicated Pelagius and almost everyone to hell who were not baptized in the Catholic church. The Popes that succeeded John XXIII follow Augustine's fabricated theory and cling to an exclusive Eucharist that is neither the product of Ambrose nor that of *our Lord*.

Might this reminder cause you to switch from church's traditions, infallible though they claim to be, and direct your diocesan bishops to return the Eucharist of Christ to the one also espoused by Saint Ambrose?

Yours in Christ,

January 13, 2011

Dear Holy Father,

Angels announced joy to the sheepherders and the world on Jesus coming. And on his parting, he again left joy to all of us. However, you and the church teach a message of grief to almost everyone because they do not "let themselves be reconciled by God" (*God Is Near Us*, p. 60) or fail to "believe in Christ" (*Lumen Gentium*, No. 9, p. 18) and are, thus, denied the real presence.

Consequently, I am not that "obedient in faith" to the teaching of the church, as my diocesan bishop wrote. As a result, he wrote that my "analysis is incorrect," in my concern for the Eucharist. However, as simplified my logical analysis would breakdown to the following calculation: God pledged to God's people, in days to come, to unilaterally teach all of them and forgive all their evildoing forever (Jer 31). Four centuries later God unilaterally performed this covenant in the death of Jesus to benefit all people created by God (1 Cor 11:23-26). Therefore, God performs God's covenant of salvation for everyone, including the unreconciled and nonbelievers, because

God so loves us as we are created to be with God forever.

I respectfully submit that my spiritual leaders need the virtue of charity to analyze scripture and to be "obedient in faith" to the teachings of God. They should realize their exclusive Eucharist is uncharitable and blatantly negates the scriptural evidence of God's saving action and purpose for Holy Communion.

Yours in Christ,

January 14, 2011

Dear Holy Father,

Hitler and his followers' evildoings toward those harmed in the Holocaust are forgiven by God in the blood of the covenant. Each of them is saved by God's unilateral performance of the new covenant (Jer 31). Still each will answer to Jesus Christ hereafter and be chastised probably to perfect each one to be more Christ like to be with God forever.

Assuming the scriptural dispensation is true, God must "remember their sin no more" (Jer 31:34). Consider the perfected Hitler in heaven, experiencing the Beatific Vision. Might he be tormented by a memory or a guilty conscience that he cannot forget for eternity?

Visualizing your own future, you know you can avoid any future similar chastisement and torment by ordering the Catholic church's Eucharist to be more charitable and open to everyone. The reasonable thing to do is be "obedient in faith," as my bishop wrote me, but to God's teachings and furnish a charitable inclusive sacrament. (See your doctoral dissertation.)

Yours in Christ,

January 17, 2011

Dear Holy Father,

I was obliged to express my opinion on those things that concerned the exclusive Eucharist for the good of the church. The suggestions that Hitler has remorse in heaven and you, too, might be sorry for your Eucharist calls for you to consider my proposed suggestions with fatherly advice and love. Our *Dogmatic Constitution on the Church* (*Lumen Gentium*), at part 37, entitles me to your response and, hopefully, dialogue "In this way, the whole Church, strengthened by each one of its members, may more effectively fulfill its mission for the life of the world" (*Infra*, p. 66).

However, God being love has presumably solved anyone suffering remorse in heaven for any evildoing done on earth. Those of the hierarchy of the Catholic church involved in harming billions, excluded from the Eucharist, will be awakened to the evil done and also be relieved by God's love somehow. Yesterday's reading (Heb 5:1-10) expressed an opinion that Christ, in the flesh, learned obedience throughout his continued sufferings to become perfect in dying to save us.

Pope Benedict, too, while alive, must keep trying to perfect himself in obedience to God's teaching and share the Eucharist. Should he artfully continue to support an exclusive Eucharist, for centuries to come he may harm many deprived people. Then, after he no longer is in the flesh, he for eternity will likely be together with *our Lord* God, Father, and Son. He will respond to their inquiries of why did he deny so many the real presence and deprive God and God's creation of love. What will he say?

Yours in Christ,

January 21, 2011

Dear Holy Father,

Freedom in the *United States* allowed us to practice hateful discrimination against our native Americans, against our African Americans, and others who were different from us. However, we try in time to love our neighbors as God urges us to do. This is likely due to the laws God puts in our hearts and writes on our minds (Heb 10:16).

We, who read, know our history and appreciate that we can do good and do evil with or without any religion's rule. The Chinese philosopher Mencus, like Pelagius, the Irish Monk of the Church of Christ, thought man is innately good. Mencus argued that if anyone saw a child falling into a well, he would impulsively feel for the child, and his commiseration proves mankind's inherent goodness. Pelagius might have attributed man's goodness to the laws of love God imprints in our conscience (Jer 31:31-34) by the new covenant's performance.

God created us to survive on earth, and the fit survive by bettering the less fit. God created us self-lovingly to survive death and later recreated us to love each other as Jesus demonstrated at the end of his life. Christians succeeded best in the world's standards by loving as evidenced in the *United States*' success over those nations of the East and Mideast according to a twenty-year study by Chinese scholars. Vatican II's Pope John and his gathered bishops, after restraining the Curia from interference, found God meant for one global Church of Christ. Their theologians and the New Testament scholars in obedience to the Council's spirit criticized the Catholic church's exclusive Eucharist. You yourself contended that the Last Supper words instituting the Eucharist were explained by the death of Jesus (*God Is Near* Us, p. 29); thus, God's presence constantly redeems the world. Jesus's words in our continuing *Lord*'s supper repeat the fact that the death proclaimed each time we consume his flesh is in context of the new covenant (Jer 31) extended to everyone by Jesus Christ (1 Cor 11:23-6).

By appropriating God's gift of Eucharist, the church negates evidence of God's salvation and denies it to most everybody in the world. In negating the evidence of God's saving action, being a unilateral performance of God of the new covenant, and assigning salvation to Catholics, makes it an anti-God principle and a blasphemy (see footnote Mt 12:31ff. of The New American Bible). You would not answer my concerns, but you will answer *our Lord*'s inquiries.

Yours in Christ,

January 25, 2011

Dear Holy Father,

Sunday on TV, I enjoyed an interview of Christopher Hitchens who is a terminal cancer victim, stage four, and is reporting his dying symptoms for the benefit of posterity. Mr. Hitchens is known for his bohemian lifestyle and open expression of convictions. For example, Christianity's compulsory love causes his dislike of our faith, and he believes abortion would relieve the poverty that Mother Teresa's mission encounters.

Monday at mass, the opening antiphon prayed about the wisdom of a just man: "The law of his God is in his heart and his steps did not falter" (Ps 37:31). It put me in mind of the outspoken Hitchens who appears not aware and does not appreciate that the love for others he has imprinted in him, to walk the talk that we Christians espouse, is by instinct from God (see Jer 31:31-34) as performed by Christ (see 1 Cor 11:23-26).

Had I his mailing address, I would send a copy of this letter to Mr. Hitchens for whatever reflection he might make. A more effective means would have been God's invitation for him to consume the Eucharist so that God's interior presence might transform the law of God written on his heart from conception that compels his compassionate work for the benefit of all of us. Unfortunately, our

Catholic church has denied him God's way of redemption.

Sincerely,

January 28, 2011

Dear Holy Father,

I read in *NCR* (1/21/11) that you agree with St. Catherine of Genoa that God's plan of creation is to have us sinners processed to be "worthy" to be with God forever. You describe a painful process of internal torment for one's sins, commonly called "purgatory." It timely, sounds like the chastisement sentences that *our Lord* Jesus Christ mercifully renders as our judge and advocate.

Probably you can find basis in tradition for your claim that "a soul stained by sin cannot present itself to God." I take issue with your argument because every one of us, present company included, are stained by our humanity. You and Catherine may be right traditionally. However, Jesus also taught us that he would eat with those stained by uncleanness from violating religious traditions, rather than violate God's law of charity (Mk 7:1-13).

Contemplating our unknown future, why don't you do God and everyone a favor and invite every person to the Lord's Supper regardless of traditional stains. *Our Lord* is big enough to want to be within the "bowels" of the worst of sinners. Your requirement that each of us must first let ourselves be reconciled by God (*God Is Near Us*, page 60) overlooks the fact that God has already accomplished everyone's reconciliation in the blood of the covenant. So give humanity the benefit of doubt and let God come unhampered to transform us by God's real presence for *love*'s sake. You may thus avoid purgatory and go straight to heaven by simply loving all of us. Just trust *our Lord* to love each one of us as God loves.

Yours in Christ,

February 4, 2011

Dear Holy Father,

Jesus prophesied how hierarchies would artfully negate God's law of love as a standard and cling to church's traditions (Mk 7:8). God demonstrates constantly God's love for us by unilaterally performing the new covenant. Pope John XXIII restrained and questioned the purpose of the curia in Vatican II. It allowed pope and bishops freedom to ressource God's love of all people, when Jesus incorporated the new covenant to relate to all people, without the curia's intervention. But on Pope John's untimely death, the curia was released to draft for Pope Paul VI's signature their forged covenant to our "*Dogmatic Constitution on the Church*" (*Lumen Gentium*), at Chapter II, No. 9, and claim only believers in Christ are saved.

Pope John XXIII and his bishops had concluded that God, in Christ, founded a global Church of Christ that included everyone created. Jesus expressly died, in the words of his last supper, to fulfill God's new covenant (Jer 31). The interdependent words and death instituted the first Eucharist to include all Jews and Gentiles (1 Cor 11:23-26). By terms of this covenant and these scriptural passages, God alone teaches us so we need no other teaching and forgives our evildoing so we need no contributing faith or good works to be saved. The Council's revelation of the global church and the performance by God alone of the new covenant is the good news that redeems us all and threatens the curia with unemployment.

What you repeatedly taught at Tübingen, of the words and actions of Jesus's last hours demonstrating Eucharist the first time, was not to form a select Church of righteous Catholics, a Church able to condemn anyone to perdition. Yet that is what the Catholic church attempts to do by clinging to age old traditions preserving the status quo of our hierarchy at the uncharitable expense of most everyone's wellbeing. The exclusive Eucharist that you so artfully establish through your diocesan bishops continues to deny your church True Church status. The Church of Christ cannot "subsist" in the Catholic church so long as it excludes most of God's people from the sacrament of love.

Yours fraternally,

February 7, 2011

Dear Holy Father,

Jesus presided at the first Eucharist and demonstrated how to memorialize it in revealing God's love for us in action and words proclaimed as God instructed him. He actually explained at supper his death was to perform God's new covenant to transform everyone, Jew and Gentile, whom God created to a new birth. Jesus, too, ordered us all as his Father instructs him to take and consume of his flesh in form of bread and wine to transform the life and faith of us as God intends.

Witness the fraud and forgery of our wise elite who drafted page 18 of *Lumen Gentium* (see attached) for Pope Paul VI's signature. It furnishes different terms of God's new covenant and ideas of Vatican II. Fraudulently, they support the traditional dogma of the church that only those who believe in Christ and are reborn not from flesh but water and the Holy Spirit (Jn 3:5-6) are the only redeemed. Thus, only the select Catholics are God's people, and all the others are damned. The boys in Rome are comforted by this wisdom of our religion, which needs their teachings and guidance to save the world, instead of God alone saving us as God pledged and Jesus performed.

Pope Benedict XVI once appreciated the ideal global Church of Christ which "subsists" in the Catholic church, a thought left by the council to be defined by popes together with bishops. Now the church elite alone, in their human wisdom, with your personal opinion, likely hold that the true church "both is and can only be, *fully* present in the Roman Church."

Understandably, when it came for you to judge the openness of the church's Eucharist, you opposed the claims of those New Testament scholars of Vatican II who insisted upon God's inclusive Eucharist, As Pope Benedict you artfully delegated the final judgment to less knowledgeable diocesan bishops after they were pre-instructed to cling to the traditional exclusive Eucharist. Consequently, the indoctrinated wisdom of bishops was combined with the biased wisdom of the boys in Rome, in conspiracy, to negate God's plan to save all human kind in the folly of the cross.

Heartfully yours,

Chapter II
On the People of God

9. At all times and in every race God has given welcome to whoever fears him and does what is right (cf. Acts 10:35). God, however, does not make men holy and save them merely as individuals, without bond or link between one another. Rather has it pleased him to bring men together as one people, a people which acknowledges him in truth and serves him in holiness. He therefore chose the race of Israel as a people unto himself. With it he set up a covenant. Step by step he taught and prepared this people, making known in its history both himself and the decree of his will and making it holy unto himself. All these things, however, were done by way of preparation and as a figure of that new and perfect covenant, which was to be ratified in Christ, and of that fuller revelation which was to be given through the Word of God himself made flesh. "Behold the days shall come says the Lord, and I will make a new covenant with the House of Israel, and with the house of Judah.... I will give my law in their bowels, and I will write it in their heart, and I will be their God, and they shall be my people.... For all of them shall know me, from the least of them even to the greatest, says the Lord" (Jer 31:31-34). Christ instituted this New Covenant, the New Testament, that is to say, in his Blood (cf. 1 Cor 11:25), calling together a people made up of Jew and Gentile, making them one, not according to the flesh but in the Spirit. This was to be the new People of God. For those who believe in Christ, who are reborn not from a perishable but from an imperishable seed

18

February 8, 2011

Dear Holy Father,

Jesus presided at the first Eucharist in thanksgiving to God for our creation and God's care for us as expressed in God's new covenant (Jer 31). The good news (gospel) Jesus tried to share, by means of his death on the cross and words at supper, was that God imprints in our hearts all we need know about God and lets us know God forgives all our evildoing because God loves us as we are.

Humans in their wisdom, however, cleverly ignore the love God manifests and God's law of love. Instead, they fabricate different relationships between God and us. Each Christian religion claims theirs to be favored by God and condemns nonmembers to perdition. The Roman Catholic Church is skilled in this art as is exemplified by its Dogmatic Constitutions' (No. 9) deceit, forgery, and fraudulent use of God's new covenant (Jer 31).

My acute concern is that people may be awakened to the *Lumen Gentium* blasphemy in our Constitution, uncharitably negating God's new covenant, to establish their own dogma that only believers in Christ and only those believers "reborn not from the flesh but from water and the Holy Spirit" (Jn 3:5-6) are saved.

I also fear the church's selection of the next pope. He likely won't be a John XXIII pope but more like his successors. Sadly, he won't be as learned as you nor have your experience of Pope John and his gathered bishops in conference, with the curia leashed, to freely resource our faith convictions. My concern is not that I will have less recognition by the next pope since I made little impact, if any, on your heart in spite of my many hundreds of letters mailed. But your centralizing power and damaging collegiality has strengthened the inner government of the church limitlessly. The Curia will secure its *status quo*.

Intriguing is the fact that ever since Jesus and St. Paul, God allowed mankind to obscure the new covenant's kingdom of God and replace it with their own church's traditional beliefs. Had we accepted the joy of being already saved by God's new covenant, the world might have evolved into loving each other so that peace on earth might have reigned over all peoples as God intended.

Sincerely,

February 9, 2011

Dear Editor,

I see that Fr. Donald Senior, C. P., is commercially advertising his book on the Fourth Gospel and still claiming it is as authoritative as those of the synoptic. The gospel does not mention the new covenant (see Jer 31:31-34) or the Eucharist in its words of the last supper, which Pope Benedict XVI says are interdependent in giving meaning to the words and death of Jesus redeeming humanity. (See 1 Cor 11:23-26.) The folly of the cross is what the Passionist Fathers focus upon. The wisdom of gospel writers, clever as they might be, is less familiar to them. Thus, the gospel, good news, Jesus proclaims in our first Eucharist sacrifice, which we brag about, is more the subject they should evaluate.

Your article *Indefensible* (2/11/11) claimed that living a morally upright life is essential for "salvation." The religions surrounding Jesus also contended the same indefensible claim as the Catholic church does today. But the good news proclaimed by Jesus, for which he expressly died, was that God alone saves us, "for I will forgive their evildoing, and remember their sin no more," and a morally upright life is not needed. By Jesus shedding the blood of the covenant, he performed God's pledges. Our only essential contribution to our salvation, and that of every human being, is that we exist as God's creation and God loves us as bad as we are.

Yours in Christ,

February 14, 2011

Dear Holy Father,

Our *Dogmatic Constitution on the Church* declares that we lay persons are "obliged" to express our opinion on those things which concern the church (citing in ftnt #7 Pius XII's quote "In decisive battles, it is sometimes at the front that the happiest initiatives originate").

My immediate concern is the "New Evangelization that you are contemplating for the World Synod of Bishops in 2012. Hopefully, my concerns for the whole church negating its mission for evangelizing the message that God, in Jesus Christ proclaimed, will be dispelled by your ressourcement to God's correct message Jesus left us from his death and interdependent words at supper. Jesus died to reveal God's new covenant, and Jesus revealed fulfillment of its objectives and which we proclaim at Mass daily in evangelizing God's new and everlasting gospel."

However, your silence to my extensive lettered concerns to date leaves me worrying that you and your fellow churchmen will continue to cling to human tradition of an exclusive Eucharist. Also, you all follow the *Antichrist* dictates of Pope Paul VI, and his supporting curia, who teach by the forgery of the new covenant and their reliance on human precepts of the Fourth Gospel that only believers in Christ are saved "not from the flesh, but from water and the Holy Spirit (cf. Jn 3:5-6)." According to you, we are saved by the baptism of John The Baptist and not solely by the blood of the covenant.

Lumen Gentium, No. 37, impliedly represented that dialogue on these concerns hopefully would occur. If I am wrong, tell me. But what if the point I make, that I believe is also what Jesus evangelizes as God's accomplishment, is the truth which you no longer need to try to improve upon?

Sincerely,

February 16, 2011

Dear Holy Father,

Last night I had a spontaneous dialogue with my pastor on the subject of taking the Eucharist to shut-ins. The booklet we are provided allows selections for "Reading of the Word." I had inserted copies of the new covenant (Jer 31:31-34) for my first reading and reporting the Eucharist is for everyone (1 Cor 11:23-26) for my second. The booklet furnishes its own sentimental Gospel (Jn 6:54-58). Recipients thus have the Gospel (good news) of the covenant that Jesus presented at his first and continuing Eucharist and the traditional Catholic one.

In our exchange, we also argued our respective opposing opinions on the openness of the Eucharist. We seemed to have agreed that our conscience is the ultimate tribunal, which must be obeyed on the choice. I am reminded of your agreement on choosing in *NCR* 4/14/06 asserting the authority of one's own conscience stands over the pope and ecclesiastical authority. Still, Father Francisco is obedient in faith to the teaching of the church and insists upon conforming to church rules regardless of my opinions.

I realized in the excitement of our argument that the new covenant, which Jesus died to perform, established God's pledge:

> "I will place my law within them, and write it upon their hearts,"

And, it is the source of God's commandment of love in every human person's conscience. Thus, the compassion we feel for the infant who falls into a well evidences the common feeling in all of us to love others as we do ourselves.

By the same unilateral performance by God of the new covenant, our evildoing is forgiven, and we are saved. Cleansed by God we are certainly worthy to receive Holy Communion simply for being created and loved by God.

Heartfully yours,

February 18, 2011

Dear Holy Father,

I did not mention that my pastor, Father Francisco, advised me to read the Bible to gain knowledge of why the Church's Eucharist is exclusive of many. I had argued that the meaning of the mystery of faith and cross were contained in God's new covenant (Jer 31:31) and Jesus performance of it for everybody (1 Cor 11:23-26). All the rest of the Bible is commentaries.

Father just does not agree, but, he's in good company with you and the bishop, too. I would respond to his advice by asking him to read again the passages I cite with an open heart for the wellbeing of the world. Also, remind him that at mass this morning, he led us to proclaim the mystery of faith, that read, in part, as follows: "When we eat this bread and drink this cup, we proclaim your death, Lord Jesus . . ." Note, by simply eating and drinking, alone, we proclaim God's constant new covenant benefits that are ours because God loves human creation.

My pastor as well as my diocesan bishop are likely unaware of your learned truths. For instance, "The true Church could not be founded on the exclusion of others." (*The New Yorker*, "Reading Ratzinger," 7/25/05); or respecting Jesus's Last Supper words: "we must regard them as being constantly guaranteed by the pledge of the blood that was his witness." (*God Is Near Us*, by Joseph Cardinal Ratzinger, p. 30.) You probably will be judged on misjudging the size of the mystical body (see 1 Cor 11:29) but still owe warning the other two of my Catholic leaders that I may be right in claiming the body as everyone.

Heartfully yours,

February 21, 2011

Dear Holy Father,

By copies of this letter, I am sharing your quoted statement by letter of Fr. Charles Finnegan, OFM, which was published in *NCR* 4/14/06, and recorded, at page 35, in my book *God's Gift To You*:

> Over the pope as the expression of the binding claim of ecclesiastical authority, there still stands one's own conscience, which must be obeyed before all else, even against the requirement of ecclesiastical authority. This emphasis on the individual, whose conscience confronts him with a supreme and ultimate tribunal, is one which in the last resort is beyond the claim even of the official church.

As spiritual shepherd of my bishops and pastor, who appear to be blindly obedient in faith to church's teachings and failings, you owe them truth. You have your opinions, conscientious as they are, that contradict Vatican II's Pope John XXIII and his gathered bishops, at times when the curia was restrained, and their theologians and New Testament Scholars were contending that God meant for the church's Eucharist to be all inclusive. You wrote *God Is Near Us* acknowledging the New Testament expert's opinions, criticizing the church's exclusive Eucharist, but you opposed them in part, as follows: "—however tempting the idea may be—it contradicts what we find in the Bible." I considered who "we" may be to include Pope John Paul II and the curia. I also believe the Bible has many opinions supporting many differences of views. The three items you submit in support, that is, Jn 13:10, 1 Cor 11:27 *ff* and Didache 10:6, I suggest, would gain a Bible scholar a failing grade at Tübingen.

Last week Father Francisco referred me to the Bible to solve the problem he saw in my thinking. But I shy from his advice because all of the human wisdom I feel is trumped by God and Jesus's words in the passages I cite. Also, I know I am not competent to analyze the churchmen's inconsistent opinions of claimed wisdom and should humbly remain with the teachings God imprinted in my heart and the faith imprinted there from the folly of the cross.

Heartfully yours,

February 25, 2011

Dear Holy Father,

Jesus, witnessing to John The Baptist, assured us that "history has not known a man born of woman greater than John The Baptizer. Yet the least born into the kingdom of God is greater than he . . . Heed carefully what you hear!" (See Mt 11:11-15.) What is meant here?

Jesus also said elsewhere in scripture that whatever he says is spoken just as his Father instructs him to say (Jn 12:49, 50). For example, "This is my body," are likely words of God voiced by Jesus. Clearly, we have a mystery here.

Understandably, Jesus, while emptied of his divinity, wrongfully thought non-Jews were "dogs" and demons inhabit desert places or the upper air as these beliefs were the accepted prejudices and superstitions of Jesus and Paul's places and times (see Fr. Raymond Brown's opinion in *St. Anthony's Messenger*, May, 1971). So Jesus may have been humanly or divinely stating a judgment about John The Baptist. Jesus's mother was born in the same period as John, and Jesus's death presumably elevated her at conception. It seems to follow that *our Lord* of love, who is not bound by time and space, redeems all created humanity. This may also be evidenced by the crucified Christ's visit to the dead to relate the good news of God pardoning their evildoing too.

The point I am trying to make is that starting with the premise of God being divine love, the scriptures should be translated by the standard of charity for the good of all created humanity. Jesus, however, may have mistakenly believed that John's untimely life excluded him from Calvary's redemption, and Jesus was not enlightened until he died.

This knowledge of God and God's law of love imprinted by God in us increasingly in life and death leave no room for my Diocese of Sacramento's maintaining Diocesan Statutes of the Third Diocesan Synod which excludes many of God's people from God's Eucharist.

You have the opportunity to correct this *Antichrist* failing of the Catholic church before or at the World Synod of Bishops that you and the inner government of the church plan for the year of 2012. I pray you do what Charity mandates.

Yours in Christ,

February 25, 2011

Dear Holy Father,

Recently you were interviewed and your comments were quoted (*Commonweal*, 2/25/11) on a world threatening climatic catastrophe, which you felt caused the recognition everywhere that we must make moral decisions. You stated: "There is also a . . . pronounced awareness of a global responsibility for it; that ethics must no longer refer merely to one's group or one's own nation, but rather must keep the earth and all people in view." This thinking is in tune to your lecture at Tübingen concerning Jesus's words of the

Last Supper; which you claimed prevents the church from becoming a select group of the righteous to condemn the wayward masses to perdition (see *Commonweal*, 4/21/06).

In the natural world, God's law of nature allows for survival of the fittest. I would assume God diminishes your moral responsibilities for advice on global climate decisions. Sunday on TV, I watched a Galapagos Island catastrophe occur in a sea bird's nest. A larger chick struggled to push its younger sibling from beneath the mother bird's protective breast. The mother unconcernedly observed the struggle and ignored the exposure to her dying chick while she cared for the survivor. God's goodness had imprinted these instincts in mother and chick, and it apparently benefits the species improving itself in the natural world. God designed an abortion or euthanasia program here for a good purpose.

Returning to the above interview, it also quotes you on the subject of the Eucharist that you are responsible for, as follows: "Every Mass is . . . an act of going out to meet the One who is coming. In this way . . . he comes, anticipatively, already now." I am struck by the fact *our Lord* is coming and anticipating that the good he ordered us to do is being accomplished for the good of humanity as a whole, that is, have an inclusive Eucharist. In the time we have yet, as a lay observer I would advise you to raise your loving views, beyond merely Catholics for the welfare of all people. Jesus's crucifixion saves all people, and Jesus's coming is to judge us on how well we cared for each other and all people.

The judgment you bring upon yourself, because of the exclusive Eucharist, falls within your continuing responsibility to all people of the world that make up Christ's global church far more than any advice on the climate. The coming *Lord* anticipates that his death, covenant, and Eucharist are not to be appropriated for your group of Catholics alone, as *Lumen Gentium* deceitfully claims but are being shared. Such is what he anticipates you are accomplishing. Please do not disappoint *our Lord*.

Yours in Christ,

February 28, 2011

Dear Holy Father,

Your fine art of setting aside Christ's open Eucharist invitation to keep your traditional exclusive Catholic Eucharist has come home to harm my young granddaughter, Eve. She is barred by the Diocesan Statutes of the Third Diocesan Synod from receiving her first communion with her parochial school classmates because she is not baptized.

Eve's parents were married in her mother's Protestant church. There they have no baptism but a ritual for nine year olds upon joining the church. Their Eucharist is an all inclusive one where everyone is invited, and baptism is not a prerequisite. The mother expects Eve to have her first Communion there because we bar her from ours.

I suggested that since baptism was not of great religious importance to them then why not have Eve baptized Catholic and allow her to receive the Eucharist with her class. Eve could easily be persuaded to this artful means of avoiding the discrimination to which she is threatened. However, the mother, who has more character than this attorney, refused to send the deceitful message to Eve and her siblings.

My son frustrated me further when he asked me what difference was there in which church she received Eucharist since ours excluded her from the sacrament. I would have objected to the relevancy of the question as a lawyer. Your opinion came to mind: "The true Church could not be founded on the exclusion of others" (see *The New Yorker*, 7/25/05, "Reading Ratzinger," p. 44), and besides I was contending for a specific Communion. I was too limited in patience and ideas to enlighten my son on his father's faith in our Eucharist. The Holy Spirit was also silent on the subject. The authenticity of the other church's inclusive Eucharist is beyond my competency to judge objectively, but my son's idea sounded sensible.

The new covenant (Jer 31:31) and its relationship to include Gentiles (1 Cor 11:23-26) invites every human creature to the Lord's Supper. If you but open your heart to the world and cease your reliance on churchmen's wisdom, you should realize that Eve is worthy to receive Holy Communion with her class because she also is baptized in the blood of the Lamb. Additionally, the judgment you bring on yourself is increased by ignoring the extent to which the Body of Christ includes her. You harm Eve by your uncharitable obstinacy. The greater competency of the New Testament scholars for an open Eucharist tempted you. However, you opposed it to cause an *Antichrist* church not a true church.

Why can't you dispense of the requirement of baptism in the case of Eve? Just pass word down to our pastor, see below, and he will obey your directions. Better yet, rid us of this statute that was squeezed out in 2006 by a bishop whose bias or ignorance matched your own in disobeying God's law of love.

Sincerely,

March 2, 2011

Dear Holy Father,

At page 29 of your book *God Is Near Us,* you teach that the words of Jesus at supper give meaning to his death hours later. Jesus's dying words at supper refer us to the good news of the new covenant (Jer 31:31).

Paul's letter of the Last Supper words of Jesus's sacrificial death and institution of the Eucharist are the first report of Jesus Christ's words after his enlightened status in heaven (1 Cor 11:23-26). All the rest of scripture and traditional teachings of the church are commentaries by men on the message revealed to mankind that last weekend of Jesus's earthly life.

My pastor, Father Francisco, referred me to scripture to find explanation for why the church has an exclusive Eucharist. The point I was trying to make, however, is that Jesus said it all above and all the rest are the opinions of men commenting on the mystery or foolishness of the cross by use of human reason and wisdom. It is a futile errand Father Francisco sends me on to overcome the folly of the cross by apparently wiser men.

Pope John XXIII and his Second Vatican Council, with the curia in restraints, correctly ressourced God's redemption of us in the performance of the covenant by Jesus on the cross. As a result, the Holy Spirit furnished us the ideal of the global Church of Christ, whose members include every human being to be further defined as we evolve. You, yourself, reported our New Testament

Scholars' criticism of the Catholic church's exclusive Eucharist and their contentions for an all inclusive one. (*God Is Near Us*, pp. 59 and 60.) Unfortunately, you artfully opposed them by use of *Sacramentum Caritatis*.

The injustices of the church's exclusive Eucharist weigh on me as a trial attorney and as the grandfather of Eve. The thought of a class suit against the corporate Diocese of Sacramento is a contemplated remedy. My studies of suing you and the Church here in the *United States* found you saved by the immunity laws protecting sovereigns. However, my diocese is not immune to a civil suit for the discriminatory application of the Diocesan Statutes of the Third Diocesan Synod. A class action and a recovery for the harm caused children denied their God-given Eucharist because of the Catholic Diocese appropriating their gifts for its own interests has jury appeal, and a case can be made for jury judgments in a monetary amount to be reasonably valued by nine of the twelve jurors.

Sincerely,

———————

March 4, 2011

Dear Holy Father,

My youngest son questions the difference, if any, of our Eucharist to his wife's church's Eucharist, which is open to everyone. I submit it takes Jesus Christ or the Spirit of God to competently answer and maybe they already have taught us.

My own faith convictions are biased for the Catholic church's Eucharist even though you and your clergy have made it *Antichrist* in distribution. I am disappointed in my son's question as it reveals I failed to teach him the difference. I hope my daily communions and constant writings, which he may have witnessed, might assure him of my sincerity or certainty. I doubt now that he could be persuaded by me, and I ask God to guide him in conscience. I am unable to help him, and my spiritual leaders won't help with fatherly advice on God's guidance.

My advice to his question is that I convincingly trust that the real presence of God is within Jesus, Jesus being God is rather a special way of being man and so communicates the meaning of God in the consecrated bread and wine I consume daily at mass. After receiving communion, I usually pray that God within me transform my life and faith as God chooses to do, and, now, I will include Eve's parents in God's transformation. I simply trust God to do what ought to be done.

Jesus ordered us to take and eat his body, not a sign or symbol of it, for divine purpose. That is what I consume. This is also the choice I want my granddaughter to have. On reflection, I do believe there is a difference in kind between having the real or actual God and possessing God in symbol or sign of God, within the substance of the Eucharist. God in actuality is far more valuable a possession than God in symbol or sign. Real gold in hand beats possessing signs of gold. We have no standards to judge the extent of the difference in value of God possessed and God symbolized but we know that a difference exists. We know also Eve is being dispossessed. We can measure a reasonable value of possessing God in Eucharist by means of the knowledge of God imprinted in every human being. No one contests God is of value, but the worth remains to be judged, and its loss should be remedied.

Consequently, we can ask a jury of twelve people to reasonably appraise and assess a monetary sum for the wrongful appropriating of my granddaughter's right to consume her gift of God with her classmates. C. K. Chesteron complimented the use of jurors for such a difficult task by noting our society uses its experts to catalogue libraries, discover space, and so on, but for truly important tasks, it selects twelve ordinary people to reasonably remedy the wrong by means of their conscience and reasoning abilities.

Sincerely,

March 4, 2011

Dear Holy Father,

Soon I will be seventy-nine years of age, God willing, and as I contemplate my faith convictions, I wonder about senility. I am concerned about your mental abilities too as you are several years older than I. My concerns are with your death my chances of effectively changing the church's exclusive Eucharist and its disregard of God's new covenant (Jer 31:31) diminishes or may even disappear. Note: I trust God in you to change you and our Catholic church.

Thus, I wrote on 1/13/06 this first paragraph "Apparently, the Holy spirit has placed upon you the responsibility to discern and define what *our Lord's* purpose was in gracing us with Eucharist in addition to redeeming every one of us to be God's children and expects you to affirm or correct the Church's tradition that has existed since its infancy."

At the beginning, I thought what upset you in Tübingen to abandon the progressives and join Karol Wojtyla's ambitions to advance the church's human traditions over God's law of universal love as manifested in Pope John XXIIII's council would decline soon. However, with *Sacramentum Caritatis,* you have made a fine art of negating the evidence of God's saving action and have delegated control to bishops who are less learned than you.

Ever since Pope Paul VI's delay in appointment, the interim papacy of Pope John XXIII and his version of Vatican II are heard. The church's traditionalists, and inner government, have fought to silence the Church of Christ and return the *status quo* to secure the curias' "Cosa Nostra" as the mafia would say. You, your predecessor, and proponents of the traditional way have actively modified ideals of a global Church of Christ and its open Eucharist by restrictive translations. Still the laity expresses their consciences by receiving together Holy Communion, without prior reconciliations. They even walk away from your church's traditions to follow God's law as imprinted in their hearts (Jer 31:31-34) as ordered to do (1 Cor 11:23 *ff)*.

While you still live, *wake up*! Do what you know God calls you to do in the message Jesus's death proclaimed, while a dead man walking, at the Last Supper and translated in his last hours. God has graced you, apparently, with another Lent to reflect on the good news (Gospel) of Jesus, incorporating by reference the new covenant, with his cleansing every human being in his blood. Remember the Gospel Jesus proclaimed and offer everyone Eucharist to be joined with Jesus's offering of love to God. Don't miss the opportunity again to imitate Christ for our annual Passover reconciliation.

Sincerely,

March 10, 2011

Dear Holy Father,

Lumen Gentium No. 37 obliges the more competent of us laity to express our opinion on those things which concern the good of the church so that it "may more effectively fulfill its mission for the life of the world." We, in turn, are assured that our spiritual leaders will, attentively in Christ, consider with fatherly love the suggestions proposed by the laity. Among things, "hoped for from this familiar dialogue" is that our spiritual leaders, aided by the lay experience, can better decide on both spiritual and temporal matters to strengthen the whole church throughout the world.

The above is taken from our *Dogmatic Constitution on the Church*, a document of Vatican II promulgated by Pope Paul VI at the end of 1964. I can personally complain that my constitutional rights have been violated by you and your inner government's oppressive silence. I agree with what you told the UN in April 2009, I believe, that denying citizens their basic rights was an "illegitimate" act. Still, you can remedy the wrong.

Paul asked that we no longer pass judgment on another, but I heartfully feel I must make judgment about the objective wrongness of your Vatican's actions in excluding almost everyone from Christ's Eucharist. Please consider the gospel that Jesus died to establish—everyone's evildoings are forgiven by God's love as Jesus's blood is shed. We repeat this good news daily while all people God created are recreated.

The Catholic church's deliberate deceit and forgery, thanks to what our inner government wrote into *Lumen Gentium* at No. 9, makes Catholicism, with its believers baptized in water members, a select community of the righteous that condemns the rest of humanity to perdition. An uncharitable church cannot be true Christian with exclusion of almost everyone from the Eucharist. Christ's church subsists elsewhere so long as our Eucharist is exclusive.

Sincerely,

March 17, 2011

Dear Holy Father,

I have been writing for years asking for response of my spiritual leader to the concerns I submit or suggest I perceive in the failings of our Catholic church. The only response I received was from my diocesan bishop writing his opinion that my analysis for an open Eucharist was incorrect, and I needed "obedience of faith" to the teachings of the church. He claimed the traditional teachings were clear back beyond St. Paul that required true Catholic faith and worthiness to receive Holy Communion. Obviously, Vatican II is ignored as is the covenant.

Thus, Catholic faith and good works are the prerequisites for worthiness to share Eucharist. My shepherd advises of his analysis from selected teachings. I would agree if I could shut my mind to the teachings of God imprinted in my conscience and my learnings from scripture of God's unilateral performance of the new covenant (Jer 31:31) fulfilled by Jesus Christ and memorialized at mass (1 Cor 11:23-26).

I have argued that God's forgiving of our evildoing secures "worthiness" in all Jews and Gentiles for salvation and their rights to receive Eucharist. The ordering of us to "Take this, all of you . . ." by *our Lord* Jesus Christ is an added indication that God calls all of us to Eucharist to be refreshed in faith and life. Like the rich young man, not giving up his loved properties, we have a calling also to perfection. This thought is of my recent consideration to me and not fully developed, but I am trying to analyze why I need good works if I am saved by covenant.

The second reading of the Second Sunday of Lent has Paul instructing Timothy (2 Tm 1:8-10) that "God has saved us and called us to a holy life, not because of any merit of ours but according to his own design—the grace held out to us in Christ Jesus before the world began but now made manifest through the appearance of our Savior." So God asks for my works.

Consequently, I must change my plans for life to conform to those of God. Instead of living life as I please, knowing God loves and forgives me as I sin, I freely give God what I could withhold. God guarantees to pardon my evildoing, with perhaps chastisements to remove the imperfections if I choose to be selfish. I am now realizing that God appreciates my loving God by doing good works that I could avoid. I should avoid sins and be holy out of a reciprocal love for God. I need God's help to do both. Likely, I will continue to sin and must receive the Eucharist as God's aid for my life and faith holiness.

Sincerely,

March 21, 2011

Dear Holy Father,

Paul's instructions to Timothy turn out to be an epiphany for me. I thought I implied distrust if I ceased sinning in view of God showing love for me in saving me as I am. But God's calling me to be holy I take as God's wish. I need not respond, but if I do answer the call, it becomes my gesture of love, to which God is entitled. I am free to deny God, so out of love I choose to give God what I feel God wants.

Timothy was left bishop of Ephesus, and his teachings were likely passed on to the authors of the Fourth Gospel who came out of Ephesus. Their *Gospel according to John* had other contributing teachers; for example, Prologue is Storic in language (*Logos*), and its prerequisite belief in Christ through the word and from water (cf. Jn 5:3-6) preserves the religion of John the Baptist for a later Augustinan water cure of original sin. In this sense, I agree with Fr. Donald Senior, C. P.'s claim to the authenticity of this Gospel. However, since it disregards the words of Jesus concerning the new covenant and the Eucharist at the Last Supper, the letter of St. Paul (1 Cor 11:23-26) and the Gospels of the Synoptic are more authentic in reporting of our salvation and recreation by God alone in redeeming us.

God implies that any other teachings on "how to know the Lord" are superfluous after God imprints in us all the knowledge "for I will forgive their evildoing and remember their sin no more" (Jer 31:34). God asserts "I will be their God and they will be my people" includes everybody to the calling to treat God as God, and people interiorly know this means to be good.

My diocesan bishop held that any human creature remains unworthy after God washes them in the blood of the covenant or believed that a church baptism is needed after we all are baptized in the blood of Jesus Christ. This belief seems stupid to my humble way of thinking.

I would suggest that your woeful argument in opposition to our post-Vatican II New Testament scholars' criticism of our church's exclusive Eucharist and their contention that God intended an all inclusive one, is why you did not rule as Pope for an exclusive Eucharist on basis of your argument citing Jn 13:10. I further worry that your bias for church's traditions and your pride to save face prevents you from declaring for an inclusive Eucharist, even though it is obvious that God's law of love calls for you to give God's gift to every human being, bar-none.

Why are you not doing what you know you ought to do? Just do it!

Sincerely,

____

March 23, 2011

Dear Holy Father,

NCR's edition of 3/18/11 has your opinions reported by John Allen, Sr., including that God will save the Jews after the gentiles are saved. I must express my concern for the good news that Jesus died to establish so dearly (see Jer 31:31 with 1 Cor 11:23-26) and restate his mission for the wellbeing of humanity.

God has performed the pledge of salvation of all Jews and Gentiles in the blood of Jesus Christ—Bernard of Clairvaux's advice and your opinions notwithstanding. All of the gentiles are to be saved first is from, at best, a self-serving Christian tradition. I respectfully submit the human tradition borders on blasphemy in negating the evidence of God's saving action in history. Jesus died to redeem the world. Obviously, you have read nothing of what I write you. Likely you will also ignore this writing to everyone's loss especially Jews.

Sincerely,

____

March 28, 2011

Dear Holy Father,

Your typescript of a lecture at Tübingen revealed your conviction that Jesus's words in the Last Supper, for example, "for many" (Mk 14:24) "prevents the church from becoming simply a select community of the righteous, a community that condemns the wayward masses to perdition." (See *Commonweal*, 4/21/06, p. 13.) Yet your present views contradict these prior ones.

Some Protestant clergymen agree with your earlier view. Chad Holz, a pastor of a Methodist church, wrote in support of a book by Robert Bell, a prominent evangelical pastor who criticized the belief that a select number of Christians will spend eternity in the bliss of heaven while everyone else, including the likes of Mohandas Gandhi, are tormented forever in hell. Pastor Chad Holz, father of four, so believes God is Love that he was terminated from his employment because he wrote he does not believe in a monster God who can torment people because of nonbelief.

Please take a lesson from these Christ-like pastors and open God's gift of Eucharist to everyone. You will still remain secure in comfort in the Vatican, although temporarily less so from your fellow clergymen, unlike Holz who suffers the cross of unemployment. If you copy Holz and Christ, himself, you will secure a comfortable reception from God in the hereafter.

Truly yours,

March 30, 2011

Dear Holy Father,

The Preamble of the US Constitution partially reads that "We the people, in order to form a more perfect union, establish justice, and so on." It is to form communion or unity with all our people.

The Introduction to the *Dogmatic Constitution on the Church* reads in pertinent parts that because Christ is the light of nations (*Lumen Gentium*), "this sacred synod . . .

desires, by proclaiming the Gospel to every creature (cf. Mk 16:15), to bring the light of Christ to all men, a light brightly visible in the countenance of the Church. Since the church is in Christ like a sacrament or as a sign and instrument both of a very closely knit union with God and of the unity of the whole human race, it desires now to unfold more fully to the faithful of the church and to the whole world its own inner nature and universal mission . . . so that all men, joined more closely today by various social technical and cultural ties, might also attain fuller unity in Christ." The introduction adds meaning to Chapter I, part 8, which defines the church to be "*One Church of Christ"* and this church "*subsists in the Catholic Church*" (emphasis mine).

In the *United States,* the people themselves form the constitution, while in the Church of Christ, the Popes and bishops constituting Vatican II promulgated the document. The Gospel to be promulgated is "the good news to all creation." The longer ending citation of *The Gospel According to Mark* adds men must believe in it and accept baptism to be saved, while others will be condemned. Such is not the good news Jesus died for.

The Gospel that Jesus proclaimed of the new covenant is unique to those of our Canon. It seems that Jesus died to proclaim God so loves us that God unilaterally imprints in our conscience what we need know, and God forgives our evildoing and forgets our sins, without need of belief, baptism, or contribution on our part. We need only be created, as parties to the new covenant because God's goodness loves us as we are.

"Interdependent" with God's covenant, Jesus's death, and testament for our salvation, has God calling us by words to be holy, to be perfect, and to nourish us to love others by consuming Eucharist for "all" to take. Thus, God's plan from the beginning is to create us free to sin or to freely love with no strings attached. Peace be to us because we are all saved for eternal life. Also, all have the freedom of opportunity, with God's grace, to love God and each other freely if we so choose. The love of God under these circumstances may be more precious. It is ours to give freely as we will likely be unable to withhold from God while overcome by God's beatific vision.

You can love God today by giving God the Eucharist God intended. God awaits your gift of love.

Sincerely,

April 1, 2011

Dear Holy Father,

I have suspected that the God of ambition tempted you to oppose the New Testament scholars' criticism of our exclusive Eucharist and their post-Council contention for an inclusive one, especially when I consider the unscholarly citation of authorities you furnished with your argument (*God Is Near Us*, pp. 59 and 60). My suspicions were strengthened when you did not rule for an exclusive Eucharist on attaining the Vatican. Instead your Vatican released *Sacramento Caritatis* to purportedly delegate the judgment for an exclusive Eucharist to bishops in Synod. However, it was a foregone conclusion that the preselected bishops, indoctrinated by the Vatican in Synod working documents, were preconditioned to exclude non-Catholics and others. Thus, as prophesized by Jesus (see Mk 7:6-13), you artfully manipulated the exclusive Eucharist to cling to traditional precepts. The dogmatic result is evidenced in our Diocesan Statutes of the Third Diocesan Synod while allowing lip service to collegiality and hypocritically suggesting God's law of love.

Whether or not my suspicions are correct, you succeeded to the Papacy. What now prevents you from remedying the church's wrong doing before you die? Donatists, who uncharitably denied the sacrament to members, you judged to be untrue to Christ in your doctoral dissertation. The Catholic church to be true to charity and the Church of Christ, thus, requires a Eucharist open for all. Remaining true to your convictions calls for equal charity for all those excluded from Holy Communion. Illegitimately denying most people their God-given rights, secured to them by Christ's performance of the new covenant, is *Antichrist.* The covenant's performance, which happened to be the good news Jesus died to proclaim, reveals God's goodness and love of us as we are. God's unilateral performance of the new covenant or New Testament, fulfilled by Christ's death, mandates for an all inclusive Eucharist.

We blaspheme against the Spirit by negating the Eucharist of God's salvation. However, you have time to repent your ambitious wrongdoing, by opening the Eucharist to everyone.

Sincerely,

April 4, 2011

Dear Holy Father,

The Gospel According to Jesus was written in his blood. Jesus died to proclaim the words of God in the context of the new covenant (Jer 31:31-34), and its explanation has Jesus redeeming all the world's Jews and Gentiles (see 1 Cor 11:23-26). The authors of our Canon tried to write and preach what happened but, unlike Jesus who walked-the-talk of the Last Supper, were incompetent. They were also handicapped by the religions and culture that surrounded them to make difficult their interpretations of the good news demonstrated by the death and "interdependent" words of Christ at the Last Supper.

Evidence of the misunderstandings and biases appear in the writings of *The Gospel According to John*. This fourth Gospel avoids reporting the words of the Last Supper concerning the new covenant and the Eucharist. Jesus's death and words gave "interdependent" meaning to the words with the folly of the cross. The universality of our redemption and communion are divinely of one piece. Irenaeus, Bishop of Lyons, favored John the Evangelist, likely because his mentor Policarp claimed that John converted him. He added it to the synoptic in his incompetent selections for the Canon and trashed the other opinions of witnesses likely because there were only four corners of the world.

Recently, the Roman Catholic Church's governmental body carried the traditionalists' view of good news mistranslations into a higher state of blasphemy. To wit, Vatican II document *Lumen Gentium's* No. 9, drafted after Pope John XXIII died and the curia was released, was promulgated. The words God expressed in the new covenant and the New Testament fulfilled by Jesus Christ were forged by the curia to negate the evidence of God's saving performance in history. Instead of God unilaterally performing the pledges, the curia drafted it to require us to help God. The promulgation by Pope Paul VI became our *Dogmatic Constitution on the Church*. It erroneously concludes that baptized believers in Christ, "a small flock," are predestined for heaven, while the rest of humanity are created for everlasting torment unless converted by the redeemed. God still forgives every human evildoings.

The human dogma negated God lovingly performing the new covenant in Christ's blood to redeem the whole world. It deceitfully misleads humans to deny *our Lord's* proof of God's love for which Christ died. The implication left is that a nonloving God created most of humanity for everlasting torment. Yet, God alone cleans and saves everyone.

Sincerely,

April 5, 2011

Dear Holy Father,

I am told that an issue considered by the Pope and gathered bishops of Vatican II was the role of the curia in the future of the Roman Catholic Church. The "brutes" described by Fr. Francis Xavier, S. J. would have been disturbed by this (see my letter of 6/21/06 or p. 45 of *God's Gift to You*). The shameful forgery located in No. 9 of *Lumen Gentium* may be a product of the disturbance. In keeping with the Fraternal Correction advised by Jesus (Mt 18:15ff.), I have tried to refer my concerns to the members of the Church of Christ; however, the shame will out to the world, and the harm to the Catholic church's credibility may destroy its mission for the life of the world. I am concerned that the truth will out, and we can add this fraud to our reputation for covering up abuses to our innocents.

Let me spell out for you the blasphemy that is obvious to me. In the *Dogmatic Constitution on the Church,* the disturbed scribes fraudulently misquoted the new covenant, (Jer 31:31-34) to read as follows:

> "Behold the days shall come says the LORD, and I will make a new covenant with the House of Israel, and with the house of Judah . . . I will give my law in their bowels and I will write it in their heart, and I will be their

> God, and they shall be my people . . . For all of them shall know me, from the least of them even to the greatest, says the LORD."

The forgers fraudulently misquote the *Douay Version* of the Old Testament by deleting the following words from verse 34: "*And they shall teach no more every man, his neighbor and every man his brother, saying: Know the LORD.*" Plus deleting God's pledge at the covenant's ending, which reads: "*for I will forgive their iniquity, and I will remember their sin no more*" (see Jer 31:34).

Based upon this negation of God's pledges in covenant and the terms of Jesus's Testament, the blasphemers distort evidence of God's salvation and substituted their own conclusions, as follows: "Christ instituted *this* new covenant, the New Testament, that is to say, in his blood (cf. 1 Cor 11:25), calling together a people made up of Jews and Gentiles making them one not according to the flesh but in the spirit." (Emphasis mine.) The lie exists in referring to the quoted forgery as identifying "this" covenant as being the one Jesus died to perform or establish, rather than the actual one that is set out in the Bible by God (Jer 31:34) and the one expressly referred to by Jesus (1 Cor 11:25).

Having fabricated the false premise, the drafter's deceit continues to misstate God's calling was "[F]or those who believe in Christ," not for all Jews and Gentiles, or for all people. The new people of God are baselessly designated to be only those who believe in Christ and only those reborn, "not from the flesh but from water and the Holy Spirit (cf. Jn 3:5-6)." Thus, *The Gospel According to John* that makes no mention of the new covenant or the institution of the Eucharist words you acknowledge to be "interdependent" with the death of Jesus, receives top billing. The good news that Jesus proved of God alone teaching and forgiving all humans God created now needs the church to make good on God's and Jesus's inept efforts.

Sincerely,

April 6, 2011

NCR

Dear Editor,

Fr. Mike Glockner of Mt. St. Joseph, Ohio wrote to the Editor (*NCR* Letters, 4/1/11) that our two recent Popes selected bishops who have steadily sinned, with the curia, against the Holy Spirit. His accusations are aimed at their undermining the Spirits' renewal of people through Vatican II. Father spells out specifies and calls upon the laity and "lower" clergy to stand up for what matters.

My hat is off to this clergyman, one of a rarity who dares to express concern for the good of the whole Church of Christ which Vatican II declared "subsists" in the Catholic church. He is like the post-Council scholars of the New Testament who publicly criticized our exclusive Eucharist and contended that the Eucharist was divinely instituted to include every human being, nonbaptized as well as sinners, unconditionally.

Pope Benedict's response to these Vatican II biblical experts was to delegate the judgment on the openness of the Eucharist to less learned and more indoctrinated diocesan bishops (see *Sacramentum Caritatis*). As a result, we have a Roman Catholic Church traditional and exclusive Eucharist excommunicating almost everyone created. It is neither a charitable or Christian practice unless the excommunicated obey Jesus and "take this, all of you."

Sincerely,

cc: His Holiness Pope Benedict XVI

April 8, 2011

Dear Holy Father,

Fr. Daniel Harrington, S. J., on reviewing your books *Jesus of Nazareth*, reported the criticism of other theologians for your excessive reliance on John's Gospel and a narrow conventional outlook. However, he recommends reading the second volume for your breaking open the passion narrative to provide us their historical information (*America*, pp. 38-29, 4/4/11).

I will pass on reading this second volume because your reliance on John's Gospel ignores the words of God at the Last Supper, indicating the historical fact of the new covenant being what Jesus died to perform. Jesus's mission was to fulfill, perfect, perform, and reveal God's pledges contained in the new covenant (Jer 31:33-34). The motivation of Jesus's seemingly foolish death was in context of God unilaterally redeeming the world. (See Mk 14:24 and 1 Cor 11:23-26.) Once before you argued John's version of the Last Supper (Jn 13:10) as authority for excluding most people from Christ's Eucharist because washing in the blood of the covenant needed further washings by men (*God Is Near Us*, pp. 59-60).

God's message in scripture plainly are the words of the covenant (Jer 31:31ff.), and Jesus's words at supper, repeated from heaven, were plainly posted on the cross for revelation to all the world (1 Cor 11:23-26). The remainder of the Bible might be deemed commentary, mostly words of men, on these mysterious divine passages. A well-known Rabbi said a similar thing about the *Torah*, the message was God's law of love, and all the rest was dismissible as commentary.

Sincerely,

April 11, 2011

Dear Holy Father,

I doubt if my writings interest you, but if you are giving them a modicum of the fatherly consideration that our *Dogmatic Constitution on the Church*, No. 37, calls for you to give my expressed concerns, Lent's ending is soon here. We face Holy Weeks when we are to celebrate Christ's *Paschal Mystery*—the foundational mystery of our faith convictions—and I again try to unfold some of the meaning of this mystery in the context of God's unilateral performance of the new covenant Jer 31) as revealed by Jesus Christ.

Using your own expressions on the subject matter may appeal to the teachings of God imprinted in your mind, heart, or bowels by *our Lord*. You lectured for years that the new covenant (Jer 31) mentioned by Jesus at the Last Supper linked Jesus to founding his church. You preached then that the words he spoke at supper represented the truth of God's love and Jesus's message in suffering. The words renew the meaning of the institution of the Eucharist in anticipation of his passionate death. "For Jesus shares himself out, he shares himself as the one who has been split up and torn apart into body and blood." He transforms his death into self-sharing love and into offering adoration to God. Both the death and words are "essentially interdependent" so that the death with the words at supper would be mere execution without any discernible purpose (see *God Is Near Us*, p. 29). Thus, we must regard the *Paschal Mystery* as being constantly guaranteed by the pledges of God's new covenant (Jer 31) and the blood of Jesus shed in witness of the performance of the covenant.

The Eucharist we proclaim daily is in the body and blood of the new and everlasting covenant (*Eucharistic Prayers*). Simply put, God recreated evildoing humanity in baptism of the blood of the Lamb. Thereby, as God pledged, everyone created has his or her evildoing forgiven and forgotten. God spells this out in *The Book of Jeremiah*, Jer 31:31-34, and God's pledges are guaranteed absolutely. Additionally, God pledges to imprint interiorly in each and everyone of us the knowledge of God and God's love so we need no teacher or church to teach us better. Furthermore, the Lord's Supper is to be continued in our universal Eucharist where everyone, unconditionally, has to share God's real presence interiorly to nourish us with God's imprintations to transform our faiths and lives everywhere until Christ comes again.

Please consider these thoughts and open the Eucharist this Easter to all God's creation as God planned.

Sincerely,

April 14, 2011

America

Dear Editor,

Sister Barbara Reid, O. P. (*The* Word 4/11/11), may cling to Catholic tradition in interpreting—"This is my blood *of the covenant* which will be shed on behalf of many for the forgiveness of sins" (Mt 26:28, emphasis mine). Sister Reid claims that "it is not by a single sacrificial act but by an entire way of life into which his followers are invited" that Jesus saves mankind. She ignores the new covenant (Jer 31), which *our Lord* pledged for centuries before God unilaterally performed it in Jesus's shedding of blood and death on the cross for human kind's salvation.

In fairness to Sister Reid, for two millenniums of Catholic tradition, the church also changed God's unilateral covenant to a bilateral one. Every human was cleansed and saved by the cross, and God wants us to freely reciprocate the love demonstrated for us by a lifetime of loving others. Often receiving Eucharist enables us to love as God wants.

We need only exist as humans to benefit and be saved by God's covenant. All people are saved by the blood of the cross. Also, God forgiving our evildoing makes all of us worthy to receive God's Eucharist. An all-inclusive Eucharist is a means for God within us to grace everyone worldwide to love others as Jesus demonstrated.

Sincerely,

cc: His Holiness Pope Benedict XVI

April 15, 2011

Dear Holy Father,

As Easter Sunday approaches, I hear God's call to Peter to share supper with Cornelius repeated to you who stand in Peter's shoes and face God's non-Catholic people whom you keep excommunicated. The first reading this coming Easter Sunday should convince you that you keep God holding for you to answer the call to share Eucharist with everyone created and cleansed by God in Jesus shedding of the blood of the new covenant.

You did not effectively put off the call as it is still ringing, when your Vatican released *Sacramentum Caritatis*, trying to delegate to lesser bishops the final judgment on whether or not to share Eucharist with all humankind, while God waits patiently for you to love God's non-baptized Catholic as you do Catholics.

You taught me that shedding the blood of the covenant was "interdependent" with the words of the Last Supper. Those words included the institution of the Eucharist. Thereby, Jesus both redeemed the world and graced its inhabitants with the teaching and forgiving real presence in Eucharist.

It has been during your watch that your diocesan bishops have promulgated statutes of human precepts setting aside God's law of love to cling to two millenniums of the church's traditional Eucharist excluding most of people from God's new covenant benefits.

As Peter's successor, you have yet to answer God's call. In the interim, our bishops continue excommunicating non-Catholic or non-Christians. Should you not answer the call this Easter, April 24, and do what you know God wants?

Sincerely,

April 18, 2011

Dear Holy Father,

If you had a loving mother, I suggest the love of a mother for her child is the closest experience we have for the love God has for each human person. God shows no partiality, and in the blood of the covenant (Jer 31:31-34 and 1 Cor 11:23-26), God imprints in everyone's heart this knowledge to the extent needed. You know it.

Jesus Christ performed perfectly God's new covenant in his words and acts that first Easter weekend. You wrote of your teachings and preachings that the words of the Last Supper were "interdependent" with his sacrificial death. The death without the words you wrote was a mere execution (*God Is Near Us*, p. 29). Since the words also instituted the Eucharist, which Jesus ordered all of us to take, the "interdependent" death plainly shows God's intent was to use the Eucharist for the education and salvation of humankind. God's motherly care plans to create us or recreate us in the words and death of Jesus Christ.

You must know the information I am here writing to you. Yet your closed heart or mind leaves the church's Eucharist continuing to exclude non-Catholics from God's plan. When you acknowledged that after Vatican II, our New Testament scholars criticized the exclusive Eucharist and contended that Christ meant for an inclusive one, you uncharitably opposed them on irrelevant scriptural, and even *Didache*, grounds. But attaining your present position of power instead of ruling as you should, you delegated the offensive task of judging for an exclusive Eucharist to your more ignorant and pliable bishops. The church today, like Donatism you wrote about, is not true church because of its exclusive Eucharist, and your negation of God's law of love makes it *Antichrist*.

You know by heart that, as Pope Benedict XVI, you easily can repair the structure God made for humanity. Regardless of what you do, God saves everyone in the blood of the Lamb just for being God's loving creation. God is being shortchanged in the deal, which God unilaterally made because you are denying God this love as a return on creation's covenant. The intimate presence of God in our bowels, to teach and forgive us, is God's means to transform us to love each other and God in Jesus Christ's Eucharist.

Sincerely,

April 19, 2011

Dear Holy Father,

This is my last letter before Easter. I am convinced that my spiritual shepherds will not read it. But I possess great joy in writing to you in efforts of proclaiming the good news of the new covenant, which Jesus died to publish. In fact, this effort has become my sole work as an advocate since my trial practice died half-a-dozen years ago when I started writing. *Lumen Gentium,* No. 37, "obliged me" to express my concerns for the good of the church in its mission for the whole world. I assumed it meant Vatican II's whole Church of Christ. I have come to enjoy my writing, not because I write well as it is obvious I do not, but because I feel I am trying to help Jesus carry his cross.

Often I am questioned as to what is my knowledge, competence, or outstanding ability to claim to be "obliged" to express my opinion on, the Eucharist or the new covenant, concerning the good of the Church (*Infra*, No. 37). My faith conviction is that God imprinted in me the knowledge of God and the law of God. Thus, I am competent as the least of God's people, to argue my common knowledge with the greatest of God's people.

I pray that you recognize the "body" of Christ includes every human being already saved by God in the new covenant's performance by Jesus and that the universal Eucharist is God's gift to every human being made worthy by Jesus's death.

Easter is a time of resurrection and an occasion for you to awaken to love God and everyone as you should.

Sincerely,

April 29, 2011

Dear Holy Father,

My latest diocese's magazine *Catholic Herald* claims that God challenges us to define our relationship with God. However, God establishes our relationship from the beginning in the new covenant (Jer 31:31) performed for all humanity by Jesus (1 Cor 11:23-26). God alone performs the covenant relationship forever and for everyone in the blood of the covenant because we prove to be untrustworthy. God in words at the Last Supper orders everyone to take and consume the Eucharist of the new and everlasting covenant. Since God pledges to forgive our evildoing forever, every human is redeemed by being the objects of God's love and goodness. Also, by terms of God's covenant every individual is taught by God to know God and God's law by conscience imprints over church teachings.

Vatican II's ideal of a global Church of Christ, which subsists in the Catholic church, was argued in the faith convictions of our New Testament scholars who criticized an exclusive Eucharist and contended that Christ meant for the Eucharist of the true church to be open to non-Catholics and mortal sinners (see *God Is Near Us*, p. 59, by Cardinal J. Ratzinger). God transforms the lives of all human beings to be one with God for eternity, and we should be at peace with God's revealed relationship.

Sincerely,

____

May 3, 2011

Dear Holy Father,

God created humanity to love God and each other. God also instilled in us the instinct to survive, resulting in our evildoing. But God's plan of creation was to pardon our evildoing and, in Jesus Christ, reveal that God forgives our evildoing forever out of God's goodness and love for us.

Few humans, however, have grasped the fact that God is a God of love. Instead, we are taught God is a God to be appeased or else suffer eternal torment. We Catholics are taught about hell, given only lip service to a God of love, and persuaded not to trust God's new covenant at God's word, even though Jesus died to proclaim it. Instead, we are indoctrinated in the standard Christian view summed up in the Gospel of John, which promises eternal life to only those baptized believers in Christ who are persuaded to do good for greater favors.

Christian writers tend to craft whatever their self-interests would have Jesus say. This has always been so as we note the authors of the last Gospel disregarded Last Supper words of new covenant (Jer 31:31), which Jesus died to establish and proclaim (1 Cor 11:23-26) because it contradicted their ideas. The Catholic church also negates God's new covenant, by deleting essential terms (see *Lumen Gentium*, No. 9), and fraudulently arguing that their forged version are God's words. Thus, Pope Paul VI concludes that only Christians, who believe in Christ and were baptized in water (cf. Jn 3:5-6), are the "small flock" redeemed by Jesus.

Vatican II, earlier when Pope John XXIII served, tried to return us to God's covenant relationship, by, suggesting a global Church of Christ and an open Eucharist presuming every human is made worthy by God's forgiving love. However, you were reported to have wielded imagined texts of Council documents to claim the Church of Christ "both is and can only be, *fully* present" in the Roman Church (*The New Yorker* 7/25/05). As for the open Eucharist, your Vatican artfully have diocesan bishops excommunicate non-Catholics and almost everyone as unworthy. You craft Christ's Gospel to your own.

My concern for the good of our church is for its credibility when the truth outs. Your decreeing an inclusive Eucharist returning matters into Christ's hands may initiate a rehabilitation of faith in the true Church when the "gnats hit the fan."

Sincerely,

May 4, 2011

National Catholic Reporter

Dear Editor,

Jamie Manson wrote an article (4/29/11) about her mother's excommunication because she was divorced and remarried out of the Church.

Father Joseph Ratzinger commented on a Vatican II's statement he witnessed on the subject of conscience: "Even against ecclesiastical authority, conscience must be obeyed before all else." (See *America*, 5/2/11, p. 5.) I have written over three hundred letters and two books about God's new covenant (Jer 31:31) forgiving everyone's evildoings and Jesus's performing it to save everyone (1 Cor 11:23-26). God unilaterally makes everyone worthy to receive Holy Communion and all should take and consume. (See *God's Gift To You*, available online.)

Note, however, that it took Jamie's mother to hear it from a priest, even a rogue one, before her Catholicism freed her misinformed conscience to take Holy Communion. It is not a matter of conscience but a God-given right for all humans to receive God's gift of love.

Sincerely,

cc: His Holiness Pope Benedict XVI

May 5, 2011

Dear Holy Father,

You personally accepted the voicing of his informed conscience by Dominican Yves Congar, O. P., at the beginning of the Second Vatican Council, acknowledging that non-Catholic Christians, are members of the mystical body. But from about 1968, you changed your mind and, coincidentally, your rise in the hierarchy of the church occurred. You became a protagonist with Karol Wojtyla in restrictively interpreting the Council's principle to fit the version that clung to pre-Council traditions of the church narrowing the "body" to Catholics.

Our consciences subtly exercise their loving power as Congar's did in Pope John XXIII's gathering, but artful exercises of politics by the successors of Pope John have killed much of the love generated at the time of Congar and your enthusiasm for Vatican II too. Presumably, you now think that the older church tradition is for the better. You evidenced this by your opposition to the inclusive Eucharist proposed by the New Testament scholars (*God Is Near Us*, p. 59) and by your writing *Sacramentum Caritatis* (a false message on charity), which causes the excommunication of most of God's human creation. The "body" you now recognize may bring judgment upon you, according to St. Paul, and delegating the judgment call to diocesan bishops does not relieve you of the obligation to feed all of God's people the new covenant's fruits.

Imprinted with the knowledge of God instilled in everyone recreated in the blood of the covenant and renewed in Eucharist likely will deprive you of the defense of ignorance in recognizing the extent of the body. God pledged that the least to the greatest of us would know God's law presumably over any contrary teachings by human wisdom. So between the both of you, Jesus Christ and yourself, your refusal to decree an open and inclusive Eucharist for all mankind becomes more culpable. Furthermore, in denying most people their gift from God, in order to use their gift, your act becomes an offense against both God's justice and God's commandment of love.

Sincerely,

May 11, 2011

Dear Holy Father,

Although I do not receive response from you to my written concerns, I am reading His Holiness John Paul II's *Crossing The Threshold Of Hope*. My impression from reading his first chapter "The Pope: A Scandal and a Mystery" is that he does play acting to satisfy his role as vicar. It raises a question of what is my faith as distinguished from superstition. Pope John Paul seems to put on the mask of the vicar of Christ in representing

God on earth, but it is an act to please us who need to believe he is more than our servant and brother in Christ.

It reminds me of Father Raymond Brown's opinion that both Jesus and Paul were believers of demons because it was the superstition of their people at the time. Father Brown, our expert on the Bible back in 1971, simply stated Jesus was wrong in his thinking, not wrong in his acting to disturb the demons, but thinking that demons existed. Or was Jesus or his evangelists acting to suit the people of God of that day?

I wonder what you really think about God's words at the Last Supper "Take this, all of you," and all are ordered to consume the flesh of Jesus Christ as sacrificed in love for everyone. Jesus's sacrifice is symbolizing the completed performance of God's pledges of the new covenant (Jer 31), the last testament of Jesus, to which we are all heirs to inherit the benefit of God's teachings, forgivings, and lovings without effort on our parts but to exist on earth.

Your role as "a dog in the manger" suits your reign, but as vicar of Christ, Jesus himself prophesied your disregard of God's commandment of love to cling to what is human tradition (Mk 7:1-13). With *Sacramentum Caritatis*, I submit, "you have made a fine art of setting aside God's commandment in the interests of keeping your traditions!" All those people saved by Jesus's sacrifice and, thus, whose evildoings are forgiven by God, you contradicted God and caused your bishops to excommunicate. You were never authorized as vicar of God to do so uncharitable a harm and must remedy your wrong as soon as you can.

I pray to God that God remind this dunce of a vicar the truths that he already knows by heart with adequate force to give him courage of his conscience.

Sincerely,

May 12, 2011

Dear Holy Father,

You agreed with St. Augustine's opinion that Donatism's ex-communication of their wayward priests disqualified them. You wrote your doctoral dissertation upon Augustine and his regarding the lack of *caritas* (charity) as the defining characteristic, which denied Donatism being true church.

Ironically, *Sacramentum Caritatis* lacks the same "charity." It allows your bishops to unlovingly exclude most of God's created people from God's Eucharist. You arranged for your Vatican to artfully control your diocesan bishops to cling to the traditional Eucharist, which hypocritically disregards God's law of love (see Mk 7:1-13).

Plainly, our Eucharist was instituted by God as part of God's new covenant relationship to feed actual God to every human. The ecumenism spirit of Vatican II caused our New Testament scholars' attempts to return us to God's open Eucharist as an "interdependent" part of God's covenant. Their opinions are the more charitable translation as a result. You enthusiastically accepted the openness of the Council's ideas until you joined Karol Wojtyla. The traditional Eucharist we have today results from the Vatican's uncharitable translation of the Bible and negation of God's law of loving others.

I am uncomfortable with calling you a "dunce" in my previous letter, but it is a term more charitable than names Jesus used, such as "hypocrites," about his churchmen acting in similar unloving ways (Mk 7:6-13). Because of your limitations in abilities, God's plan for man's redemption lies buried in the vincible ignorance of men like you who cling to other men's ideas because of a lack of moral courage to love God and all other people as they should.

Sincerely,

May 13, 2011

Dear Holy Father,

You agreed with St. Augustine's opinion that Donatism's ex-communication of their wayward priests disqualified them because of the movement's lack of the fundamental Christian virtue of charity. You wrote your doctoral dissertation upon Augustine and his regarding the lack of *caritas* (charity) as the defining characteristic, which denied Donatism being true church.

Sacramentum Caritatis lacks the same "charity." It allows your bishops to unlovingly exclude most of God's created people from God's Eucharist. The "truth" of Christ cannot exist in the thinking of the individual or the institution that lacks *caritas* or "charity" for all people created by God. In your apostolic exhortation of the "Sacrament of Charity," you allow our traditional discrimination in Eucharist. You planned for your Vatican to artfully control your diocesan bishops to continue excluding almost everyone from the Eucharist. My diocese, by statute, now is being true to our uncharitable Eucharist. As acting vicar you hypocritically acted untrue to Christ's law of love. You seem not to care about negating evidence of God's saving action in Eucharist.

The Eucharist was instituted by God as an "interdependent" part of God's new covenant to save every human. The ecumenical spirit of Vatican II enlightened our New Testament scholars' movement to return us to God's open Eucharist making each human being one in Christ. You enthusiastically accepted the openness of the Council's ideas until you opposed the scholars and joined Karol Wojtyla as protagonists of Vatican II and then argued stupidly (*God Is Near Us*, p. 60).

I am sorry for having called you a "dunce" in my last letter, but it is softer than names Jesus used, such as "hypocrites," with his churchmen who were acting in a similar way (Mk 7:6-13). By authority of God's words in the new covenant and Christ's orders, which you choose to disobey, I feel I should use an appropriate attention grabber for those who govern the church and deny people their God-given rights. The title of illegitimacy commonly used for the illegitimate, arguably was suggested by you to the UN on April past, as might be used to define those who deny God-given rights for the real presence to be consumed by each human being as God intends. I hope it is ignorance rather than a Church god influencing you all to sin against *our Lord*'s deal.

Sincerely,

May 17, 2011

Dear Holy Father,

"Woe to me if I do not preach the Gospel!" (cf. 1 Cor 9:16). Paul of Tarsus voiced this obligation that we followers of Jesus Christ have to the rest of the world. But which Gospel?

The Gospel according to Jesus was likely revealed in the period he spoke and the actions he demonstrated at the last weekend of the first Easter. Mainly it deals with God's new covenant (Jer 31:31), which Jesus incorporates by reference in the words of the Last Supper (1 Cor 11:23-26) and the revelation that our God of Love redeems the whole world from death simply because we are created by God to be loved as we are. This is the good news and the peace that Jesus expressed without being conditioned on our reciprocating with faith or good works. God loves us all as we are.

The Eucharist is, as you described, an "interdependent" element of Christ's last words and Christ's death. Just as the death would be a mere execution without the words, the words instituting the Eucharist receive their universal meaning from Christ's shedding the blood of the covenant. Thus, at every mass, we proclaim God's good news, the new covenant, and thank God for it as fulfilled on the cross.

The Gospel of John, however, ignores the words of the new covenant and the words instituting the Eucharist to speculate on the philosophy of the Greeks and has Jesus as a standard of the word of God exemplifying behavior based on his culture or wisdom of his people. The standard view of Christianity today is, thus, summed up and accepted as authenticated by John's writings. The Gospel's author(s) promises eternal life to those who believe in Christ if they also are baptized in water (Jn 3:5-6). We are to believe that our God of Love created most of us to suffer eternal torment, unless we change our nature. Salvation is up to us and not a unilateral performance by God.

Vatican II's ideal global Church of Christ and its New Testament scholars' espousal of an open Eucharist for each and every human being unconditionally was the Spirit's attempt to return us to the Gospel of Jesus Christ. God has in mind a universal purpose for both church and Eucharist, but it is being negated by the Vatican during the watch of each successor to Pope John XXIII. Pope Benedict XVI is presently our last hope to remedy the church's wrongdoing. But he seems to have his head in the traditional darkness and refuses to translate the Bible in a charitable way for all people as Christ's Gospel plainly reveals.

Sincerely,

May 20, 2011

Dear Holy Father,

Please imagine that you are in Saul of Tarsus' shoes when he receives the good news from the risen Jesus Christ that Paul repeats to the Corinthians (1 Cor 11:23-26). Since this is the first written report of the Last Supper words, which words you agree are "interdependent" with the passion and death of Jesus, we ask you to draft from God's words God's good news for publication. *The Gospel According to Pope Benedict XVI* would not be influenced by the hearsay of our Canon and should most likely mention God's Eucharist and God's new covenant (Jer 31:31-34) as essential parts of your Gospel. St. Paul and the evangelists tried to explain our redemption with human wisdom and negated God unilaterally saving human creation in the folly of the cross to fulfill God's covenant. God alone forgives and teaches humankind without our contribution and forgets our sin forever as God pledges. The real presence of God is with us intimately in daily Eucharist for God's purpose, and, mysteriously, the love of God within us all is to transform humanity. God does it all, and we need only take, eat, and enjoy it all. Perhaps some will reciprocate lovingly and give God a true gift, which may be the goal of God's creation.

I cannot prove it to be true in the world today, but I submit that God, in God's goodness and love for all of us humans, creates no one for eternal torment. God creates everyone to share love and everlasting life with God and each other. God, ever optimistical, hopes humans will love God spontaneously. Considering that I may be correct should make peaceful tidings on earth. God's peace on earth would be far more assured today, however, if we had shared the new covenant's Eucharist for the previous millenniums. To return to God's way for our redemption, I submit, is mainly your obligation. I am "obliged" to express my concerns to my spiritual shepherd (No. 37, *Lumen Gentium*). Otherwise, "the-buck-stops-with-you" to make the church correctly fulfill its mission for the good of the world.

Yours concernedly,

May 24, 2011

Dear Holy Father,

Jesus's death introduced the new covenant relationship of God with us, but the relationship always existed. Our awareness resulted from Jesus's words fulfilling God's new covenant (1 Cor 11:23-26) in Jesus's blood. From the beginning of creation, God creates us as one in God's image, imprints us with the knowledge of God and God's law, forgives our evildoing, and remembers our sin no more (Jer 31:34). We are all one in Christ.

Evidence of God's unilateral performance of this covenant, I suggest, is perceived in the faith and life of an aboriginal tribe in the Australia outback who call themselves the "real people." The perceiver, Marlo Morgan, a medical doctor from Kansas City, wrote "*Mutant Message Down Under*" about her fourteen hundred miles "walkabout" with the tribe, sharing their life for months and reporting their ancient philosophy. These people believe in God as the "oneness" of creation wherein we are a global family evolved by learning from each other. Also, they feel our beingness is enhanced by our giving care to others, and we all are meant to be together for eternity. Jesus, the Divine One in human form, is venerated, but Christianity does not apply to them because they never forgot and are always living the truth of God, Jesus, and oneness is everything.*

The only thing that I would think God might wish for these people of God on earth is God's Holy Eucharist that Jesus instituted at the Last Supper and directed that all people take and consume to nourish us with actual God. I can see where it would not improve their lot as God is with them always; however, Christ did order all to take and consume.

The Roman Catholic Church would not share Holy Communion with these "real people," anyway, because they are only baptized in the blood of Christ and not the Church's additional water rite. Besides, the priest's numbers are lacking in Australia as you are informed by Bishop William Morris, to serve the Eucharist to all Australians, let alone aborigines in the outback. Traditionalist's teachings include *Didache's*,(16482)

"Give not that which is holy to the dogs" to further rule out God's commandment of loving these "real people" as equals.

Sincerely,

---

*(I was told later that *Wickipedia* reported the author, Dr. Morgan, admitted she wrote the book fictionally.)

May 25, 2011

Dear Holy Father,

Readings at mass today had to do, in part, with the traditionalists arguing we had to be circumcised to be saved. We still have teachings in the church that we must be baptized in water to be saved, ignoring the fact that our baptism in the blood of Christ has God forgiving our evildoing and forgetting our sins forever (see Jer 31:34 with Cor 11:23-26).

God's unilateral performance of the new covenant (Jer 31:31) is manifested in the knowledge of God's law of love practiced virtuously by the aborigine "real people" mentioned in my last letter. God imprints in our hearts and minds God's knowledge, and they acknowledge this fact in action. The extent to which the "real people" cared for creation as they care for themselves is a lesson well planted in everyone's "bowels" but fully acknowledged only among "real people."

God's purpose for the Eucharist may have been added for the rest of us, who need reminding of the new covenant and the price Jesus lovingly paid for it, a refreshing that the "real People" do not need. God's performance of the covenant by God alone may require Eucharist in addition to the teaching and forgiving God fulfills in redemption. Because we misunderstand, we add circumcisions, baptisms, and repentance, but God is satisfied in saving us simply for being ourselves or like these "real people."

You opposed the New Testament scholars' "ideal" of an open Eucharist. In your argument, you squeezed your own "gnats" of cited authority (i.e., Jn 13:10 and 1 Cor 11:27ff.). You even grasped for a straw in submitting *Didache* 10:6 which states: "May grace come and may this world pass away. Hosanna to the God of David. If any man is holy, let him come; if any man is not, let him repent. Maran Atha. Amen." (*God Is Near Us*, p. 60.)

However, when you became Pope Benedict XVI, you lacked courage of your convictions and delegated the judgment on the open Eucharist to diocesan bishops (*Sacramentium Caritatis*). As Jesus prophesized: "You have made a fine art of setting aside God's commandment in the interests of keeping your traditions!" (Mk 7:9.)

I suspect that you know by heart to care for all people God created, as Christ did, and know you should open Eucharist to everyone unconditionally.

Yours concernedly,

May 26, 2011

Dear Holy Father,

My *St. Joseph Weekday Missal* had an introduction for Thursday of the Fifth Week of Easter that read: "We should always remember that we are all one under the Good Shepherd. We cannot bar anyone from our circle of friends. All human beings are our brothers and sisters, and our belief in the Father is proof that we are related to every human being. Faith imposes upon us this underlying unity and is the foundation of lasting peace. Christ our Lord showed charity and love in the salvation of all human beings."

Fresh from reading Marlo Morgan's *Mutant Message Down Under* and the philosophy of the fifty thousand year old aborigine culture, which sounds the same as the quote above, I wonder how God's imprinting the knowledge of the new covenant (Jer 31:31) works in all human beings created as God pledges to occur. Jesus's death changed the lot of us, even the souls of the dead, and his fulfillment of the new covenant likely had an effect on every human God created out of love. We Catholics accept the immaculate conception of Mary affected mysteriously by way of her son's glory; so God having immaculately created mankind from its inception by reason of Christ's glory is conceivable. Even though Jesus praised John the Baptist's birth, he was likely in human error to add that even the least of humans born to the new covenant kingdom is greater than John. John the Baptist was also imprinted with the common knowledge we see in the aborigines that were imprinted in "bowels" by God at the same time God's pledge of forgiving his evildoings took place, perhaps at John's conception, thanks to the loving sacrifice of Jesus Christ for all.

We won't know the truth of these thoughts and philosophies until our veils of ignorance are lifted after death. However, in the interim, we must exercise the love of God's law imprinted in our hearts and treat everyone on earth impartially. Personally, you know as well as I do that the "tempting idea" you expressly felt on being informed of the New Testament scholars' open Eucharist for everyone, non-Catholics and mortal sinners too, was an appeal from God's Spirit in your heart and mind.

All the changes called for by God, a few hinted at in Vatican II, may be too much for

Catholics to swallow. So I suggest we start with you opening up our Eucharist and allow the Spirit of God to transform us to whatever extent God feels would be the church's more effective mission for the life of the world's people.

Sincerely,

May 31, 2011

Dear Holy Father,

I am constantly concerned about your wrongdoing in respect to the Eucharist.

I presume Pope John Paul II and you were so close to returning us to God's way of redemption by means of an all-inclusive Eucharist that it is a crying shame your limitations prevent you from agreeing with the New Testament scholars' contention on an open Eucharist. As Cardinal Joseph Ratzinger you wrote *God Is Near Us* and, at p. 59, reported the New Testament scholars' criticism of the church's exclusive Eucharist. They also contended, in the Spirit of Vatican II, that Christ's last words and actions meant for a universal and all-inclusive Eucharist to fulfill God's new covenant relationship with humankind.

You expressly wrote of how "tempting the idea of every human being coming to encounter the universal God," without any limit or denominational preconditions, would be. But, you wrote, in part, as follows:

> But then again—however tempting the idea may be—it contradicts what *we* find in the Bible. (Emphasis mine)

Presumably the "*we*" includes you and His Holiness Pope John Paul II, for whom you spoke then and with whom you joined as protagonists rejecting the Council in part by your own restrictive interpretations of principles (see *My Hope For The Church*, p. 93, by Fr. Bernard Haring C.Ss.R). However, when you succeeded to John Paul's throne, you shied from ruling on the matter and delegated the judgment on the Eucharist to our pre-selected and pre-indoctrinated diocesan bishops (*Sacramentum Caritatis* or "Sacrament of Love"). The hypocrisy

Jesus prophesized (Mk 7:6) appears in your "Caritatis" title for an uncharitable cause.

You wrote in your doctoral dissertation on St. Augustine that lack of charity denies the church from being true to the Church of Christ. You do these things in the face of Jesus Christ's prophesy that you churchmen artfully cling to church's traditions and negate God's commandment to love everyone impartially (Mk 7:1-13).

Time is running out, but we still can right the wrong by simply loving others as we do ourselves.

Persistently yours,

June 1, 2011

Dear Holy Father,

I am still disturbed by how near you came to doing the greatest good in your life, that is, make our church's exclusive Eucharist into an all-inclusive one as the post-Vatican II New Testament scholars supported. (See *God Is Near Us*, p. 59). You can still obtain the glorious act by a mere use of your pen to correct your error.

As a lay partner of the Passionist Fathers, I read prayers at bedside from *Living Wisdom For Every Day* by Bennet Kelley, C. P. on May 30, St. Paul of the cross offered the following to Obey the Spirit—always be obedient to the inner indications and attractions the Holy Spirit gives you. Jesus desires a complete detachment from all that is created, a true mystical death to all that is not God, and a great nakedness and poverty of spirit in order to be completely clothed with the most pure faith and love of Jesus Christ.

Assuming that the feeling you had on acknowledging the New Testament scholars' contention for an open Eucharist, which you confessed was a "tempting idea" (see p. 59), was actually of an inner indication and attraction from the Holy Spirit to you. To obey the Spirit or reject the message Jesus expects a compete detachment from personal interests and attachments to the world temptations. Killing of such thoughts that are not God, not charitable to all humanity, is what the Spirit called for before you selfishly rejected the idea of an open Eucharist. I suggest you were aware of what you were doing and did not pursue the rejection upon attaining your present power. However, as Jesus prophesied (Mk 7:1-13), your hierarchy artfully and hypocritically drafted your letter of Sacrament Charity (*Sacramentum Caritatis*) to cling to church's tradition and excommunicate almost everyone from the Eucharist in a non-charitable way.

As protagonists of the global Church of Christ, which "subsists" in the Catholic church, and the new covenant (Jer 31) relationship that reveals all people created are one and cleansed with Christ, your dioceses have taught *Antichrist* dogmas of mere human precepts in distribution of God's universal gift of Eucharist, a blasphemy against the Spirit of God!

Disturbingly yours,

June 3, 2011

Dear Holy Father,

In or about 1938, Adolph Hitler, your nation's leader, explained God's work in causing Austria to cease to exist as a nation. He explained in a speech his thinking:

> There is a higher ordering, and we are all nothing else than its agents. When on 9 March Herr Schuschnigg broke his agreement then in that second I felt that now the call of Providence had come to me And that which then took place in three days was only conceivable as the fulfillment of the wish and will of Providence. I would now give thanks to Him who let me return to my homeland in order that I might now lead it into the German Reich! Tomorrow may every German recognize the hour and measure its import and bow in humility before the Almighty, who in a few weeks has wrought a miracle upon us.

The Catholic church today, as posed by Pope Paul VI and his scribes in No. 9 of *Lumen Gentium*, is led by similar sentiments to Hitler's Master Race invading Austria. Today, as the spiritual leader of Catholicism you have a church mission, to lead a select community of the righteous to convert the best of humanity to your church. Those you leave unworthy, apparently most of people created, you contend are not to be allowed in their Creator's presence by some kind of Christian fulfillment of the wish and will of providence.

You, who concluded Donatism is not "true church" for its lack of charity in excluding members from the Sacrament, know that *Lumen Gentium* states that the Church of Christ "subsists" in the Catholic church. By charitably inviting its members made up of all humanity to share its Eucharist Catholicism remains "true church." So long as it excludes no one from Jesus's order to take and consume his Eucharist, it is Christ's church. Consider, with an open heart and mind, the power you have to conform Catholicism to the Church of Christ by freeing its Eucharist and have God's presence embrace God's creatures as God always desires.

Persistently yours,

June 6, 2011

Dear Holy Father,

The Gospel of John lectures by Rev. Donald Senior, C. P., STD, are a masterful work of theology and eloquence, but the Gospel overlooks God's personally guaranteed salvation of all.

The Gospel and Senior's translation, I suggest, negate the common knowledge that God imprints in our hearts and minds to confuse even the least to the greatest of us. God pledges that we need no teaching, other than God's, on how to know God and God's law (Jer 31:31-34). Also, Jesus's words at the Last Supper insure completely God's new covenant performance in his Eucharist (1 Cor 11:23-26). Consequently, everyone created is covered by God's pledges to teach and forgive us solely on God's goodness. The only contribution required on our part is to be created living human beings and consume the Eucharist.

God's new covenant that Jesus died to fulfill is his good news traditionally mistranslated by disciples. I am at peace knowing God saves each of us even if Catholic traditionalists reject our God-given knowledge of God and God's law of love, "for I will forgive their evildoing," says God, which obviously overcomes any refusal to agree with God's agreement.

My take on *The Gospel of John* is that it was written by those of a group out of Ephesus, whose parents were re-baptized and confirmed by Paul (Acts 19:5-6). The offspring added Hellenist and Stoic ideas, plus contributions from other traditions and surrounding cultures or religions, to bridge human wisdom in a Gospel to explain the folly of the cross. They constitute the common mindset of the times and place, certainly influenced by the knowledge God imprints in everyone but lacking in love and deliberately disregards God's words of the new covenant and Jesus's dying orders to share God's Eucharist with all people. The Gospel to believe (or else) implies a monstrous god who condemns most people created to everlasting torment (see *Time*, 4/25/11, at pp. 38 *et seq*), while its accumulated wisdom leave the mystery unsolved.

Jesus's good news, in his performance of the new covenant, is proclaimed at the Lord's Supper, especially on ingesting the real presence of God in Eucharist. Jesus instituted the Eucharist at the Last Supper, in obedience to instructions, because God wants to intimately be with each of us. We, thus, benefit from the new covenant as God planned from the beginning of creation; plus, God may get a spontaneous reaction of love on occasion.

Persistently yours,

June 7, 2011

Dear Holy Father,

The issue that I am trying to put in controversy with my spiritual leaders is the exclusive Eucharist of the Catholic church. The matter is so important that I feel I should take the gloves off and simply put my inner convictions to you all.

God's words in the new covenant (Jer 31:31-34) are the words of God and we should believe this to be true. Jesus's words at the Last Supper gives meaning to the new covenant words as he dies to perform the covenant for Jews and all Gentiles (1

Cor 11:23-26). Whether Jesus speaks as instructed by God (see Jn 12:49) or speaks as God somehow being in Jesus, the words are those of God creating us to be one with God forever. Jesus died to proclaim this good news and even its unawareness should put us at peace in trusting God so loves us to save us as we are (see *God's Gift To You* and its *Sequel*).

From whenever humans exercised their wisdom to explain God and Christ, instead of relying on God's work as pledged, they insist on improving on God's doing, teaching, and forgiving. God, however, loves us nonetheless.

The Eucharist is an "interdependent" part of God's redeeming us (*God Is Near Us*, p. 29). Jesus instituted it by ordering that we "all" take and consume his flesh for God's purposes. This is not imprinted as law within us nor in God's law—but is an obligation ordered by Jesus at the Last Supper. On the other hand, the exclusive Eucharist is a man-made job that deprives us of God's presence within us, and our way of loving and thanking God in reciprocation of all our gifts because it lacks fundamental charity.

Also, "it negates the evidence of God's saving action in history." My Bible states it is a blasphemy against the Spirit that will not be forgiven. (See footnote Mt 12:31ff., p. 1084, of *The New American Bible For Catholics*). I mention it, not to suggest its truth, but as an opinion that overlooks the fact that our God is Love. God being Love and God's commandment prevents the Church of Christ to subsist in the Catholic church so long as it excludes anyone from Eucharist or forgiveness.

Sincerely yours,

June 7, 2011

Dear Holy Father,

Anthony Grafton, the journalist who authored "Reading Ratzinger" (*The New Yorker*, 4/25/05) characterized your misrepresentations as "wielding proof texts that in his hands are as powerful, and as malleable, as articles of the constitution in the hands of an ideologically partisan jurist." The basis for his criticism was your argument against Brazilian Leonard Boff's teaching of "liberation theology" and his claim that it was justified by the definition of the true church "subsists" in the Catholic church as defined in *Lumen Gentium*, Chapter 1, No. 8, which allows for a qualification of the church's traditional exclusivity to have "liberation theology" as one of its many elements of a sanctification and truth outside the church's visible confines. However, you silenced his teaching by claiming when the council used the term "subsists" it stated it in the strongest terms that the true church "both is, and can only be *fully* present" in the Roman Church. But Grafton reported you reframed the council's debate well beyond the historical circumstances of the document's origins, and nowhere had the drafters mentioned the terms asserted by you to have occurred.

Hans Küng also investigated the terms and made inquiry of one of the drafters in writing. He asked the secretary of the theological commission, Msgr. Gerard Philips why they used "subsists in" rather than "is." He received the reply that "we wanted to keep the matter open." Kung, a colleague at Tübingen, stated you were always fixed on tradition and, as Pope, told him "I have to keep the tradition," meaning the Catholic tradition (*NCR*, 11/12/10, p. 17).

Recently, a clearer case evidencing a deliberate misrepresentation to win a point is in your letter misquoting your predecessor to justify your demand of early retirement for Bishop William Morris of Australia. You wrote: "The late Pope John Paul II has decided *infallibly* and irrevocably that the church has not the right to ordain women to the priesthood" (emphasis mine). In 1994 when this apostolic letter was written, you probably participated in its drafting. It actually reads: "I declare that the church has no authority whatsoever to confer priesthood ordination on women and this judgment is to be definitively held by all the church's faithful." No word of infallibility was used, and you must have known this and the difference it makes in authority to characterize the bishop's wrongdoing. It tells me, as a trial attorney of much experience discerning liars, that your credibility is not to be trusted as an ideological partisan.

This brings us back to Jesus condemning members of hierarchies for clinging to tradition uncharitably and denying people their rights to supper with Christ (Mk 7:1-13). Christ forewarned you in prophecy, in New Testament scholars, and in all the various ways my writings reminded you. Still you persist. Stupidly I would suggest in brotherly love.

Sincerely yours,

June 8, 2011

Dear Holy Father,

On Paul's departure from Ephesus, he warned "from your group, men will come forward perverting the truth" (see Acts 20:30). *The Gospel of John*, at the same daily mass, has Jesus saying that he protected his disciples "and none of them was lost except the son of destruction," (Jn 17:12) who was destined to be lost. Paul prophesied what John's writers misunderstood.

Pause and reflect on this Gospel's passage, using the knowledge of God and God's law of love imprinted in us by Christ's execution of God's new covenant, and ask: who would believe that a God of love could create Judas knowing Judas was predestined to loss or everlasting torment? Think also the injustice to Judas, who was obviously ignorant of the risk of eternal torment, if he chose wrong.

But Judas possessed the pre-forgiven deal or pardon that God's covenant guarantees. The history we have from scripture of the new covenant, which John's Gospel negates, lovingly assures us and Judas of true good news.

Analyzing the above passages of John's writers, they simply misstate the truth because they do not accept that God forgives evildoing as the new covenant pledges. Accepting, however, the new covenant benefiting Judas too, Judas is forgiven and is not lost. Thus, our God of love creates us all in God's image to be forgiven and be together forever. Consequently, the authenticity of John's Gospel is lacking, and likely a perversion inadvertently caused by those from Ephesus and carried on by you traditionalists since.

Popes and bishops at Vatican II tried to return us to God's covenant relationship. Their idea of a global church for everyone on earth, for example, and their New Testament scholars' espousing an open and inclusive Eucharist describe benefits of our God of love. You antagonists of the council's principles, like Judas, pursue your own interests rather than agree with the new covenant relationship wherein God does it all, and we need only remain at peace and enjoy God's benefits. Instead, you give us an exclusive Eucharist, negating the evidence of God's loving action of all humans because of your closed minds and hearts.

Sadly yours,

June 10, 2011

Dear Holy Father,

A few minutes ago, we prayed this *Prayer After Communion* "God our Father, the Eucharist is our bread of life and the sacrament of our forgiveness. May our sharing in this mystery bring us eternal life where Jesus is Lord for ever and ever." *Amen*

I am trying to represent the rights of my siblings who you choose to refuse Eucharist, even though it is their God-given right. Jesus died to reveal God's covenant, wherein God teaches us that we need no church as God alone teaches us and forgives us each and all by including an inclusive Eucharist.

I wish God would give me insight into your thoughts on the topic of my writings to persuade you to do what God imprinted in you of common knowledge (Jer 31:33-34) which your typescript of lectures evidence you even taught: "Mark 14:24 prevents the church from becoming simply a select community of the righteous, a community that condemns the wayward masses to perdition." But that is exactly what you and the antagonists of Pope John XXIII and his bishops' portion of Vatican II do. (See *Dogmatic Constitution*'s *Lumen Gentium*, Chapt II, No. 9). From being an enthusiast of the openness of Pope John's council, you swung like a weather vane with the wind of opportunity, to return us to the traditional exclusive Eucharist. I thought it might have been in response to the 1968 students revolt, but I suspect your motivation is likely more self-interests. I am not supposed to judge you or your motives, but the traditional Eucharist appears to be *Antichrist*. Arguably it is a defensive measure to protect the occupations of clergymen against the covenant's exclusive teaching provision.

I read that the weakness and strength, as a nation, of Germans is their lack of imagination. They are found incapable of putting themselves in anyone else's place and, thus, hurt people unreasonably. The strength of this quality allows Germans to behave inflexibly and without faltering. (So, wrote Irène Némirovsky in her novel *Suite Franscaise*, at pp. 567 and 568, of WWII's occupied France from where she was taken to Germany and exterminated, preventing her finishing the story.)

Unless you repent from clinging to tradition, most of us human beings are left to the Catholic church's perdition by depriving us of our bread of life and the sacrament of forgiveness or most of us face chastisements and delay to "eternal life where Jesus is Lord forever and ever" whether or not perdition exists.

Anxiously yours,

June 13, 2011

Dear Holy Father,

The issue that I am trying to put in controversy from my monologue concerns the exclusive Eucharist of the Catholic church. The matter is so important that I chance offending you to put my inner convictions before you. My argument becomes less persuasive but may make you awaken because I believe you have retained a guilty conscience on the matter for decades.

God's pledges in the new covenant (Jer 31:31-34) are the express words of God and are spoken to each of us personally. Jesus's words at the Last Supper you heard to be "interdependent" with the new covenant terms as Jesus dies to perform the pledges for Jews and all Gentiles (1 Cor 11:23-26). Whether Jesus speaks as instructed by God (see Jn 12:49) or speaks as God somehow in Jesus, the words reveal God making us one with God forever. Jesus died to proclaim this good news and reminds us in Eucharist his words are to be accepted literally. In contrast, all other relevant scriptural and traditional teachings are human precepts and commentary on God's revelation in Jesus to humanity. Those human precepts and traditions, that you insist upon clinging to, are mostly incompetent opinions on the Eucharist of God (*God's Gift To You* and *Seque*l).

The Eucharist and its institution are essentially "interdependent" with Christ's words and death (*God Is Near Us*, p. 29). I agree with your "interdependent" point and add that Jesus, at the Last Supper, ordered that we "all" take and consume Christ flesh. It is God's command to love others, thus, as Jesus reveals. In contrast, the exclusive Eucharist is uncharitable, deprives most people of appreciating God's love, and absents God's real presence within them. Excluding anyone from Eucharist has repercussions on everyone loving God spontaneously and in reciprocation for our benefits from God—*Denying many of us ability to love each other in unity*. Under the circumstances, the Roman Catholic Church's practice of loving neighbors is a hypocrisy, and we remain globally ununited.

Scripturally, "it negates the evidence of God's saving action in history." And may be deemed to be a blasphemy against the Spirit that, according to man, may not be forgiven. (See footnote Mt 12:31ff., p. 1084, of *The New American Bible For Catholics.*) The Church's present Eucharist (*Sacramentum Caritatis*) prevents the Church of Christ to subsist in the Catholic church whenever it excludes anyone from Eucharist. Remember, you wrote this truth in your doctoral dissertation on St. Augustine and the Donatists. (*The*

New Yorker, 7/25/05, "Reading Ratzinger.") You should practice what you preach.

Sincerely yours,

June 15, 2011

Dear Holy Father,

The Gospel According to John is reputed to be written by the son of Zebedee. It was actually published at Ephesus, Timothy's diocesan community. Its writing's tradition essentials were founded by Bishop Iraneous who selected it to be in our Canon. Iraneous had a prejudice favoring this fourth Gospel because his mentor, St. Polycarp, claimed to have been converted by John the son of Zebedee. Thus, though likely written by many authors, in about AD 200 the Bishop of Lyon, France, identified John, "the beloved disciple," to be the source of this traditional writing.

My critical analysis finds it hard to accept this Gospel as authority because it negates God's pledged new covenant relationship with humanity, which is established by Jesus. The

Prologue's *Logo* is of the Stoic school and introduces biblical scholars to the mishmash of traditions that the writers collected from surrounding religions and cultures to make up this Gospel. Personally, I sensed the writings attacked Peter and other apostles for failings politically, as though "the beloved disciple" was ambitiously presented by this Ephesian cult to lead the church. Chapter 21 shows change when Peter is acknowledged to be Christ's choice while their favorite is given another role never having to die.

The major factor that rules out this Gospel as being as authentic as the traditions of the synoptic is its disregard of the words of the new covenant and the Eucharist at the Last Supper. Besides negating God's forgiving our sins, it ignores the words instituting the Eucharist to share the fact God alone has saved us. Instead the sayings of Jesus are entered in two different discourses neither mentioning the words of God in context of the new covenant (Jer 31) nor salvation occurs as Jesus died for everyone (1 Cor 11:23-26) whether any believes, are baptized, and so on.

Christianity, however, erroneously summed up salvation through the death and resurrection of Jesus to be mainly in the Gospel of John, which promises salvation to those of faith and good works, and hell to those who do not act to save themselves. It implies a monstrous God who creates many to everlasting torment. Rev. Don Senior, C. P., commercially advertises in his book that this Fourth Gospel is equally authentic with that of the synoptic. He, like you, refuses to respond to my letters of concern in order to correct them and point out any erroneous analysis of my argument on the church's Eucharist and God's new covenant. As a result, we maintain our church in an uncharitable tradition with our Dogmatic Constitution (see *Lumen Gentium* No. 9) and exclusive Eucharist without dispute.

Sincerely concerned,

June 17, 2011

Dear Holy Father,

Whatever happened to you in or about 1968 when the student's revolt may have contributed to your change of mind or heart on the subject matter of openness in the Catholic church? The times triggered your changing camps from the progressives to the traditionalist non-movement. Coincidently, the charismatic and rising star of Karol Wojtyla may have influenced you. Your colleague Hans Kung claims that you were frightened into leaving Tübingen by the students' revolt, but he also said that you always were fixed on Catholic tradition. (*NCR* 11/12/10, p. 17.)

Recently, French Vatican writer Jean Marie Guénois was reported to have written that Pope Benedict XVI's core aim is to promote "a Catholic church that is more Catholic" (*NCR*, 6/10/11, p. 16). Obviously, I am being confronted with your preconvinced confirmation that the traditional Eucharist of the church, which excludes so many, is good enough for human kind and authorized by *our Lord* if your diocesan bishops judge it to be their Eucharist of choice. (*Sacramentium Caritatis*—"Sacrament of Charity.")

My recently informed conscience tells me it's all wrong, and the church is *Antichrist* and uncharitable in its exclusive Eucharist practice. As far as I know my spiritual shepherd, Pope Benedict XVI refuses to consider my concerns. Still, I feel I am obliged by Christ and the church to express my opinions, which I am dutifully doing through the only organs available to me. However, I fail to perceive any spiritual leader respectfully acknowledging my efforts or recognizing any dignity or responsibility on my part as a layman trying to do my obligation in expectation of leaders, responding with love to my efforts. Our *Dogmatic Constitution on the Church* represents that I am to receive such leaders' attention and hopefully even a "dialogue between the laity and their spiritual leaders" to aid the whole church to effectively fulfill its mission for the life of the world (see No. 37 of *Lumen Gentium*, Document of Vatican II). The Constitution as thus used is a lie that has misled me to write in spite of my misgivings but in hopes of a change of heart on your part.

Sadly yours,

June 21, 2011

Dear Holy Father,

Bible scholar Fr. Raymond Brown hinted that the "historical Jesus" was most likely not the "real" Jesus because of distrust of the shifting historical construct. You are reported to have developed his hint in your *Jesus of Nazareth* (see Cavadini's "History and Mystery," *Commonweal*, 6/17/11). I, too, used Fr. Brown's opinion in trying to know Jesus. Brown had written that Jesus and Paul were wrong in believing in demons, but they were creatures of their culture and accepted superstitions as true. (*St. Anthony's Messenger*, March 1971.)

Today at Mass's Gospel of Mathew (7:6), he quotes Jesus as saying the following:

> Do not give what is holy to dogs or
> toss your pearls before swine.

You taught that the charitable standard we must use to translate the Bible would rule out Jesus calling non-Jews "dogs," as he did with the non-Jew mother who pleaded for the crumbs from his table, when it comes to recipients of God's Eucharist. However, you argued *Didache* in opposing the post-Vatican II scholars of the New Testament in their contention that the Church of Christ includes everybody created as called to receive God's real presence in an open Eucharist. (*God Is Near Us*, pp. 59-60). Bluntly, Jesus is wrong again in being a creature of his culture if you represent him in clinging to your church's traditions so uncharitably to allow an exclusive Eucharist.

The hypocrisy of your letter's title "Sacrament of Charity" (*Sacramentum Caritatis*) is reflected in the fine art you and your hierarchy practice to set aside God's law of love in the interests of clinging to your traditions as is prophesied by Christ (Mk 7:6-10). *Didache* 9.5 deals with the Eucharist too and furnishes you some precedence in ruling: "Give not that which is holy to the dogs" but you are wrong.

I know that I am treated as a "dog" by my spiritual shepherds on the subject matter of my concern, and I am including the whole lot of you in hopes someone sees that the words of Jesus at the Last Supper are the words of God as distinguished from his many human words empty of divinity.

Sincerely concerned, I am

June 22, 2011

Dear Holy Father,

You wrote and preached that Jesus's words at the Last Supper were "interdependent" with his death, and without the meaning they gave it was a mere execution (*God Is Near Us*, p. 29). Jesus's words also gained meaning from the death whereby Jesus redeemed the world and fulfilled God's unilateral performance of the new covenant to bring us God's kingdom.

But what was the meaning for the death. Jesus may have been God's "scapegoat" in carrying all human sins upon the cross, but this reveals a less than loving God. Jesus's death redeems or rescues us from worldly pursuits ignoring God, perhaps by revealing God is love in the loving efforts of Jesus to benefit God and us. My spiritual leaders should advise me of their opinions or dialogue with me if they too struggle to know why Jesus had to die so horribly to fulfill God's new covenant. But these are not the concerns that risk Catholicism being true church.

The crucifixion's universal result gives "interdependent" meaning to the words instituting an open Eucharist and the global "body" to include all humanity. Essential to both the words and the death is the expression of Jesus that the Eucharist is of the new covenant (Jer 31) and, thereby, God's relationship in the baptism of blood covers all humans (1 Cor 11:23-26). Such, in effect, is the "good news" of Jesus Christ that should take precedence over all the traditional gospels especially that attributed to John, in any dialogue my spiritual leaders might have with me.

Our *Dogmatic Constitution on the Church,* No. 37, obligates me to express my concerns for the good of the church. Thus, I have dutifully written over three hundred letters to Pope Benedict XVI, two books compiling them, and even hand-delivered many to gain the fatherly advice I was entitled to receive, with hopefully any dialogue, as represented by our dogmatic constitution's provisions. Instead, I received an oppressive silence from the Vatican as one would expect from a lord to his vassal. I admit I did receive a letter response from my diocesan bishop in August 2007. It informed me that my analysis was somehow incorrect, and I was in need of obedience to the teaching of the church. The teaching, Bishop Wiegand wrote: "is very clear since the time at least of St. Paul. To receive Holy Communion requires true Catholic faith and worthiness." I already knew the teaching, and it is the topic of my concern. Because Jesus's human errors reveals that on critical analysis the church too errs especially when it clings so to tradition to secure its *status quo* against God's covenant relationship wherein God is doing it all as God pledges in the new covenant. The negation of the covenant is what denies Catholicism being true church.

Sincerely,

June 23, 2011

Dear Holy Father,

If you would practice what you preached before 1968, we would have Holy Communion correctly distributed as *our Lord* ordered: You progressed in learning to write your doctoral dissertation on the people of God and understood the Donaticism movement excluded priests from the church to disqualify Donatists of being true church.

At Tübingen, typescripts of your lectures claim the words of the Last Supper (Mk 14:24) prevents the Catholic church from becoming the people of God while condemning the nonrighteous to perdition.

You wrote in *God Is Near Us* that the crucifixion gives meaning to the words of the Last Supper, as words and death are "interdependent." Thus, the Eucharist instituted necessarily includes all the world Jesus redeemed by the cross.

In 1964, you published an earlier book on Vatican II in which you wrote enthusiastically of the church's new openness in translating that the mystical body "subsists" in the Catholic church to include those existing elsewhere or outside of the church.

However, in 1968, you changed your views. Some attribute the change to shock from the effects of the students' revolt, while others cynically attribute the change in heart to your rise in hierarchy within the company of Karol Wojtyla.

Later when confronted by the New Testament scholars' criticism of our traditional Eucharist and the contention that Christ meant for an all inclusive Eucharist, you suggested the idea to be "tempting" but opposed the experts on the opinions of "we." I assumed "we" to include Pope John Paul II (see *God Is Near Us*, p. 60).

When you became Pope Benedict XVI, however, instead of asserting your preexisting convictions you passed the judgment on an open Eucharist to preselected and preconditioned Synod of Bishops. Today, as a result, we continue with the traditional closed Eucharist that excludes almost all people from God's real presence. Christ prophesied this hypocrisy occurring (Mk 7:1-13). However, you can still "recognize the body" of Christ to include all people created by *our Lord*, as I suspect you want to do, and avoid the judgment St. Paul mentioned in his letter to Corinth.

Sincerely,

June 24, 2011

Dear Holy Father,

My friend and pastor of years past, Father Joseph Bishop, told me of how Pope John

XXIII slipped into the papacy. The world of humanity obtained this blessing of Pope John by the grace of God. Serendipitously, we found in him Christ's gospel, which was not being sought for by the world and certainly not by the Roman Catholic Church.

Pope Paul VI was supposed to immediately succeed Pope Pius XII, but he was delayed in obtaining his Cardinal ranking by serving the poor excessively according to the opinions of authorities in Milan. While his position was being corrected, Pope John XXIII was selected as an interim representative of Christ.

We were fortunate to have him as Pope, with bishops in council trying to return us to the new covenant (Jer 31) relationship as presented by God, through Jesus, in that weekend of the first Easter. Everything else written about the events of Jesus's last hours are in human commentary and of value if they translate the words and acts of Jesus with a standard of charity for all. Jesus died to fulfill the new covenant whereby God teaches and forgives every human one of us that God loves us just as we are at any moment of our creation. God created us to love us and to be with us as intimately as we allow while on earth and fully thereafter forever.

Vatican II, while Pope XXIII was alive, succeeded in revealing Christ's church to include everyone created and its Eucharist to be for these people of God. But the Roman Catholic Church has closed ranks and excludes most everybody. (See reverse page of Xerox copy from *Dogmatic Constitution on the Church* promulgated by Pope Paul VI as a document of Vatican II.)

Sincerely,

June 27, 2011

Dear Holy Father,

My immediately prior letter has Pope Paul VI promulgating a forged version of the new covenant (Jer 31:31). The forgery fraudulently purports to support the good news of salvation of the people of God for which Jesus died (1 Cor 11:25). Plainly, the false foundation is a construct for the fabrication that only "those who believe in Christ" and are baptized in water (cf. Jn 3:5-6) are the people of God.

Part *No. 9* continues in deceit to define the saved as a small flock of the whole human race, and a messianic people to convert, as the Church of Christ, all the rest of humanity. Obviously, the writers are followers of the *Gospel According to John*.

Pope Paul VI and his scribes include the above as Chapter II, No. 9, of the *Dogmatic Constitution on the Church* (*Lumen Gentium*). It is expressly located to immediately follow and affect Chapter I, No. 8, where the Council of Pope John describes the church, "globally," as follows: "This is the one *Church of Christ* . . . . This Church constituted and organized in the world as a society, *subsists in the Catholic Church* . . . , although many elements of sanctification and of truth are found outside of its visible structure. These elements, as gifts belonging to the Church of Christ, are forces impelling toward Catholic unity" (emphasis and selections are mine).

Pause for a moment and reflect on these contrasting two parts of a dim *Lumen Gentium* (light of the world). *No. 9* implies a Creator who created humanity in divine image only to have most of created people condemned to everlasting torment. God, as I draw inference from *No. 9*, is a monster, but the creator of this God does a monstrous *Antichrist* thing to the Roman church.

No. 8 allows for a charitable inference to be drawn from the global Church of Christ description. The mystical body characterized includes all humanity saved by the blood of the covenant and implies a loving God. The Church of Christ "subsists" in the Catholic church. But not always, as when it drafts a Constitution like the one written by the scribes in *No. 9* (see attached to the reverse page of the prior letter). The Lord's Supper Jesus proposes according to *No. 8* gives proper regard to God's commandment of love (see Mk 7:1-13) and invites everyone created (1 Cor 11:23-26) as renewed in the blood of the covenant (Jer 31:31) to share as one body.

Your Vatican, however, squeezed out a gnat of a letter, hypocritically entitled *Sacramentum Caritatis*, to artfully set aside God's law of love in the interests of clinging to church's tradition. How long are you going to persist in this evildoing or allow our church to condone it?

Sincerely,

June 28, 2011

Dear Holy Father,

Sunday, the feast of the body and blood of Christ had the *Gospel of John's* Discourse on the bread of life, a part of it lodged in my ear. It claimed Jesus said in a synagogue instruction in Capernaum:

> "Let me assure you, if you do not eat the flesh of the Son of Man and drink his blood you have no life in you."

Considering that we have more credibility in the charitable words Jesus said at the Last Supper, which are repeated in Eucharist prayers daily, Jesus died and fulfilled the new covenant (Jer 31) whereby God forgives and forgets our evildoing and sins, and every living human is worthy and entitled to eat the flesh of Christ and drink his blood and have life in us forever with God from the moment of Jesus's death.

However, you and the Roman Catholic Church permit diocesan bishops to deny almost everyone alive Holy Communion with us. You do this by letter *Sacramentum Caritatis*

(Sacrament of Charity), which actually allows bishops to do your uncharitable work of depriving God's life in others.

It reminds me again of Jesus's prophecy (Mk 7:1-13) but also your own words to the United Nations a couple of Aprils past. You stated that governing bodies who withheld the civil rights of their people were acting illegitimately. The greater illegitimacy in withholding the Eucharist from any human being, a God-given right, appropriated for your uncharitable purposes or mere selfish clinging to tradition, bastardizes our Catholic hierarchy directly and yourself indirectly until you quit the blasphemy.

Think of these wayward children as a breed to themselves. They squat in the Church and call to their non-Catholic mates:

We piped you a tune and you did not dance!
We sang you a dirge but you did not wail!

They sing the song of repentance in the face of God's accomplished unilateral covenant salvation. God made us to be selfish and pardons us as sinners. "Yet time will prove where wisdom lies." (Mt 11:16-19.)

Hopefully, in Pope Benedict XVI, we have a knowledgeable teacher who appreciates the covenant and God's commandment of love, in order to still choose Christ's way. I question, however, has he the courage to trust God and overcome his vice of dancing or clinging to the traditionalists' tunes?

Sincerely,

June 29, 2011

Dear Holy Father,

God's promises are provided in God's new covenant (Jer 31:31-34) and performed by Jesus for all humanity (1 Cor 11:23-26) as he expressly represented in his testament, incorporating the covenant by reference, and dying to fulfill God's pledges. God hereby establishes God's relationship with all human beings. God's kingdom has come and is coming moreso to us as we evolve to be one, with Christ forever.

In *God's Gift To You,* I describe that this covenant relationship indicates God loves each of us regardless of our sinning. There is no covenant commandment to do anything or not do anything. Nor is there a law to love God or love each other. Hopefully, if we love it is our free doing. God leaves us alone to do good as we choose to do or as Jesus demonstrated to do. Thus, if we come to love God, it will be because God appeals to us in creation or in Christ. God loves us because God is love and not because of our merit.

Vatican II's spirit caught the essence of God, in that there are no shalls or shall nots in the product of the Council of Pope John XXIII. Its product of a global church, the Church of Christ which included as membership everyone created, was left open to fill God's new kingdom of everyone created. The new covenant relationship that Jesus left us is Christ's testamentary bequest to be filled as needed in our evolution. The only command or law detectable, which is in controversy in the Church, is the order Jesus gave to all people "Take this all of you," and consume of the Eucharist. The Eucharist of the new covenant is for everyone. The command or order, however, is being blocked by the Roman Catholic Church, and all churches that follow the church's lead, to deny God to be present within everyone unconditionally. Catholics cling to manmade reasons to exclude others and, their dam has effectively blocked God's way for millenniums of humanity's loss and God's loss.

Sincerely,

July 1, 2011

National Catholic Reporter

Dear Editor,

Your June 24 issue had a lot about theologians. Our *Dogmatic Constitution on the Church*, promulgated by Pope Paul VI as a document of Vatican II, provides, at No. 37, that "The laity have the right" as brothers in Christ to express our opinions. By reason of knowledge, competence, or outstanding abilities some are "sometimes even *obliged* to express their opinion" (emphasis mine) on theological things which concern the good of the church (see *Lumen Gentium*, No. 37). The *Dogmatic Constitution* declares our spiritual shepherds are to respect and promote the dignity of the laity in these efforts. Also, spiritual shepherds are to consider with fatherly love the suggestions proposed, respectfully acknowledge them, and, hopefully dialogue with the laity.

As an aged trial lawyer, competent to distinguish unilateral from bilateral agreements, God's new covenant (Jer 31:31-34) is performed unilaterally by God, in Christ, to teach and forgive every human being (1 Cor 11:23-26). Thus, Vatican II acknowledged everyone is baptized into the Church of Christ which "subsists in" the Catholic church. New Testament scholars contended that Christ meant Eucharist to be open to everyone. God's goodness purifies everyone baptized in the blood of the covenant, and we need no church forgiving or teaching to be saved or nourished.

I have mailed over three hundred letters of my concerns to Pope Benedict as recorded in my books entitled *God's Gift To You* (available online) and received oppressive silence in response.

Where are the theologians and others in these efforts to Christianize our church?

Charitably concerned,

cc: His Holiness Pope Benedict XVI

July 5, 2011

Dear Holy Father,

Jesus too was our father in the sense of a founding father or the father of the founding fathers who instituted the Christian church. I write this letter on our Independence Day (July 4) when we revolted from rule by a king denying our divine rights. I had thoughts during Mass, a little while ago, that Jesus instituted the church in the Last Supper words that were interdependent with his first Eucharist and the cross and freed us from earthly rule by a hierarchy denying our God-given rights to Eucharist and salvation.

Jesus asked his disciples to repeat the Eucharist meal in remembrance of him. Among the apostles a hierarchy competition arose, to which Jesus said: "Earthly kings lord it over their people . . . yet It cannot be that way with you. Let the greater among you be as the junior, the leader as the servant." (Lk 22)

In your teaching and preaching days, you agreed that the words of Jesus at Supper gave meaning to his death and vice versa his crucifixion defined the breath of words instituting the Eucharist and the Church in service of everyone. Since both words and death were God's expressions, in context of fulfilling God's new covenant, God forgave the evildoing of humanity in the blood of the covenant.

As founded, you churchmen are meant to serve, not rule. Christ made clear to Peter, even in the Gospel of John, he is to serve God's sheep in the numerous flocks to which they strayed. Plainly, as the New Testament scholars taught you after Vatican II, the Eucharist is God's gift to everyone, and the Church must serve it to everyone unconditionally.

However, *Sacramentum Caritatis* is your artful way to shift judgment on the subject matter of serving the Eucharist. But your emotional clinging to Catholic tradition makes you incompetent to judge charitably. You lack the fundamental Christian virtue of charity and uncharitably wrote *Sacramentum Caritatis*. So in the face of Jesus's prophesy you still disregard God's commandment of love and cling to the church's traditional Eucharist (see Mk 7:1-13). You artfully passed the judgment to more biased, indoctrinated, and controlled bishops in Synod to cause in my diocese's denial of God-given rights, by law, to almost everyone living here. My diocesan bishop excommunicates most people created and pardoned by God. People living in the Sacramento Dioceses should revolt against the rule of the church preventing people's participation in the Eucharist. Our national founding fathers did to the king, who discriminately barred our participation in 1776 God-given rights, what we should do to our unjust rulers—rebel!

Sincerely,

July 8, 2011

Dear Holy Father,

One far more knowledgable about you than me is your fellow theology professor and colleague, Hans Küng. He got you the job at Tübingen and reportedly commuted with you to work. You both participated in Vatican II and were enthusiastic progressives in the council's ecumenism and open ideas while Pope John XXIII presided. Küng also witnessed your clinging to Catholic tradition and flight in 1968 from the students' revolt. Since then he visited you at the papacy and exchanged views to hear your bias to Catholic tradition. When Küng expressed concern to your refusing to accept responsibility for the sex abuse cover-ups because as Cardinal Ratzinger you "enjoined secrecy on the episcopal" in your 2001 letter, you terminated exchanges and left him devastated by the 1979 withdrawal of his license to teach as a theologian.

Hans Küng wrote of your conduct (see *NCR*, 11/12/10, p. 17) in concern for the church in crisis. To overcome your bishop's cover-up of clerical sexual abuse, Küng says "we need to go on again in the line of the (Second Vatican Council)." However, I personally fear that the successors to Pope John XXIII have changed the episcopate and the magisterium to prevent the line of thinking that existed while Pope John was alive and had the curia restrained.

The performance of God's new covenant (Jer 31:31-34) in Jesus's words and death that last weekend is memorialized in Eucharist (1 Cor 11:23-26) and establish the true relationship God has made with humanity within the Church of Christ. We are all baptized in the blood of the Lamb and saved as one with Christ forever. I would, thus, agree with Hans Kung to return to the line of thinking of Pope John XXIII and his bishops and continue with their Church of Christ idea which subsists in the Catholic church. Secretary Msgr. Gerard Philips told Hans Küng it was so drafted because "we wanted to keep the matter open." Finally we might return everyone who exists to the true gospel and Church of Christ in lieu of the Catholic Church founded on exclusion of others.

Yours in Christ,

July 11, 2011

Dear Holy Father,

Your colleague Hans Küng wrote to you suggesting that you admit to the blame with bishops in the cover-up scandal on the sexual abuse crisis since you at the congregation for the Doctrine of Faith enjoined secrecy on the episcopate in 2001. You treated Küng to no reply (as I have experienced for my three hundred letters) and ended exchanging views with him. Apparently, you are a rule to yourself and the admonition of Jesus at the Last Supper, to serve and not rule as the Gentiles or kings do, simply rule us out.

Hans Küng, interviewed by John Wlkins (*NCR*, 11/12/10, p. 17), characterized you as an "antimodernist in the deepest sense of the word." However, you wrote a book on Vatican II enthusiastically supporting the Church's new openness toward non-Catholics. Küng reported symptomatic changes came with your rise in the hierarchy. We see the change against the openness of the Church of Christ, a global church for everyone. You narrow the global church down and identify it with the Catholic church and condone exclusive Eucharists. Recently, in argument with Australian Bishop William Morris's suggestion to ordain women for the good of the whole Church and his dioceses in particular, you misrepresented that your predecessor exercised "infallibility" in preventing ordination of women. This implies you believe in infallibility. Küng thinks you are by nature a humble man but one clinging to human traditions of the Roman Catholic Church. I submit the virtue of charity, love of others, may be choked off by your feelings for human traditions and institutions as you experienced with the Master Race in your youth.

Küng's ideal pope is always John XXIII, who I favor too for constancy in practicing what he preached. Pope John and his council's ideal Church of Christ subsists in the Catholic church when the latter acts charitably, and the ideal was kept open for later definitions. You, too, agreed with Pope John, his council and Hans Küng, thinking we're on the right track at the time you all were expecting it to be settled. However, you did not take into consideration, what Jesus prophesized about hierarchies who cling to church's tradition and ignore God's law of love. Unfortunately, Pope John's successors, each, turned out to be one of those and felt Catholic church's traditional Eucharist of old must be kept. In *Sacramentum Caritatis,* I witness your clinging to tradition but hope that you'll repent. I sense a caution on your part not to rule as Pope Benedict XVI favoring an exclusive Eucharist or denying the body of Christ to be everyone created in God's image.

Sincerely,

July 12, 2011

National Catholic Reporter

Dear Editor,

Your article on the Vatican's efforts to revive Eucharistic adoration ignores mention of the new covenant (Jer 31:31) relationship established by God in the words and death of Jesus Christ (1 Cor 11:23-36). By disregarding the gospel of Jesus for which he died to proclaim, Pope Benedict XVI contradicts the principles of Vatican II and its New Testament scholars' contentions that every human person is to eat the Eucharist meal unconditionally.

Pope Benedict quotes St. Augustine that we sin if we do not adore the flesh we eat, but, Augustine, too, ignores the basic gospel of Christ wherein God's pledge of forgiving our evildoings occurs in our Baptism in Christ's crucifixion. Instead, Augustine fabricated the theory, out of whole cloth, of original sin to win an argument but taint us all. We are all made worthy by God, however (Jer 31:34), and need not adore the Eucharist we eat. For Eucharist, as well as salvation, God unilaterally forgives us because God loves what God creates, even sinners.

Jesus ordered all to take and eat, take and drink, unconditionally, without any strings attached. That's why our theologians are concerned about the pre-Vatican II human traditions being renewed to distort the Eucharist.

Sincerely,

cc: His Holiness Pope Benedict XVI

July 13, 2011

Dear Holy Father,

The seeds of revelation that fell from the hands of Pope John XXIII and his council onto your mind and heart apparently were enthusiastically received but then chocked by your needs to cling to the traditions as Jesus prophesized. (Mk 7:1-13.)

Ressourcement to God's plan for human salvation in Jesus's fulfillment of the new covenant (Jer 31:31-34) at the sacrifice of Calvary and in Communion (1 Cor 11:23-26) resulted in the global Church of Christ, which merely subsists in the Catholic church until it acts uncharitably. Additionally, the ideal of the open Eucharist to allow Christ's real presence to be ingested in everyone, to transform them into loving others, was an accompanying Holy Spirit awakening us to God's love of all.

The good news (gospel) of Jesus, proclaimed by his death and resurrection, was again choked off, however, by well-meaning Christians who misunderstood and stuck to their own traditional thoughts, which constituted the status quo.

The good news renewed by Pope John and his gathered bishops at Vatican II, while the Curia was restrained, was juridically again choked off by a frightened curia released by Pope Paul VI. As antagonists against the principals of the new covenant (Jer 31:31), these traditionalists fraudulently deleted its terms and stole Christ's bequest provisions inherited by all humanity. (See *Lumen Gentium*, No. 9.) You personally contributed as a major negator of God's evidence of love that graced everyone created with the Eucharist (see *Sacramentum Caritatis*) to deny most of people access to Holy Communion.

I write to you of these concerns not to "rub it in" but to attempt fraternal correction and, hopefully, a dialogue to clear up our differences for everyone's good. You, as my spiritual director, have an obligation by our *Dogmatic Constitution on the Church* to respond. "Attentively in Christ," (No. 37).

Yours in Christ,

July 15, 2011

Dear Holy Father,

"Boobies" are the Galapagos sea birds I earlier wrote about, whose chicks instinctively struggled to push its siblings out from beneath the mother's breast to die in the equatorial sun. The law of survival of the fittest was explained as being good for the species.

The providence of God directed the behavior for the general good that the one die for the many.

God made the human person in God's image presumably to live forever. Mysteriously, to improve our lot, God also had Jesus tortured and killed. God informed us of improving God's relationship with God's people by a unilaterally performed covenant to be fulfilled in days to come (Jer 31:31-34). Four centuries later, Jesus expressly died to perform God's spelled-out pledges, and thereby reveal the providence God has for mankind even when God is denied by so many (1 Cor 11:23-26). Somehow Jesus had to die to fulfill the non-bargained for deal God made, which seemingly left lacking consideration for God while benefiting evildoing humans with so much. Like the "boobies," Jesus was allowed to die for the benefit of all, but, unlike the "boobies," it was for our mysterious supernatural gain that requires God to reveal when our veil of ignorance lifts hereafter. Jesus himself, however, died in an act of love and trust of his Father, whom he believed scripturally wanted him to sacrifice himself. Jesus also died for all of us thinking we were doomed unless he carried our sins upon the cross and died to ransom us.

My reflections and concerns on these divine mysteries are fed by daily Eucharist. Consider how many similar thoughts are being denied to people because your diocesan bishops choose to cling, like "boobies," to tradition in disregard of God's law of charity.

Yours in Christ,

July 17, 2011

Dear Holy Father,

The "boobies" mentioned earlier were named by sailors for their stupidity. *Sacramentum Caritatis* delegates final judgment on an exclusive Eucharist upon diocesan bishops who you know are likely to act "Booby" like with the assignment. The Vatican artfully coached and controlled the bishops in Synod to assure that the Catholic Eucharist would remain in the traditional exclusiveness for Catholics. Denying the Eucharist to most human beings is plainly uncharitable, a fact Pope Benedict appreciates, but now my particular concern is that "boobies" ignorant of Vatican II's ideals of a global church and its New Testament scholars' criticism and contentions that Christ meant for an inclusive Eucharist have final judgment on the subject matter (see *Sacramentum Caritatis*).

Your conduct also reminds me of the bishop of Hippo who you hold in esteem. He fabricated the theory of original sin, disregarding God's New Covenant that made everyone worthy in Christ's blood. Augustine's opinion made dogma and stains all human infants with sin, which God already forgives and forgets (see Jer 31:31-34 and 1 Cor 11:23-26). Sadly, you personally followed suit and clung to the tradition of an exclusive Eucharist because recipients you judged soiled. In an artful way, you share with bishops' denial of nourishment to the body of Christ, the saving bread of life, but you still bring judgment on yourself.

You have time to remedy your wrongdoing before you answer to Jesus Christ, and I pray God aid you to overcome your misguided love of Catholic traditions, to do so.

Yours in Christ,

July 19, 2011

Dear Holy Father,

In my lifetime, the only ideal pope known to me is John XXIII, who opened the Second Vatican Council and left us the truths of a global Church of Christ which at times "subsists in" the Roman Catholic Church. The Council, its theologians, and New Testament scholars criticized the Church's exclusive Eucharist and contended that Christ meant it to be a meal open to everyone created. To enable open discussions with those at council, Pope John prudently restrained the curia who, true to tradition, constantly tried to retain the status quo. Pope John even threatened to make an issue of the curia's role, if any, in the church.

Obviously, the fear upon the curia was their threatened extinction, and when John died, Pope Paul VI returned with a traditional rule and the curia struck back vehemently. What had transpired with Pope John XXIII and bishops, in council, remained of record, but little had been declared final. Left intact were ideas submitted for later definition, for example, the above-mentioned phrase "subsist in" rather than "is" (see Msgr. Gerard Philips explanation, "we wanted to keep the matter open," at p. 17, *NCR*, 11/12/10). Instead of explaining them, the curia scribes drafted the forgery of the new covenant (Jer 31:31), which His Holiness, Pope Paul VI, promulgated into our *Dogmatic Constitution on the Church*, a document of Vatican II (see No. 9 of *Lumen Gentium*), to deny us God's proof of salvation in Jesus performing God's agreement.

It is shocking to me the ends my church hierarchy will go to preserve their comforts in the church. Not only do they deliberately distort God's words of covenant but delete God's pledges to humanity, which Jesus bequests us by shedding his blood on the cross. The testament of Jesus Christ, to which we all are entitled by gift of God, was embezzled from each human being by the pen of Pope Paul VI and his curia scribes. Arguably, this is blasphemy against the Spirit because it negates God's new covenant and the testamentary fulfillment of God's pledges by Jesus's passion and death. The evidence of God's unilateral saving of God's human creation, simply out of love for humans as they are is negated by these stupid men leaving gnats of their teaching to preserve their jobs.

Like the forgery made dogma, the church's exclusive Eucharist is man-made, and today your authored *Sacramentum Caritatis* is a comparable hypocrisy for which you will answer for the harm you are doing.

Yours in Christ,

July 20, 2011

Dear Holy Father,

My faith conviction is that I am already saved for everlasting life with *our Lord* God. I take God at his word fulfilled by the blood of the covenant (Jer 31:31-34 and 1 Cor 11:23-26).

Why, then, do I receive daily Eucharist? It is because I want to thank God for my life, and it is the best way I know to give God, from my free will, a gift God may not otherwise receive. Besides, Jesus ordered me to take of the Eucharist and consume it. Thus, in thanksgiving, I take God intimately within myself to nourish me to love others each day.

I tend to do selfish things because I enjoy doing them. I try not to harm others who are less capable than I. But I enjoy my efforts to confront the establishment especially the Roman Catholic Church and its spiritual leaders in matters that are *Antichrist*, for example, the exclusive Eucharist and the negation of the new covenant relationship as Jesus established it for all humanity. Vatican II's global Church of Christ and New Testament scholars' support of an open Eucharist, both opposed by you, are Christian charitable concerns that I somehow became obliged to write about to you personally.

I await your fatherly advice on any of the over three hundred letters I mailed you.

Yours in Christ,

July 25, 2011

Dear Holy Father,

Hans Küng told us that he wrote Pope Benedict XVI "at the time when we were still exchanging views" asking why he let the bishops carry all the blame for the sex abuse cover-ups "when he himself as Joseph Ratzinger at the (congregation for the Doctrine of Faith) enjoined secrecy on the episcopate in his 2001 letter." Küng a colleague at Tübingen and commuted together by automobile received no reply to his letter, but you, instead, ended exchanging views.

I, who have never received any response from you, hopefully write on. I feel like Hans Küng, who trusted you to consider his request for "a mea culpa" admission of fault for contributing to this scandal and crises of the Catholic church. Your letter to Bishop William Morris misrepresented that your predecessor wrote "infallibly" on not having authority to ordain women to the priesthood. It lessens my hope if papal powers are corrupting you into believing popes are infallibly divine. So demented you give me despair for changing your mind on *Sacramentum Caritatis*. But nothing is impossible for God, so, I persist.

"Reading Ratzinger" (see *The New Yorker*, 7/25/05, at p. 45) by journalist Anthony Grafton reveals you "at work, wielding proof texts that in his hand are as powerful, and as malleable, as articles of the constitution in the hands of an ideologically partisan jurist," provided correct views of your attitude. As Pope,

Benedict XVI, you have disregarded God's commandment and cling to human tradition by releasing *Sacramentum Caritatis*.

In my youth, I could not believe this of any pope, but the hypocrites that Jesus prophesized about (see Mk 7:1-13) appear in the hierarchy of the Vatican acting in concert since Pope John XXIII. Pope Paul VI proved by his curia scribes drafting No. 9 of *Lumen Gentium* fraudulently forging the new covenant to suit their traditions, willingly to negate God's new covenant. The embarrassing act of evil that I wish would never see the light sits as a gnat in our church bowl. The Roman Catholic Church maintains this odious provision in the form of our *Dogmatic Constitution on the Church*. Where are the bishops, theologians, and clergymen who claim to be Christians to prevent this evildoing among the "Documents of Vatican II"? Specifically, how do you dare leave this blasphemy to exist in your church? The futility of these actions remains in the fact that God's covenant exists in the Church of Christ no matter how uncharitable the Catholic church acts.

Yours in Christ,

July 26, 2011

Dear Holy Father,

God blessed you with understanding that the words Jesus spoke at the Last Supper represented the shaping of Jesus fulfilling the new covenant (Jer 31:31) of God. The words reveal anew that the institution of the Eucharist is anticipating Jesus's spiritual death. Jesus shares himself out in communion to bring us together with God. Jesus undergoes a spiritual death, transforming an act of self-sharing love into adoration to God and reacts in human beings upon consuming the flesh of Jesus. In Eucharist's bread and wine, humans are transformed from our self-loving selves into God-like loving others. By Jesus's death, God is made available, in actuality, to human individuals. Both words and death "are essentially interdependent" giving meaning to each other. As you wrote the death without these words would be a mere execution without any discernable point to it (*God Is Near Us*, p. 29).

Your writings (at p. 29, *Infra*) echoed the theme of Pope John XXIII and his bishops at Vatican II describing God's people globally as a result of Jesus performing God's pledges

(Jer 31:34), forgiving and teaching every and all human beings (1 Cor 11:23-26) in the blood of the covenant. God unilaterally established a new relationship, a new communion, a global Church of Christ, which included everyone of God's creation made in God's image.

The Eucharist instituted in words "interdependent" with Jesus's death continues to proclaim Jesus's spiritual death and brings God intimately within us to transform our lives and faiths. And, at pages 59 and 60 of *God Is Near Us* you acknowledge that the scholars of the New Testament criticize the church's exclusive Eucharist. Eucharist is instituted interdependent of Jesus's death, which is meant to redeem sinners. The Eucharist logically cannot be conditional on worthiness, which God's covenant already resolved. Yet, you opposed it stating "—however tempting the idea may be . . . it contradicts what we find in the Bible." You added your feelings we must let ourselves "be reconciled by God" before receiving God in Eucharist.

Later, as Pope Benedict you did not rule for the pre-reconciliation condition. Instead you released *Sacramentum Caritatis* and passed final judgment on the matter to more ignorant diocesan bishops. Presumably they could have an inclusive Eucharist, but every diocesan bishop, knowing your sentiments, did not dare follow Vatican II and have open Eucharist, as you artfully schemed.

Yours in Christ,

July 27, 2011

Dear Holy Father,

John Julius Norwich comments on you as Pope Benedict XVI in his book *Absolute Monarch* (*NCR*, 7/27/11, Books). He notes that in an earlier incarnation, as liberal theologian Joseph Ratzinger, you wrote in (*Theological Highlights of Vatican II*) that you were disturbed by the monarchical aspects of the papacy. You contended that the synodal system must always "correct the monarchic idea." But once you became the monarch, I see you now enjoy the monarchic imbalance and artfully misuse synods in applying *Sacramentum Caritatis*.

Norwich writes of Pio Nono (Pius IX, 1846-78) who he characterized arrives as a liberal and departs infallible. I am reminded of your letter to Australia Bishop William Morris about Pope John Paul's statement that he was not authorized to allow women into the priesthood. You misrepresented it was "infallibly" made. At the time John Paul spoke, you wore his mantle of authority and likely drafted the statement. I would humbly submit your recall now that it was "infallible" is a symptom of the corruption the papal monarchy is having on you.

The fact you believe anyone but God to be infallible, I submit evidences the extent of your clinging to Catholic tradition to be idolatrous. It is Christ we worship and not Catholicism. At Vatican II, you found a pearl as a liberal or progressive theologian, but instead of buying that treasure with all you had, you sold out the kingdom of God to obtain your own monarchy. Look around you and tell us whether or not it was worth selling out the Church of Christ for the uncharitable church you now rule.

The little time you enjoy your reign will be nothing to the eternity you spend with God sorrowing over your insanity. There is still time and power for you to surrender to the will of God and realize God along saves us in Christ. I again suggest you start with inviting everyone to Holy Communion as your token of letting yourself, be reconciled by God.

Yours in Christ,

July 29, 2011

Dear Holy Father,

The Anchor Bible (1966) on *The Gospel According To John* as commented on by our recognized biblical expert Raymond E. Brown, at page 293, reads, that while the Synoptic Gospels record the institution of the Eucharist, John explains what the Eucharist does. In Eucharist, Jesus gives us a share in God's own life. Surprisingly Brown commented on the Eucharist itself, as reported by the writers of John, echoes the theme of the new covenant ("Blood of the covenant"—Mk 24:24). The mutual indwelling of God (and Jesus) and the Christian may be a replica of the covenant promise and theme (citing Jer 24:17 and 31:33) "you will, be my people and I shall be your God." Brown gives us recognition of God's new covenant, negated by John's writers in the Gospel itself, by stretching inferences to do so.

Otherwise, the Fourth Gospel blasphemed the Spirit in disregarding God's new covenant. Vatican II (1962-1964), however, seemingly paralleled Brown's thoughts, and in its own themes of a global Church of Christ, whose membership included all humans, the new covenant's existence is implied if not expressed. Its New Testament scholars included an open Eucharist as interdependent with the Covenant's performance where every human, bar-none, is worthy to share God because God forgives everyone in the blood of the covenant.

You, like Father Brown back in 1966, restricted Christ's bequest only to Catholics or to Christians. You should know by heart and charitable reflections, if any made since, that the Eucharist and new covenant, established by God in Jesus Christ, charitably must include every human being created by God. God (and Jesus) from the beginning of creation designed the breath of both covenant and Eucharist to benefit all of us created as sinners. God pledged, and Jesus died to perform the pledge of God, to forgive each individual human being's evildoing forever (see Jer 31:34). In other words, we are all saved by God in the blood of the covenant while not volunteering to do anything in consideration on our own behalf.

Yours in Christ,

August 1, 2011

Dear Holy Father,

Bishop William Wiegand wrote me in August, 2007, stating that "You are incorrect in analysis." I was left ignorant of what specific analysis he was referring to; except that I differed from the traditional Church's teaching. We differ in more than analysis.

France's difference of analysis resulted in revolution ending its monarchy. We in the *United States* got rid of our king but drafted a radical written constitution for a system of Republican governmental checks and balances. The French instituted none but relied on logic to serve for law. Our republican government survived while that of the French proved logical analysis was not enough.

Bishop Wiegand accepted that church teachings have been clear since the time of St. Paul; at least, "To receive Holy Communion requires the Catholic faith and worthiness." He likely rejected that some at Vatican II analyzed that Christ's Eucharist was meant to serve everyone. However, you radically authored *Sacramentum Caritatis* to purportedly give diocesan bishops, such as Wiegand, final judgment on who would receive the Eucharist to counter the analysis of the Vatican II experts. Hypocritically, the synod system was artfully used by the Vatican to dictate to the bishops to cling to our traditional teachings. Our *Diocesan Statutes of the Third Diocesan Synod* is an exemplary product of your Vatican's artful deviousness to avoid the checks and balance of your monarchial form of government and deny most people Holy Communion. I doubt if any diocese has a different statute than any other.

In your earlier incarnation as a biblical theologian at Vatican II, you wrote in your book *Theological Highlights of Vatican II* of being disturbed by the monarchical aspects of the papacy. As Joseph Ratzinger, you contended that the synodal system must always "correct the monarchic idea." As Pope Benedict XVI, your release of *Sacramnetum Caritatis* patently delegates final judgment on the subject matter of the Eucharist to bishops, proved to be untrue in the way you used the Synods. The cowed bishops, selected as was Wiegand, were easily controlled by the Vatican in their synod meetings and directed by Vatican working documents ordering, for instance, that only Catholics were to receive the Eucharist.

Sacramentum Caritatis, as evidenced in your oppression of the bishops in Synod, evidences the hypocrisy Jesus prophesized at Jerusalem (Mk 7:1-13). Also the church demonstrates the increased monarchic imbalance in your Machiavellian rule. Hans Küng warned that your centralized absolutism is a crisis calling for reform (*NCR*, 11/12/10). I suggest a worse scenario in the loss of the Roman Catholic Church, similar to what occurred to France's republic, because it relies on human logic or wisdom.

Yours in Christ,

August 3, 2011

Dear Holy Father,

I heard at mass this morning that Jesus may have made the same error you make in excluding others from the Eucharist. Jesus, likely on a narrow but literal reading of scripture, believed he was sent for only the lost souls of Israel. He, thus, rejected the Canaanite mother's plea to cure her daughter of a demon. He uncharitably indicated that the bread he had to offer was not for "dogs." The mother persisted, however, and argued that even dogs ate the crumbs that fall from the table. Our sermon then explained she was appealing on a broader basis than the narrow one Jesus was using, and her faith in the higher law of God persuaded Jesus to change his mind and cure her child.

I do not recall the citation of *Mathews* being read, but it struck me that Jesus being wrong and charitably correcting his wrong thinking may help you correct yourself and the Catholic church to share God's Eucharist with all humanity. You can do so as Jesus demonstrated and still save face in that your reading of scripture remains as true as those of the New Testament scholars who, you acknowledge, criticized the church's exclusive Eucharist and contend that Christ intends an open and all-inclusive distribution of the Eucharist (see Cardinal Joseph Ratzinger's *God Is Near Us*, p. 59). But either translation of scripture must defer to the higher authority of God's law, which God imprints in each heart and mind simply by Jesus shedding the blood of the covenant (see Jer 31:33).

Yours in Christ,

August 5, 2011

Dear Holy Father,

I am having fun in expressing my concerns to have you charitably analyze the Gospel of Jesus Christ and apply it in your operation of the Roman Catholic Church. His Holiness Pope John XXIII and his bishops in the Second Vatican Council did so by ressourcement, while restraining the curia, and more correctly described our church as the Church of Christ which subsists in the Catholic church. The use of "subsists in" rather than "is" was deliberate according to the Belgian secretary of the theological commission, Msgr. Gérard Philips, "we wanted to keep the matter open." (See *NCR*, P. 17, 11/12/10.)

Karl Rahner also complimented the idea of the global Church of Christ, made up in membership by all human beings, as the best idea that came out of Vatican II. I respect Karl Rahner's opinions, and I do not really know how he phrased his complement, but I would classify the New Testament scholars' support of the inclusive Eucharist as a better product of Vatican II. It leaves the church to be defined by God within all of us by God's new covenant's standards.

My personal gift was the cause of my writing to express my concerns to you. I felt obliged by *Lumen Gentium,* No. 37, to express my concerns for the good of the church, initially, but when I became subject to your oppressive silence, I discovered the joy in futilely writing you of my concerns in fraternal correction. I figure it is the best gift I will ever be able to give *our Lord*, something which God cannot receive but for my furnishing it to God. Once I am with God's Beatific Vision, I assume I will be overcome with loving God as I will not be able to help it. Here on earth I have found a pearl, and I have, in effect, sold out my practice to write to my spiritual leaders of the miss-defined role of the Catholic church's Eucharist they choose to distribute uncharitably and of the new covenant which they seem anxious to disregard. What began as an obligation on me has changed to a labor of love. I am told

I am an unpaid servant, but I feel I am well paid and, rather than in service, have a game to play with holy ones who ignore me.

I charitably translate scripture, particularly Jer 31:31-34 and 1 Cor 11:23-26 to conclude that I and all human beings are saved by God's goodness alone in the blood of the covenant. However, I suspect that Pope Benedict XVI finds himself in a tragic state of affairs, clinging to a definition of church that obviously disregards God's law of love and God's covenant too. But he can remedy it all if he lets his conscience be his guide and obey what God imprinted in his heart and mind.

Yours in Christ,

August 6, 2011

Dear Holy Father,

I have another bone of contention. Jesus said that it was better Judas had never been born. Jesus spoke as a man, and it was not God speaking. If Judas' birth was bad, then his conception and the idea of his conception in the beginning were worse than God not conceiving him at the beginning.

God is love. God cannot create Judas in God's image to be separate from God forever, and, certainly cannot create him for everlasting torment. So, likewise, it is for all humanity who God foresaw would sin if given the free will to do selfish and evil things. Designing humans with self-survival and self-satisfaction instincts, a God of love could not justify punishing them for acting the way God foresees them to act.

God, thus, created us for everlasting life, or, in other words, pardoned us of our evildoing as God created each of us. Because God created us to love God freely, God taught us God's law so every one of us would know enough to choose good over our instinctive evildoing. We know from Socrates, Confucius, and other mental giants of God's law of love being imprinted. God in scriptures communicated the law through learned men. Jeremiah, an example, was used by God to communicate the new covenant relationship God promised us through Jesus Christ. God is within all of us created in God's image but is mysteriously more-so in Jesus Christ, who died to perform the new covenant (Jer 31) and instill the knowledge of God and

God's law in each and every one of us. Jesus extended the new covenant to all Jews and Gentiles (1 Cor 11:23-26), and, in turn, by his New Testament instituted a universal Eucharist to intimately place God and the law of love in everyone. We need no church or other teacher to know these truths.

Catholics accept the Immaculate Conception of Mary. The blood of the covenant cleanses her of evildoing. So, likewise, it is believable that God conceives Judas, as well as any other human, to be saved from the instance of conception. God's law of love is greater than any scripture, any church, and even most thoughts of Jesus Christ. This law of God is imprinted in the conscience of Pope Benedict XVI, and he need only open his heart and mind to invite everyone to God's supper.

Yours in Christ,

August 8, 2011

Dear Holy Father,

Mathews, the apostle and evangelist, told the story of Jesus sending Peter to fish and find the coin needed to pay the temple tax. Mathews being a tax collector by occupation made a living exaggerating the value of estates to obtain his income from the excess evaluation; so, his relating this story to me would raise the thought of a "tall tale."

In his gospel, Mathews was trying to persuade Jews to accept faith in Jesus as prophet successor to Moses or as Messiah. I have suspected that he made up tales to sell the Jews, using their faith in Moses, to accept Jesus, for example, Jesus too came out of Egypt. Within the last year or so, the *National Geographic* also questioned his story on King Herod's mass murder of infants. Their research of history finds no mention of the event, even though Josebus (sic), the historian of the period, did a bibliography on Herod and the magazine authors implied it evidenced the killings never occurred.

Besides, Luke wrote on the period, likely having interviewed Mary, who kept all these things close to heart, and he also made no mention of it or the trip to Egypt. The tax collector's stories conflicted with Luke's presentation of Mary at the temple as there is no way the family could have fled to Egypt and be timely present at the temple before moving back to Nazareth.

As you know, if you read my letters, I question the authenticity of the Fourth Gospel because it negates God's unilateral performance of the new covenant (Jer 31:31) and the words at supper instituting the Eucharist. Mathew's gospel concludes with Jesus commissioning the apostles, similar to Peter's commission to feed his sheep, to teach and baptize disciples everywhere "in the name of the Father and of the Son and of the Holy Spirit." However, New Testament scholars who wrote my Bible question Jesus's words here since the Trinitarian understanding did not evolve until after Mathews wrote, and they claim it was added later.

Since Jesus died to fulfill the new covenant in his death, and God thereby performed the forgiveness of sins, like circumcision baptism served no purpose, and Jesus knew baptism was not to forgive what God already purified (see 1 Cor 11:23-26). But Mathews was a creature of his culture, and the baptism of disciples of John the Baptist was a tradition he clung to in disregard of God's baptism in the blood of the new covenant.

Yours in Christ,

August 9, 2011

Dear Holy Father,

Yesterday I attacked the credibility of Mathew's Gospel mainly because it disregards evidence of the new covenant even though he related Jesus dying words indicating his dying was to fulfill the covenant "for the forgiveness of sins" (Mt 26:26). Today he purportedly quoted Jesus saying unless we became as little children we could not enter the kingdom of heaven. Jesus may have said this, and Mathew may have sentimentally reported his own opinion of what was said. Because his writings otherwise disregard the new covenant, he fails to realize that the New Kingdom came with the new covenant's fulfillment, the benefits of which we receive because of God and Jesus's doings and not in exchange for us acting as little children or any other response, than being ourselves, in return.

God still calls us to trust like little children and to love God and each other as Jesus demonstrated, preferably, not for gain but spontaneously because God wants us to be childlike. As my spiritual leaders, you are obliged by *Lumen Gentium*, No. 37, to respectfully consider my concerns and suggestions and respond with fatherly advice, even hopefully with a dialogue, to enlighten me if I err in these matters of faith and morals. After one-half dozen years and over three hundred letters, you should be ashamed for your lack of response.

But, then again, who am I to complain. Someday we will meet face to face, and you can explain to me how wrong I am or how right you are to leave me questioning. Perhaps, with our veils of ignorance lifted, *our Lord* will reveal how good you are to keep me in my vincible ignorance and humble state of fallibility. I can wait patiently, relieving my animosity by persisting in expressing my opinions on these things which concern the good of the church to fulfill its mission for the lives of all humanity not just Roman Catholics, in the world.

Yours in Christ,

August 11, 2011

Dear Holy Father,

One of my fellow communicants, fooling with his computer, discovered a Saint Malachy who prophesized that there were to be only 112 popes, and he counted you as number 111. My response to him was "Long live Benedict!"

Yesterday, a lay partner of mine in the Community of Passionist Partners (CPP) phoned and reminded me that our facilitator, Father Neil Parsons, C. P., taught us his faith conviction that everyone was saved (see Intro to my book *God's Gift To You*). He refreshed my memory that the basis for Father's conviction was that God, as Love, could not create anyone to be lost or tormented.

Considering, the scripture that we proclaim daily of Christ fulfilling God's new covenant, forgiving and forgetting our evildoing, we are back at the beginning of my writing to you. I always figured you knew by heart what my expressed concerns were about, especially our exclusive Eucharist. Now the news that you might be the next to last pope may be persuasive to reconcile what is between you and *our LORD*.

I pray, in your long life with God, you remedied your wrongdoing on earth and carry not the memory of burdening your church with your *Antichrist* traditional convictions.

Yours in Christ,

August 15, 2011

Dear Holy Father,

"By their fruits you shall know them."

Two fruit products of Vatican II, that portion before Pope John XXIII died, are (1) the global Church of Christ and (2) its inclusive

Eucharist. As Cardinal Ratzinger, you acknowledged the New Testament scholars' ideal of an all-inclusive Eucharist but you disagreed with them on basis of the Vatican's traditional translation of the Bible. (See *God Is Near Us*, pp. 59 and 60).

But you contended that one's conscience has the final judgment on whether or not one should receive Holy Communion. Likely you referred to law which is imprinted in us by Christ's execution of God's new covenant provisions, for example, "for I will forgive their evildoing and remember their sins no more" (Jer 31:31-34). Since every human is by God made worthy and ordered to take and consume Eucharist, Jews and Gentiles are also God's intended recipients (1 Cor 11:23-28). Men's opinion on the Bible should not be ruling the issue; so, on becoming Pope Benedict XVI, you did not rule for an exclusive Eucharist but respected God's law of love.

However, as Jesus prophesized, you artfully released *Sacramentum Caritatis*, under the guise of delegating the final judgment to diocesan bishops in synod. Hypocritically, after espousing the synod system as a check on the monarchy of the Vatican, you had the Vatican dominate the collegiality of the system by dictating to the bishops in session, working documents, such as declaring only those of the faith were worthy to receive the sacrament. How accurate Jesus and Isaiah were in foretelling our hypocrisies to disregard God's commandment and cling to traditions denying most people access to the Lord's Supper (Mk:1f).

I challenge you to reflect on my suggestion: Your favorite Saint Augustine fabricated a theory of original sin to counter Irish Monk Pelagius' argument as to God making men good. Since God recreated them in the blood of the covenant, to be forgiven of evildoing, Augustine overlooked God's pardon. Irish Saint Malachy centuries later warns us that you may be our last chance to do God's will in evidencing God's saving action of everybody in human history and rid us of *Sacramentum Caritatis*, Augustine's fabrication, and other blasphemies of churchmen.

Yours in Christ,

August 17, 2011

Dear Holy Father,

The missal furnished us in the pews states, at the "Liturgy of the Eucharist," in part, the following: "*Christians* are baptized into the paschal mystery of Christ's death and resurrection for the forgiveness of sins and fullness of salvation." The mystery is celebrated at every mass, remembering Christ's loving deed and giving thanks and praise to God. (Emphasis mine.)

Actually, not only Christians, but all Jews and Gentiles, bar-none, are baptized in the blood of God's covenant and its paschal mystery. Jesus Christ, glorified, declared from heaven to Jews and Gentiles, through St. Paul, that Jesus's death is to be proclaimed in mystery at every Eucharist where we thank God and consume God's gift of Jesus's body and blood to transform the knowledge of God and God's law imprinted in us from conception (see 1 Cor 11:23-26 and Jer 31:31-34).

The Roman Catholic Church's quotation above implies that Christians baptized from water (cf. Jn 3:5-6) are the only ones worthy, forgiven of sin, and fulfilled for salvation. I respectfully suggest that the implication negates God's sole performance of God's covenant in the sacrifice of Jesus fulfilling God's unilateral execution of the covenant. Establishing God's covenant relationship is why Jesus died in loving obedience. I submit that the *Dogmatic Constitution on the Church* (*Lumen Gentium*) blasphemes against the Spirit, at part No. 9, because it negates evidence of God's unilateral saving action in God's idea for human creation (see footnote Mt 12:31ff., *The New American Bible*, p. 1084).

The contradiction is in human words struggling to explain paschal mysteries and the words of God, explaining the death of Jesus as imprinted in our hearts. Unfortunately, our pope chooses human traditions because he loves church's traditions that have survived millenniums. The alternative is the folly of Christ's Cross and the truth that God loves us as we are.

Yours in Christ,

August 18, 2011

Dear Holy Father,

How evil is the man who negates the evidence of God's saving action in the new covenant (Jer 31:31) that Jesus died to perform for all Jews and Gentiles (1 Cor 11:23-26)? My Bible's footnote (*The New American Bible*, Mt 12:31ff.) states, in part: "This is the blasphemy of the Spirit that will not be forgiven, because it negates the evidence of God's saving action in history." I suggest, however, this unforgiving is grounded on scriptural exaggerations of Jesus, Mathews, or the scribes who drafted the footnote and, besides God already forgives the sin.

Still, you would think the footnote is a warning to Roman Catholics, especially those in the bureaucracy of the Vatican. Instead, the popes who succeeded Pope John XXIII conspired with the Vatican to reject in principle John, and his gathered bishops' ideas of (1) a global Church of Christ, which subsists in the Catholic Church, and (2) a universal open Eucharist to feed all human creatures nourishment to know God and God's law.

My suggestive letters of concern, if you read any, target you with challenge because you are so highly gifted in knowledge and scripture. But I have inferred that you also uncharitably cling to church's traditions at the expense of God's law of universal love. At the moment you alone have capabilities to remedy and republish the new covenant relationship and open the Eucharist, both of which Jesus died to establish.

Yours in Christ,

August 19, 2011

Dear Holy Father,

News of God having forgiven everyone's evildoing in exchange for nothing on our part, or simply because we all exist is *The Gospel According to Jesus Christ* (see 1 Cor 11:23-26 and 1 Jer 31:31, referred to in scripture). The Glorified Jesus announced this news to Paul before he launched his mission to tell all Jews and Gentiles of God's new covenant relationship with all of created humanity.

Whatever inroads Vatican II made in our hearts and minds were apparently erased by you from about 1968 to cling to ambitions and traditions of the Roman Catholic Church that preexisted to negate *The Gospel According to Jesus Christ*. Both Jesus and Isaiah prophesized your hierarchy will cling to tradition in disregard of God's law of love (Mk 7:1-13). Jesus called it hypocrisy, but his warning has had little effect on your hierarchy of the Catholic church. In the face of the warning of lack of reverence in teaching as dogmas, mere human precepts Pope Paul XVI and his scribes advanced clinging to the extreme of forging their own covenant, in the place of God's new covenant, to support their own opinion that only baptized believers in Christ are saved by God, and destine the rest of humanity to perdition unless the saved convert them to their deceitful fictions in the *Dogmatic Constitution on the Church* (*Lumen Gentium*, No. 9).

As Professor of theology at Tübingen, you revealed the goodness that exists in you, when you taught the words of Jesus were interdependent with his death and charity. You taught the meaning of Jesus saying "This is my blood, the blood of the covenant, to be poured out on behalf of many" (Mk 14:24).

Armed with the typescript of your lectures, Ronald Modras, a professor of theological studies at St. Louis University, and a student of yours in 1968, revealed your lesson in an article in *Commonweal* (4/21/06) quoting you:

> That for "many" (Mk 14:24) prevents the church from becoming simply a select community of the righteous, a community that condemns the wayward masses to perdition.

I am starting to read *The Pope's War* by ex-Dominican Mathew Fox, which appears to be depicting you as a most evil person. I suggest that you take advice from another sinner and change your evildoing to return to the Joseph Ratzinger who taught the above.

Yours in Christ,

August 22, 2011

Dear Holy Father,

I am too limited in abilities to persuade you

to become the greatest pope in Christendom. But hear this idea and reflect on it.

Jesus spoke from heaven the last words of his mission to perform God's new covenant (Jer 31:31) and extends its coverage for all Jews and Gentiles (1 Cor 11:23).

Your charitable readings have these words, being interdependent with Jesus's death, redeeming the world and preventing the church becoming a select community of baptized believers to condemn the rest of humanity to perdition (see *Lumen Gentium*, No. 9).

God may have planned for you from the beginning, to take over the Roman Catholic Church and be a rule to yourself, capable to return its basic principles to acknowledge the salvation by God alone in Jesus fulfilling God's new covenant. You now have the power to perform this return to the gospel of *our Lord.*

God being love saves everyone in God's plan of creation. At first, it may seem to be devastating to Catholicism as God's teaching and forgiving imprinted in us at conception and renewed in Eucharist graces us, but likely there still is need of the church. God in Jesus entrusted God's Eucharist to the Church of Christ, peopled by all God's created and baptized in the blood of Christ, to consume as divine life and light giving nourishment.

Vatican II touched on this global Church of Christ (made up of everyone) that subsists in the Catholic church. The definition awaits you to define charitably. It may be that the Holy Spirit has you to overrule the uncharitable traditions and return us to God's new covenant relationship. In heaven and on earth, you may make an impact second only to *our Lord* in evidencing God's love and God's unilateral saving action is creation.

Yours in Christ,

August 23, 2011

Dear Holy Father,

No one in the church dares to tell you that you are stripped of truth in not acknowledging God's new covenant (Jer 31:31-34) as established by Jesus's death, and Eucharist

(1 Cor 11:23-26) is the Gospel you are supposed to proclaim.

Ex-Dominican Father Mathew Fox has characterized you as a scoundrel and non-Christian pope of the Roman Catholic Church. Conceding you may be a fellow scoundrel and sinner, I think he is wrong to argue that our church is not the means to cure the disaster. I personally contend that not only the church but you as its shepherd are the way the Holy Spirit best may solve the problems Fox sees and any *Antichrist* of Christendom.

The Church of Christ which subsists in the Catholic church or the Church of Christ that is and "can only be, *fully* present in the Roman Church . . ." (*The New Yorker*, 7/25/05, p. 42) is where I place my trust, conditional on trying to return to Christ our Catholic church. You are in control to dictate the changes, and Catholics will accept your fascistic direction. You know the words of God as scripturally stated in the circumstances of the paschal mystery (see Jer 31:31-34 and 1 Cor 11:23-26). Jesus died to fulfill God's new covenant relationship and save every Jew and Gentile created. You are asked to enforce the same by feeding all

God's sheep, under God's commandment of love, this good news in Eucharist.

This may not win you fame on earth and certainly not with your cronies in the Vatican. But the glory of Jesus Christ will be shared with you, for recognizing the body of Christ to be everyone and bringing the church home to God's kingdom.

Yours in Christ,

August 26, 2011

Dear Holy Father,

In your doctoral dissertation on our favorite Saint Augustine, you both agreed that the fundamental virtue of charity is the defining characteristic of the church of Christ. Donatism was not true church because it evidenced a lack of the virtue of charity in excluding others from sacraments.

The Second Vatican Council, when Pope John XXIII and his gathered bishops were in session, presented the idea of the Church of Christ which subsists in the Catholic church to include all God's people. It was left open for future definitions, but it was presumably to be charitable and not exclusive, until you uncharitably ruled.

Unfortunately, you suffered a traumatic emotional experience in 1965 of a surge of ambition to become pope and converted to a being less charitable. Your colleague Hans Küng thought the revolt of students at the time frightened you to change. By hindsight, I would attribute the conversion to disregarding God's law of love and clinging to a seemingly more secure church's tradition as Jesus prophesied (Mk 7:1-13). Now as Pope Benedict XVI, you have changed the church to be more to your liking of exclusiveness and isolated your rule. Noncharitable as the church has become in excluding communicants, theologians, and most people who disagree with you can be easily returned to be true to God's covenant relationship and law of charity.

I have written reasons you should return to Christ. Some bear repeating (1) God is love and imprints in our hearts this knowledge and the knowledge of God's law, (2) God spells out the new covenant relationship in the mystery of Christ's words and death in scripture (1 Cor 11:23-26 or Mk 14:27) to which all the rest of the Bible and tradition are commentary, and (3) we proclaim in Eucharist daily that Jesus died to establish the covenant relationship and save everyone. Our God of love is proved to us as God who loves us as we are. God's love, mercy, and justice control, but we are free to love or not and should love God thankfully and not for gain. Jesus tried to tell us this, but the news became obscured by incompetent human hearsay.

Your record of discipleship to date awaits God's judgment, but you can improve on it divinely if you would only open the Church's Eucharist and surrender to God's virtue of charity.

Yours in Christ,

August 29, 2011

Dear Holy Father,

God created you and loves you as you are. Our God has no favorites in loving us. All that you were and all that you evolve into,

God loves as God loves those whom you excommunicate.

I suggested that what you made of yourself and made of the Catholic church was wrong, but who am I to judge especially judge one of God's loved subjects. Imprinted in me by God is God's commandment to love you as I love myself or moreso, as Jesus Christ loves you and loves everyone else.

I ask *our Lord* to grace me with the ability to love you as I ought. Trusting in the *Lord*'s patience and benevolence I pray for you to open your mind and heart to include every human being created and invite them to share the Eucharist. Opening your mind, you know they are all made worthy by God's unilateral performance of the covenant (Jer 31:34) and *our Lord* ordered us all to take and eat, take and drink (1 Cor 11:23-26).

May God grace you to obey your conscience and exercise love, the love of God's law, in thanksgiving for God loving you. Not for gain or merit, but freely love God and do God's will. It may be your last chance to do something for God, freely loving God because once you are with God in the Beatific Vision, I predict, God's love will overcome any free will you may try to exercise in the rapture of God's presence.

Yours in Christ,

August 30, 2011

Dear Holy Father,

I admit to being an active sinner and in your opinion unworthy to receive the Eucharist, but, as St. Ambrose confessed, because he sinned, he also often received Holy Communion. My conscience informs me that God wants me to consume the Eucharist in order to have God actually within me to transform me intimately to know, love, and serve God and God's humanity.

Comparing the harm of my sin, which I believe God alone is constantly forgiving and forgetting without any contribution on my part, as God and Jesus revealed in the performance of God's covenant on Calvary, to the harm your *Sacramentum Caritatis* does, and will obviously do after you die, the residual of my evildoing is a scintilla of the apparent cosmic harm you are guilty of causing.

However, God's goodness with Christ saves everyone for eternal oneship with Christ. So the evildoing you cause, too, will be absorbed by the love of God somehow. Still I feel I must answer for my evil residuals by chastisements from *our Lord* judgments. In loving mercy you too, I imagine, will face the judgment St. Paul predicted facing Corinthians who denied the body of Christ included all people even those being discriminated against for sinning like ours.

Thus, we experts in the law hold many to be unworthy to share the Lord's Supper, because they failed to cleanse themselves with traditional washings, should listen to Jesus's prophesy (Mk 7:1-13), and choose instead to obey God's law of loving every human being as we love ourselves or as Jesus Christ loves us. The obvious hypocrisy of your mistitled letter "Sacrament of Charity" (*Sacramentum Caritatis*) will realize the *Antichrist* blasphemy that you and your hierarchy have made of it. You previously appreciated the synod system as being a restraining check on the monarchy of the church running amok. But when you cowed the bishops and reigned as

Pope Benedict XVI, you twisted the system and used your letter delegating power to diocesan bishops, to control their choice and their Synod by Vatican working documents, for example, "only those of the faith are to receive Eucharist" and then secured the bishops' compliance. The deviousness of your conduct over mine is remarkable and deserves a different chastisement.

Sadly yours,

August 31, 2011

Dear Holy Father,

Jesus in the public ministry tried to depart Capernaum while the impressed crowds tried to detain him that he might not depart from them. But Jesus said to them, "To the other towns also I must proclaim the kingdom of God for this is why I have been sent" (Lk 4:42-44). Jesus purpose for living and dying was to proclaim the kingdom or reign of God. In words at the Last Supper, he gave the same meaning to his sacrificial death fulfilling God's new covenant, whereby God would be our God, and we God's people. These meanings are proclaimed in every Eucharist sacrifice. "[T]his is the cup of my blood, the blood of the new and everlasting covenant. It will be shed for you and for all so that sins may be forgiven."

In death, Jesus fulfills God's unilateral new covenant (Jer 31:31ff.) and his words of the Last Supper are interdependent with the death. Death and words give mutual meanings to each other. Jesus Glorified repeats the words from heaven to again reveal God's covenant relationship or God's kingdom extending to all Jews and Gentiles, those "all" whom Jesus orders to take and eat, take and drink of his flesh (1 Cor 11:23-26.) Jesus continues his mission today of proclaiming the good news of Christianity established by God's performance of God's new covenant. Our Creator forgives our evildoings and forgets all sins out of goodness and love in the blood of the covenant, and God imprints in our minds and hearts how to know God and God's law of love, so we need no other teacher but Jesus Christ proclaiming the mystery of what seems foolish to our reasoning.

Pope Benedict XVI does not grasp this lesson, which God imprints in his conscience. He and his Catholic church hear the proclamation of Christ constantly but disregard it for traditional wisdom. Pope John XXIII and his gathered bishops counseled to resource the proclamation of good news so dearly made by Jesus. Vatican II succeeded in defining the global Church of Christ to include everyone and to declare it subsists in the Catholic church. However, Pope Paul VI, Pope John Paul II, and Pope Benedict XVI, each negated evidence of God's saving action according to Christ's proclamation and prevent the real presence to dwell in souls of others than baptizing Christians. Thereby they prevent Catholicism being true church for excluding many uncharitably from Eucharist and the Church of Christ.

Yours in Christ,

September 1, 2011

Dear Holy Father,

Continuing with the thoughts of the last letter, today we heard Paul's writing to the Colossians about God performing the new covenant: “he rescued us from the power of darkness and brought us into the kingdom of his beloved son. Through him we have redemption the forgiveness of our sins (Col 1:13-14).” How many more people would be at peace knowing God already forgave and forgot their evildoings, in the sacrifice of Jesus? Especially had they obeyed Jesus’s invitation to consume the real presence. Would Mohamed need to seek salvation elsewhere, had he known he was being saved by Aliah? Over two millenniums of Christian divisions may not have occurred if Eucharist was shared with everyone to allow God’s real presence to transform consumers’ lives and faith.

God solely performs the new covenant without any merit needed on our part. Our contribution is not needed for God’s covenant is a unilateral deal, performed by God alone, because God loves us. Additionally, the knowledge of God’s law is imprinted in each human’s conscience so we need no further teaching “for” God forgives our evildoing and forgets our sins (see Jer 31:31-34). Jesus even proclaimed from heaven (1 Cor 11:23-26) the universality of the covenant and the Eucharist of Christ.

The cult that authored *The Gospel According to John* is a prime sample of what we substituted of human reason in place of the covenant's proclaimed mystery. In fact, the curia, frightened by the Second Vatican Council's Pope John XXIII, forged its own new covenant for Pope Paul VI to promulgate (see No. 9 of the "*Dogmatic Constitution on the Church*" (*Lumen Gentium*). A malicious deceit and an *Antichrist* blasphemy to God's Spirit is now proclaimed whereby only baptized believers in Christ are saved and the remainder of people damned.

You have made the Roman Catholic Church a kingdom of its own with little limitation on your power and no guarantees of our rights. As a result, the obligation I obey to write these letters of my concern for the good of the church are of no value to you, and you reject them illegitimately (see No. 37 of *Lumen Gentium*). My spiritual shepherd won't give me fatherly response, but I hopefully rely on God alone to more effectively fulfill the Church's and Jesus Christ's mission for the life of the world. Meanwhile, I see humor in your telling the UN that governments who deny given rights to citizens are illegitimate actors or, in my words, "bastards."

Happily yours,

September 2, 2011

Dear Holy Father,

Because God distrusted us to keep an agreement, God solely performs the new covenant, the terms of which Jeremiah spelled out (Jer 31:31ff.). Centuries later, God unilaterally commences the performance of the pledges promised in the mystery death of Jesus (Mk 14:24). Jesus believed his mission on earth was to proclaim this new and everlasting relationship God make with men. God's pledges are thus constantly being performed, and we are taught by God to know essentials by heart. God's covenant, I suspect, has retroactive effects to pardon Judas and all humans ever created.

The new covenant is fulfilled in the sacrifice of Jesus Christ to save all people "for I will forgive their evildoing and forget their sins forever" (Jer 31:34). Jesus, fulfilling God's performance of the Covenant, spoke at his Last Supper and from heaven (1 Cor 11:23-26) interdependent words with his death, giving mutual meaning to words and death as you wrote (*God Is Near Us*, p. 29). Death and words give universality to the Eucharist being one piece in our redemption of one Body whose members include everybody.

Jesus's mission was to proclaim by death and words the new covenant relationship of God, the kingdom or reign of God, and mankind. Therein, God provides for the enlightenment of every human being by imprinting in consciences the knowledge of God and God's law of love. Jesus's proclamation fulfilled the deal so we need no other teachings and even the least of us knows as much as the Pope, at least what God wants each to know.

The illusion you possess of ruling a Catholic kingdom should be dispelled by the fact that God sits on the throne. You, at most, are not to rule but serve mankind by feeding the Eucharist and its teaching to everyone. An obvious start is to withdraw the anti-Christian *Sacramentum Caritatist*, which denies most of humanity the gift of Eucharist that God presented them and which gift was so dearly purchased for us by Jesus, the true head of the church.

Happily yours,

September 7, 2011

Dear Holy Father,

Saint Augustine has an influence on you. He taught you that the fundamental Christian virtue is charity, and the true Church could not be founded on the uncharitable exclusion of people. Yet, as Bishop of Hippo, he showed that his treatment of Pelagius, the monk of the Church of Christ, was despicably uncharitable. Pelagius viewed human nature as essentially good, which it was, considering God had pardoned all evildoings in the blood of the covenant. The monk may have based his argument on this knowledge God imprinted in us. Augustine, however, altogether disregards the new covenant established by Jesus Christ and uncharitably argued that Adam's sin remained corrupting man. (Augustine believed man, not woman, was created in the image and likeness of God and predestination was a mysterious selection of some), but all are damned unless baptized in the Catholic church. Augustine's power influenced the Council of Carthage to condemn Pelagius' teachings, excommunicate him, and run him out of the area to the East, where he was conveniently murdered. Augustine's theology influenced the Council of Trent to make dogma of his original sin theory, and today Pope Benedict XVI walks in his footsteps to champion Catholic tradition over God's commandment and God's new covenant relationship with humans.

You departed, recently, from the way of Augustine, in centralizing your rule. His study of Plato influenced the elite of the Catholic church to rule as the Gentiles and Constantine did and not the way advised by Jesus in service of the people of God. At Vatican II, you were arguing the people of God were participants in the Eucharist. Thus, you were conditioned to oppose the New Testament scholars' Vatican II's concepts of the global Church of Christ and its universally open Eucharist to include unconditionally everyone created. They did not suit your narrow and uncharitable understanding of scripture, as you wrote in *God Is Near Us*, page 60, citing

John 13:10 (a water absolution), 1 Corinthians 11:27ff. (Paul's commentary on selfishness in the meal preceding the Eucharist) and *Didache* 10:6 (nonscripture traditions). Of course, you did not establish your opinion for an exclusive Eucharist as dogma once you became Pope Benedict XVI but artfully had diocesan bishops do your uncharitable works in *Sacramentum Caritatis* (Sacrament of Charity), a hypocrisy according to Jesus Christ (see Mk 7:1-13).

I am obliged to express my concerns for the good of the Catholic church, as anti-Church of Christ, when it is uncharitable and excludes most of the people created by God from the gift of the Eucharist. (See No. 37 of our *Dogmatic Constitution on the Church* aka *Lumen Gentium*.) The same Vatican II Document entitled me to your consideration and a fatherly enlightening.

Patiently yours,

September 15, 2011

Dear Holy Father,

Last night, I saw a TV movie about the Mafia or Cosa Nostra. The blood oath the members made was to their "thing" first and expressly "before God, nation, and family." It raised thoughts of our Catholic magisterium or curia. They evidenced their allegiance to themselves first in the Documents of Vatican II. Our *Dogmatic Constitution on the Church* (*Lumen Gentium*) No. 9, at Chapter II sits a fruit of their "thing." It is more to secure their pre-Vatican traditions that the scribes of Pope Paul VI have fabricated this welcome to their race, selected by God to know and serve God and set up a new covenant to be ratified in Christ. However, to secure their "thing," the scribes forged a "new" new covenant, falsely claiming to be the same that Jesus died to fulfill, but actually a forgery that deleted God's pledge, to wit,—"for I will forgive their evildoing and forget their sin forever" (see Jer 31:31-34).

The deliberate deceit and misrepresentations in this part No. 9 of *Lumen Gentium* (the light of the world) is a brutal, rather than artful, setting aside of God's commandment of love to keep these hypocrite clergymen their "thing" based on pre-Vatican II traditions negating God's plan of the new covenant salvation by God, solely performing in the blood of Christ, to save all people for everlasting life. Instead, a small flock of baptized believers in Christ are uncharitably selected while damning most of humanity to everlasting torment.

I had high hope that our professor in theology and enthusiast at Vatican II, Joseph Ratzinger, now known as Pope Benedict XVI, would acknowledge God's kingdom spelled out in the new covenant (Jer 31:31*f*) and ratified from heaven by Jesus Christ (1 Cor 11:23-26) saves every human created. But he evidently "cowered" out and is led blindly by his curia to release such "gnats" as *Sacramentium Caritatis* which in the manipulated hands of his cowed diocesan bishops, excommunicates most everyone.

Still if someone in our Catholic "Mafia" would share my writings of concern with Pope Benedict, it may awaken his heart and mind to do what God already has imprinted in his conscience to do—follow Christ and share the real presence with everyone.

Prayerfully yours,

September 19, 2011

Dear Holy Father,

In my futile struggle to persuade you to allow every individual human being receive Holy Communion, as Jesus ordered all to take and as the New Testament scholars of Vatican II concluded Christ meant it to be for everyone unconditionally. I have made no progress. Meanwhile, Jesus Christ has been constantly proclaiming that the Eucharist the Catholic church shares is "of the new and everlasting covenant" as fulfilled on the cross with the salvation of all human beings. Since Jesus's words instituting the Eucharist are made "interdependent" as you say, with his death, Jesus saves the world no matter what you do or fail to do. My insignificant efforts cannot improve on his delivery of the news or his salvation. However, my fellow Catholic clerical brothers are blindly obedient to your ignorant teachings and clinging to church's traditions. Ignoring consciences they continue to deny the Eucharist to many simply because they disregard God's imprinted law and cling to human traditions and precepts (Mk 7:1-10).

I have made no progress in writing constantly on rights, vested in me by the *Dogmatic Constitution on the Church* (*Lumen Gentium*, No. 37), which expressly "obliged" me to express my opinions for the good of the church. Instead the Eucharist distribution today, pursuant to *Sacramentum Caritatis*, uncharitably continues to deny most humans created the nourishment of God's gift of life and real presence. At the moment, it is Pope Benedict XVI, whose *Antichrist* guidance and disregard of the common knowledge God imprints in him, who is maintaining the blasphemy. God's new deal (Jer 31:31ff.) incorporated by reference and authenticated in Jesus's redemption of the world of mankind (2 Cor 11:23-26) exists untouched to daily remind the Pope that his *Sacramentium Caritatis* is being used as an uncharitable hypocrisy as prophesied by Jesus above.

Pope Benedict XVI faces a future with the Beatific Vision possessed of the memory of how he fed God's sheep. His death will awaken him the consequences of his actions—to feel the suffering or joy caused in his lifetime. If he continues excommunicating, I foresee his name carved in history as the *Antichrist* Pope. Thank God that the debris he may leave behind on earth will not damage the Church of Christ but harm the credibility of the Roman Catholic Church, for lacking the virtue of charity in its Eucharist, as he wrote about Donatism's denial of it sacraments.

Yours in Christ,

September 16, 2011

Dear Holy Father,

I have mailed you over three hundred letters expressing my concern for the Catholic Church's exclusive Eucharist and enclosed most copies of them in two books entitled *God's Gift To You*. The books were published, lodged in the Library of Congress, and in a half-assed effort of "Fraternal Correction" (Mt 18:15ff.) referred them to the members of the global church. It is the Church of Christ, which does not subsist in this case, in the Roman Catholic Church because the latter uncharitably excludes so many from its sacrament of Eucharist. Catholicism unjustly and uncharitably withholds God's Gift to every human being created.

At mass today, St. Paul tells Timothy that religion is a means of contentment, a great gain to those who possess it (1 Tim 6:6). Jesus died proclaiming that in his religion, God's kingdom, every human being is saved by God according to God's new covenant pledges, and God imprints in even the least of us God's law of love so we need no religion teaching more (1 Cor 11:23-26 and Jer 31:31ff.). Such is also the Gospel according to Jesus.

But purported Christian gospel writers give lip service to the new covenant, and instead of a unilaterally performed covenant by God in Christ, they insist on humans assisting God to save themselves. Since the Spirit allows these traditions to persist for millenniums, I figure I should leave the matter to God. But I also feel for Jesus, who paid so dearly to proclaim his Gospel, that I should write, even though I feel it's futile to reach your mind or heart, I still must imitate Christ.

However, I also feel I should not disturb people who are content with their religions. So, I focus on trying to penetrate your Mafia and your heart or mind. I think there is still a scintilla of hope with you to change back to your mental condition before 1968. I pray that God overcome your obstinacy to return to that opinion which, "prevents the church from becoming simply a select community of the righteous, a community that condemns the wayward masses to perdition." So wrote Prof. Ronald Modras, your student in 1968, using the typescript of your lectures (*Commonweal*, 4/21/06).

Yours joyfully,

September 19, 2011

Dear Holy Father,

In my futile struggle to persuade you to allow every individual human being to receive Holy Communion as Jesus ordered all to take and as the New Testament scholars of Vatican II concluded Christ meant it to be for everyone unconditionally. I have made no progress. Meanwhile, Jesus Christ has been constantly proclaiming that the Eucharist the Catholic Church shares is "of the new and everlasting covenant" as fulfilled on the cross with the salvation of all human beings. Since Jesus's words instituting the Eucharist are made "interdependent" as you say, with his death, Jesus saves the world no matter what you do or fail to do. My insignificant efforts cannot improve on his delivery of the news or his salvation. However, my fellow Catholic clerical brothers are blindly obedient to your ignorant teachings and clinging to church's traditions. Ignoring consciences they continue to deny the Eucharist to many simply because they disregard God's imprinted law and cling to human traditions and precepts (Mk 7:1-10).

I have made no progress in writing constantly on rights, vested in me by the *Dogmatic Constitution on the Church* (*Lumen Gentium*, No. 37), which expressly "obliged" me to express my opinions for the good of the church. Instead the Eucharist distribution today, pursuant to *Sacramentum Caritatis*, uncharitably, continues to deny most humans created the nourishment of God's gift of life and real presence. At the moment, it is Pope Benedict XVI, whose *Antichrist* guidance and disregard of the common knowledge

God imprints in him, who is maintaining the blasphemy, God's new deal (Jer 31:31*f*) incorporated by reference and authenticated in Jesus's redemption of the world of mankind (2 Cor 11:23-26) exists untouched to daily remind the Pope that his *Sacramentium Caritatis* is being used as an uncharitable hypocrisy as prophesied by Jesus above.

Pope Benedict XVI faces a future with the Beatific Vision possessed of the memory of how he fed God's sheep. His death will awaken him the consequences of his actions—to feel the suffering or joy caused in his lifetime. If he continues excommunicating, I foresee his name carved in history as the *Antichrist* Pope. Thank God that the debris he may leave behind on earth will not damage the Church of Christ but harm the credibility of the Roman Catholic Church, for lacking the virtue of charity in its Eucharist, as he wrote about Donatism's denial of it sacraments.

Yours in Christ,

September 20, 2011

Dear Holy Father,

Pope John XXIII authored *Journal Of A Soul* and offered some prayers, one of which was "To Jesus In The Eucharistic Mystery" which went, in part, as follows:

> You are our elder Brother; you have trodden our path before us, O Christ Jesus, the path of every one of us, you have forgiven all our sins; you inspire each of us and all to give a nobler, more convinced and more active witness of Christian life. O Jesus, our true Bread, and the only substantial food for our souls, gather all the peoples around your table. Your altar is divine reality on earth, the pledge of heavenly favors, the assurance of a just understanding among peoples, and of peaceful rivalry in the true progress of civilization.
>
> Nourished by you and with you, O Jesus, men will be strong in faith, joyful in hope, and active in the many and varied expressions of charity. Our wills will know how to overcome

the snares of evil, the temptations of selfishness, the listlessness of sloth. And the eyes of men who love and fear the LORD will behold the vision of the land of the living, of which the wayfaring of the Church militant is the image, enabling the whole earth to hear the first sweet and mysterious voices of the City of God.

O Jesus, feed us and guard us, and grant that we may see the good things of the Land of the Living! Amen. Alleluia.

The above was part of Pope John's prayer recited months before Vatican II opened in October, 1962, when Pope John was looking forward to see "in the Ecumenical Council, the reflection of (Jesus) loving face in the features of your church, the mother of all, the mother who opens her arms and heart to all, and here awaits, trembling and truthful, the arrival of all her Bishops."

Pope John and the Bishops gathered in Council and presented us with the global Church of Christ, which subsists in the Catholic church and the inclusive Eucharist whereby all God's created souls are to be fed the true bread and intimately transformed by God.

Pope John's prayers may have some impetus on you to open Eucharist to everyone created.

Prayerfully Yours,

September 21, 2011

Dear Holy Father,

God in Jesus Christ has loyal members of the global Church of Christ, which subsists in the Roman Catholic Church, laboring in the church for the salvation of all. Theologians and New Testament scholars from the Second Vatican Council of Pope John XXIII and his gathered bishops, since silenced, contended that the Eucharist must be for every member of the church of Christ as God intended to nourish every human being and those transformed by God to love everyone impartially.

As a Roman Catholic since a month of my birth, I appreciate being a citizen of the

Catholic church, but I have come to learn, since Vatican II, that I am moreso a Christian and a citizen of the Church of Christ. God conceived me as such from the beginning of creation when God opted to make me with defects, and God later graced me to learn of my being perfected in Jesus Christ via God's new and everlasting covenant (Jer 31:31*f*) and rebirth in the blood of Jesus Christ (1 Cor 11:23-26, Mk 14:24, etc.). The mystery of God in Jesus so redeeming me also revealed that all human beings without merit become one in Christ. Such is my religious faith and trust that awaits my death to confirm the truth.

Among Documents of Vatican II is an *Antichrist Dogmatic Constitution on the Church* (*Lumen Gentium*), part No. 9, which fraudulently distorts God's version of the new covenant (Jer 31:31-34) by deleting portions, the last of verse 34—to wit: "for I will forgive their iniquity, and I will remember their sins no more." The remaining forgery, distorted by the Vatican scribes for promulgation by Pope Paul VI on 11/21/64, stupidly claims "this" covenant is what Jesus died for. The scribes knowingly lied while writing "Christ instituted *this* new covenant, the New Testament, that is to say in his blood (cf. 1 Cor 11:25) . . ." (emphasis mine). The scribes jump then to conclude on a false basis that salvation was only "[f]or those who believe in Christ, who are reborn . . . from water and the Holy Spirit (cf. Jn 3:5-6), . . ." By disregarding God's new covenant, as the author(s) did in the Fourth Gospel, the Roman Catholic hierarchy substitutes, for our God of love, a traditional god who creates those like Judas to dangle in torment for eternity. This deceit is so blatant that we need not await our deaths to perceive the truth.

Sadly yours,

September 22, 2011

Dear Holy Father,

My competence in the subject matter of my written concerns to you, I trust, is based on the knowledge God imprints in all of us so that even the least of us know God and God's law of love. Raised Roman Catholic, I was taught the church's teachings, and again by Christian Brothers at St. Mary's College and Jesuits at the University of Santa Clara. But it was not until Vatican II ecumenical lessons in my diocese and as a lay partner with the Passionist fathers that critical thinking was added to the teachings. I possess no religious library but with renewed readings of the Bible and the writings I collected in the last two decades, I wrote to my spiritual leaders seeking fatherly guidance. I felt I had to express concerns and suggestions because I was "obliged" to write pursuant to No. 37 of *Lumen Gentium*. I received one response from my diocesan bishop who wrote that from the time before St. Paul the problem I see was solved by the church, and I was advised "To receive Holy Communion requires true Catholic faith and worthiness. You are simply incorrect in your analysis and need the 'obedience of the faith' to accept the teaching of the church."

My problem is that I have gained a faith conviction that takes precedence, the teaching of Christ over teachings of the church. Also, the common knowledge imprinted by God in me contradicts the teachings of the present Catholic church or, as I realize, that to which I was conditioned before Vatican II. I now hear Jesus Christ at every mass I attend informing me that he died to perform God's new covenant. Had I listened before I would have heard the same words in the Eucharist prayer but ignorantly ignored them. I suspect even now most Catholics, even the vowed, cannot identify the specific covenant Jesus refers to at his Last Supper and every supper since.

The first written report of the words Jesus spoke instituting the Eucharist and incorporating by reference the new covenant in his death so as to make the meanings of death and words interdependent, came by vision to Paul (Saul) (see 1 Cor 11:23-26). "Thereby everyone, all Jews and Gentiles, are intended by God to be beneficiaries of God's unilaterally performed new covenant. By pledge of God we each are imprinted in conscience with knowledge of God suitable for each of us, so we need no Church teachings, for I will forgive their evildoing and remember their sins no more." (Jer 31:31-34.)

My spiritual shepherds should take heed and seek "obedience of faith" to the teachings of God first and foremost and let God's Eucharist be delivered to everyone as God intends.

Yours in Christ,

____

September 23, 2011

Dear Holy Father,

When Cardinal Joseph Ratzinger was presented with the part No. 8 of *Lumen Gentium* stating that our Church of Christ "subsists" in the Catholic church rather than "is" in it, he misconstrued the text beyond the origins of the Second Vatican Council's historical discussion to identify the true Church of Christ to be "and only can be, *fully* present" in the Roman church. In 1984, Ratzinger read the text this differently so that the institutional church had to coincide with the church's essence (see *The New Yorker*, p. 42, 7/25/05).

However, returning from 1984 to 1964 until 1968, Professor Ratzinger, now known as Pope Benedict, XVI, taught a different tune according to Professor Modra's article "In His Own Footsteps" (*Commonweal*, p. 13, 4/21/06) in part, as follows:

> The Ratzinger of 1968 acknowledged that some Catholic apologists misconstrued the body of Christ image by merely identifying the

church with Christ, thus discounting the church's historical failings. Ratzinger, however, connected the body of Christ and bride of Christ imagery, seeing the church as a bride who has not always lived up to her calling. To put it another way, the church, by the grace of God a community of saints, is also a company of sinners. With language reminiscent of Protestant theologian Paul Tillich, Ratzinger did not absolve the church of the ambiguities that bedevil all religion, where one can find "the most awful fanaticism, self-alienation, and human degradation." And with a nod to Jesuit Henri de Lubac, he even conceded that heretics and atheists provide a service when they criticize dubious religious thinking and practice. As Ratzinger put it bluntly: "The institutional church does not coincide with the church's essence.

Professor Ratzinger participated in the Second Vatican Council as a theologian and enthusiastically endorsed its new openness, even publishing a book, about its considerations of non-Catholics being members of the mystical body. But then he seems to have had a conversion to gain the fame of ambitions and ascended thereby after 1968. However, the views of the professor at Tübingen gives me hope, in continuing to write to have him retract *Sacramentum Caritatis* and open Eucharist to all members of the mystical body of Christ before he faces the judgment St. Paul warned us about "for not recognizing the body" (1 Cor 11:29).

Yours in Christ,

September 26, 2011

Dear Holy Father,

At the consecration today, we prayed the mystery of faith prayer, in part as follows:

> when we eat this bread and drink this cup we proclaim your death Lord Jesus . . .

It reminded me of your woeful service to God and mankind, in allowing *Sacramentum Caritatis* to deny the Eucharist to most of the people existing on earth. God is denied by you to be in real presence intimately with all those God intended to consume the bread and cup mentioned. Thus, also, any pleasures God receives from communicants denied God by your stupidity.

Federico Lombardi, S. J., or whoever else might be reading and discarding my letters to Pope Benedict XVI is not doing favors for God or anyone by doing so, except perhaps their own bureaucracy. Orders that should take precedence are those of Jesus; to wit, "take this all of you, and eat it . . . Take this all of you and drink from it . . ." If you dispute what I write, have the heart to write and advise me where I err. I have a constitutional right to a response from my spiritual leader (see No. 37, *Lumen Gentium*).

Meanwhile, I must continue to write because I believe what I am writing with authorities cited, and in good conscience, are truths that Pope Benedict XVI should consider for the good of the church. I see Jesus died a horrible death to tell the news of God's new covenant relationship, which he died to perform. He on the cross and in Eucharist proclaims this Gospel years before any of the Canon was written on hearsays and opinions of others. I am so frustrated by the oppressive silence of our Pope Benedict, and his hierarchy, that I list you among my trespassers whom I ask God to forgive. At least tell me the Pope considers them.

Yours hopefully in Christ,

September 27, 2011

Dear Holy Father,

The mystery of Jesus Christ redeeming the world includes God renewing God's human creation. The sacrament of the Eucharist has God's personal involvement in the teaching and forgiving of human individuals so all are saved.

You and I have differences of opinions expressed on how God performs our salvation in the blood of the Lamb. I submit that God unilaterally performs the new covenant (Jer 31:31*f*) without any meritorious contribution by us. You, at least since your change of mind at Tübingen, require each of us to let ourselves be reconciled by God in some act of faith. For similar differences of opinion you contended, in opposition to the New

Testament scholars' criticism of our exclusive Eucharist and contention that Christ meant for an all inclusive Eucharist, that scripture supports your claim that the Eucharist is only for those "who have let themselves be reconciled by God." (*God Is Near Us*, pp. 59-60).

Since you released *Sacramentum Caritatis* delegating final judgment on the matter to less learned diocesan bishops, the issue in controversy appears to remain open. The predecessor of my present diocesan bishop promulgated in 2006 our Diocesan Statutes of the Third Diocesan Synod which exclude almost everyone in the world from our Eucharist as was the tradition before Vatican II. Bishop Wiegand wrote me: The teaching of the church is very clear since the time at least of St. Paul. To receive Holy Communion requires true Catholic faith and worthiness. You are simply incorrect in your analysis and need "obedience of faith" to accept the teaching of the Church. Seemingly at Synod, the Vatican directives were not needed by this traditional biased bishop, and he promulgated the statutes even before you released *Sacramentum Caritatis*. One wonders what authority, if any, have God's words to my spiritual leaders in pledging the new covenant provisions, cleansing everyone of evildoing or in the last words of Jesus that are conceded by you to be "interdependent" with his death and authenticating the new covenant as God's design for salvation of all.

"Obedient in faith" to Jesus Christ and his gospel which simply is spelled out in God's new covenant (Jer 31:31*f*) and its performance (1 Cor 11:23-26 or Mk 14:24) is proved by demonstration. No wonder Jesus call our hierarchies "hypocrites" for clinging to their traditions that secure their occupational comforts at the expense of humanity deprived of love in violation of God's law of love and established covenant relationship (see Mk 7:1-13).

Sadly yours,

September 28, 2011

Dear Holy Father,

God created me mostly ignorant of God and God's law, a vincible ignorance that will be removed as a veil after I die. I take this on faith and in the interim trust God to care for me in my ignorance, that God will guide me so that I do not commit great harm in my writing to you. In faith I believe I know more by heart that knowledge God imprints in me (Jer 31:31*f*), to write heart to heart.

Cardinal John Henry Newman felt heart-to-heart talks with others truly reflected the loving heart of God, attuned to each recipient's varied individuality. Thus, I try to trust that God created me to do God some definite service in writing you from the heart.

I have a mission in expressing my concerns for the good of the church, initiated by *Lumen Gentium*, No. 37s "obliged" duty. I won't know its extent in this life, but both of us will be told it in the next. I trust I do good and trust that I do God's work. I do not understand it fully and seek your advice that No. 37 represented you would furnish, to keep God's commandment and serve God and our siblings in this calling for the church to serve the world.

I place my trust in the love God has for all humanity. In my perplexity, I use a prayer of John Henry to assist me because he certainly knows, most of what it is all about. However, our prayer is with God and God in

Jesus Christ who knows always that even if my efforts are futile, God will make good of them in you or elsewhere as God knows from the beginning and always.

The prayer I make here also is to Cardinal Levada, Father Federico, and whoever else may be preventing these messages reaching Pope Benedict XVI. I ask each of you to allow God our Creator to open up your hearts to pay attention to what God has to say heart to heart to our Pope Benedict. *"Let my people go, to Holy Communion."*

Yours in Christ,

September 28, 2011

Dear Holy Father,

Writing *God Is Near Us* by Cardinal Joseph Ratzinger, especially about the New Testament scholars of Vatican II criticizing the Roman Catholic Church's exclusive Eucharist and contending that Jesus Christ intended an all-inclusive Eucharist be shared with every individual human being, proves that you already knew of what I have been trying to tell you in all my letters and books *God's Gift To You* and *Sequel*.

In no way will I ever be able to better express my concerns to you as Pope Benedict XVI, even if the letters and books I mailed or the hand deliveries of my message to Father Frederico and others were actually delivered and read by you. Jesus too foretold about experts like you paying lip service to him, but your heart being far from him. "Empty is the reverence they do me because they teach as dogmas mere human precepts" (Mk 7:1-10). Your book's response, at pages 59 and 60, to the New Testament scholars contention, even cited *Didache* as scriptural authority which "we find in the Bible" ("we" presumably being you and Pope John Paul II) is more brutal than an artful setting aside of God's commandment of love in the interests of gaining your ambitions of keeping church's traditions than Jesus foretold.

Truer to Jesus and Isaiah's prophesy are my diocesan bishops who act blinding "obedient to the faith" of your traditional Church teachings. Since 2006 we have dogma established in Diocesan Statutes of the Third Diocesan Synod complying with Vatican rulings which you dictated. You remain their prime architect and later released a hypocritical exhortation.

Sacramentum Caritatis is your personal *Antichrist* work of art. It reads as though diocesan bishops had final judgment on the subject matter of the Eucharist. However, no diocese in our realm dare have an open Eucharist as proposed by Christ initially and the New Testament scholars of Vatican II. Surprisingly, your doctoral dissertation concluded that the true Church of Christ could not be founded on the exclusion of others (see *The New Yorker*, page 44 7/25/05) and at Vatican II you enthusiastically wrote supporting Dominican Yves Congar's inclusion of Protestants in our Eucharist.

I remain obligated to proclaim the gospel of Jesus Christ. After daily Eucharist, I write you to remind you of Christ's mission to fulfill the new covenant (Jer 31:31*f*) and have it proclaimed by everyone consuming the Eucharist (1 Cor 11:23-26). I pray, too, that God awakens you to your conscience and law of God imprinted in you.

Yours in Christ,

September 29, 2011

Dear Holy Father,

You have made the Catholic church a monarchy because of personality faults in you, and now as a Pharaoh, God's memorialized words are appropriate "Let my people go!" God's command should be repeated in the halls of your Vatican and in every diocese where *Sacramentum Caritatis* restrains any human created from consuming God's bread of life.

The Catholic church, in my faith conviction, has appropriated the possession of Jesus Christ in the Holy Eucharist for its own purpose. Christ's charitable purpose of giving himself free to others preempts any other end for God's gift to humankind, and it is plain that to misappropriate God's gift, or have beneficiaries merit it, is a blasphemy to God's plan for creation. God being our God of love awaits you to release God's Gift to benefit both God and created individuals just as they exist. You must release every child born of woman to consume of God's self as their God given right of heritage entitles everyone to the real presence.

You, who in ignorance uncharitably deny God's real presence to any sibling in Christ, must be informed of what evil you do someday, and, unfortunately, you will have all of eternity with God to be sorry. I am just trying to tell you of my concern for you and the church so you can avoid an eternity of sorrow by performing a bit of love.

Yours in Christ,

October 3, 2011

Dear Holy Father,

Gaudium et Specs, a document of Vatican II, expresses that the church has "one sole purpose—that the kingdom of God may come and the salvation of the human race may be accomplished." So wrote Fra. Richard P. McBrien, Professor of Theology at the University of Notre Dame (*NCR*, 9/16/11). This conciliar teaching sharply contrasts with preconciliar assumptions that the church is the kingdom of God on earth, but the tendency to equate the church with the Kingdom of God was denounced as a "Triumphalism" at Vatican II.

Article 5 was added to *Lumen Gentium* precisely to counteract this tendency to equate the church with the kingdom which mission the church has to proclaim and to spread among all people of the kingdom of Christ and of God . . . . While it grows, the Church strains toward the completed kingdom . . . with its king. God Almighty.

The implications of the church as an eschatological community includes the readiness of members to criticize that leaders publicly in exposure of church faults and in efforts to suggest structural changes in the church. Church members, such as yours truly, challenge the church because we care about it. I disagree with McBrien that we can only trust in the Holy Spirit to bring about the church's New Pentecost soon.

I part ways with Father McBrien because I am convinced that our pontificate Pope Benedict XVI has not made a good-faith effort to serve *our Lord* as faithfully as he should. In his efforts to cling to church's traditions with God's gift of Eucharist for all of humanity, his pastoral leadership of the Roman Catholic Church is plainly not true to the Church of Christ. He ignores God's covenant relationship, the evolving kingdom, cleansing everyone of evildoing to be worthy even for Pope Benedict's standards to receive Holy Communion.

When the Holy Spirit spoke up at the Second Vatican Council, you heard as theologian. Also New Testament scholars heard and criticized our church's exclusive Eucharist because Christ meant for an all inclusive Eucharist. Yet, you silenced them by manipulating the Vatican, diocesan bishops, and dumbing up theologians throughout the church. Father McGuire says we must wait; change is not going to happen without a New Pentecost. I disagree, we must try while waiting to return the church to the new covenant kingdom because Vatican II was so close to Christ's beginning and people cannot wait again for God's gift of enlightenment.

Yours in Christ,

October 4, 2011

Dear Holy Father,

After mass, a parishioner told me he heard on the internet of a conference of Catholic bishops reporting that the new covenant makes no mention of Gentiles. I tried to dispel what the parishioner said by pointing out that the OT literally mentions only Israel and Judah as the people of God to whom God is promising the benefits God intends to deliver in days to come. (See Jer 31:31-34 or *Lumen Gentium* No. 9). The deal is intended by God for all God's people as evidenced centuries later in the Synoptic words of Jesus at the Last Supper asserting his death is for salvation of "many" (Mk 14:24 and Mt 26:28). From heaven, the glorified Jesus Christ reports the words to Saul (St. Paul) while sending him on mission to all Jews and Gentiles (1 Cor 11:23-26). Jesus's words give meaning to his death and incorporate by reference God's new covenant provisions so that Gentiles are necessarily covered. As I now write, I wonder if the bishops said what the parishioner reports.

Tragically, the scribes of Pope Paul VI distorted the new covenant wordings in part No. 9 of our *Dogmatic Constitution on the Church*. Thus, I can believe the Vatican working over the bishop's conference are proclaiming their gospel to the world by control of the bishops and the media.

Jesus prophesied the power-play of our hierarchy, like his hierarchy, in turning away guests from *our Lord*'s Supper who were not cleansed in traditional ways. Jesus called them "hypocrites" and went on to say "you have made a fine art of setting aside God's commandment in the interests of keeping your traditions!" (See Mk 7:1-13.)

I sadly attribute the responsibility as chief artist for the Catholic church's exclusive Eucharist to Pope Benedict XVI. I would, however, not define his *Antichrist* activity concerning our Eucharist to be "a fine art" as it is more a brutal exercise of power and deceit by his Vatican manipulating the synod system to force the bishops to surrender their judgment of *Sacramentum Caritatis* to the will of the pope. Our exclusive Eucharist today is a product of his modified vision and self-interested interpretation of the principals of Vatican II's global church and all-inclusive Eucharist.

Sadly yours,

October 5, 2011

Dear Holy Father,

Yesterday, I was honored to receive a phone call from Jane Via, recently retired from the San Diego District Attorney's Office and practicing as a priest in or about Jamul, California. Immediately I thought she was like Pelagius, the Irish monk, who was another excommunicated clerical person in the Church of Christ "which subsists in" the Catholic church when the latter is true to God's law. In Jane's case, she believes she is one of those women you excommunicated by general fiat or by traditional church law. As I write, your doctoral dissertation comes to mind wherein Augustine and you concluded that Donatism could not be true to the Church of Christ because of excluding from the sacraments those in their priesthood who surrendered their copies of scriptures to Roman persecutors, and you agreed the lack of showing the fundamental Christian virtue of charity disqualified Donatism from being true church (*The New Yorker*. 725/05).

Because Pelagius disagreed with the Bishop of Hippo on the evil of human beings, he too was excommunicated by Augustine and the Council of Carthage. Aware that St. Augustine is your favorite, his conduct may give you comfort in your excommunications of so many Catholics. Your recent claim of "infallible" inability to ordain women priests, as you argued while demoting Bishop William Morris of Australia, evidences an un-Christian lacking of fundament Christian virtue of charity separating Catholicism from Christianity.

Our sister in Christ Jane Via told me that you and your hierarchy or Vatican is attempting to rule that the Second Vatican Council's workings were heresy committed by heretics. Wow! Or may be more appropriately said—Woe!

Tell me it isn't so. I easily believe what she said to be true because I see the forgery of the Vatican scribes, as promulgated by Pope Paul VI in part 9 of *Lumen Gentium*, showing the extent to which traditionalists immediately attacked the global Church of Christ's ideal by the successor of Pope John XXIII. The Vatican's conspiracy, with Karol Woytla and Joseph Ratzinger joining soon after 1964, subtly and secretly refused to accept Vatican II's principles to cling to prior church's traditions and human precepts. The Vatican "brutes" are setting aside God's commandments of love and artfully pursuing personal pursuits see St. Xavier words, *God's Gift To You*, p. 45). How accurately Jesus prophesized your "hypocrisy" (Mk 7:1-13).

Yours in Christ,

October 6, 2011

Dear Holy Father,

The credibility of the papacy, most particularly in the person of His Holiness Pope Benedict XVI, has deteriorated markedly. The "straight arrow" theologian Hans Küng has told John Wilkins, former editor of the Catholic weekly, *The Tablet*, that you as Cardinal Joseph Ratzinger, at the congregation for the Doctrine of the Faith, enjoined secrecy on the episcopate in your 2001 letter to them. Practicing the science you preached, you have since let the obedient bishops carry all the blame in Ireland, Belgium, and so on. Küng personally asked you to confess your involvement in the sex abuse cover-up crisis. We have to resolve it with your *mea culpa*, but, instead, you ended the exchange of views you had with your colleague up until then. Küng thinks we need another Vatican Council to overcome the crisis. I disagree, unless we have a change in the attitude of the present leadership.

Those who attended the last Council were not the pre-selected and indoctrinated lot that we have today. I have been told, and believe, that our present hierarchy wants to deem Vatican II to be a heresy and erase its principles in order to return us to our pre-counciliar traditions or, in plainer words, to dumb us down to be as little children. Küng's idea will serve this lot with the opportunity to formally usurp Vatican II's principles, as they are artfully doing today, with the pope alone illegitimately acting.

Fr. Richard P. McBrien, Professor of Theology, at the University of Norte Dame, likely has a better idea than Küng's. He expects us to wait to experience a New Pentecost by trusting in the Holy Spirit (*NCR*, 9/16/11). I disagree with his opinion too because I suspect we waited for millenniums of the church militant to be enlightened by Vatican II and the Holy Spirit.

I respectfully suggest we realize that the Church of Christ does *not* "subsist in the

Catholic Church while it is excluding most of human beings from Eucharist and its membership. It is lacking the fundamental virtue of charity to be true Church for humanity. The global Church of Christ is membered by all of humanity since God unilaterally performed the new covenant (Jer 31:31*f*) as extended by Christ's shedding of blood for all Jews and Gentiles (1 Cor 11:23-26). The passages cited constitute the gospel of Jesus, and all the rest of the Bible should be considered as human commentary on the good news proclaimed by God. Let us try God's way by simply loving each other as demonstrated by Jesus Christ that last weekend.

Yours in Christ,

October 7, 2011

Dear Holy Father,

Ever since I recently talked to Jane Via (she does "not deem equality . . . to be grasped at"). I reflect about her with the Eucharist. Jesus said at the Last Supper and repeats at every Mass: "Take this, all of you, and eat it; Take this all of you, and drink from it." Jane, in sharing Eucharist, certainly takes it in response to Jesus and according to her own conscience's imprint with the knowledge of God's law of love (Jer 31:33, 34). I sent you a copy of a letter I wrote to *NCR* (9/21/10) stating: "Jane Via and any others who feel excommunicated by Church authorities," should listen to their own conscience and receive Holy Communion often because they need God's graces. I submit everyone should "take" because Jesus Christ orders us "all" to take, and there are no conditions added. The words from Jesus are made "interdependent" with his sacrificial death as you wrote in *God Is Near Us*. The death without the words is a mere execution, you also accurately taught; so the death without Eucharist seems meaningless.

In my own book, *A Sequel* of *God's Gift To You* at pages 15 and 16, I discussed receiving the Eucharist at a funeral mass from an Episcopal woman priest and questioned the authenticity of it because of being prejudiced from my Roman Catholic indoctrination. Now I am considering Jane Via's consecration of Eucharist of the Body and Blood presumably made divine by the Holy Spirit. If pressed by circumstances, I would obey Jesus and take Eucharist from Jane and eat or drink, but, my informed conscience or bias normally would have me shy from the venture. Jane, being excommunicated, has been forced by the Catholic church to take and eat or take and drink on her own. Jane seems like the unbaptized St. Ambrose, also a lawyer who sinned much and received Eucharist often, before they made him bishop. I too would continue taking Eucharist if ever excommunicated, say for disagreeing with Pope Benedict. Our New Testament scholars proclaimed Christ's intentions that every human being is to take regardless of being Catholic or unworthy or, I assume, even excommunicated. They clearly are of the spirit of Vatican II. In *God Is Near Us*, Cardinal Joseph Ratzinger wrote in opposition, at pp. 59-60, to the New Testament scholar's criticism of our exclusive Eucharist and contention it should be all inclusive. But the Roman Catholic Church, with Pope Benedict XVI at the helm, choose human tradition, such as was cited by Ratzinger, that is, Jn 13:10, 1 Cor 11:27ff.; and *Didache* 10:6, over the words of God to take Eucharist with no preconditions attached.

Yours in Christ,

October 11, 2011

Dear Holy Father,

While at Mass yesterday, I was praying for my spiritual shepherds to consider my concerns. The first readings had Paul referring to Jesus and wrote:

> Through him we have received the grace of apostleship, to bring about obedience of faith, for the sake of his name, among all Gentiles, among whom are you also, who are called to belong to Jesus Christ, to all the beloved of God in Rome, called to be holy (Rom 1:1-7).

Since I hold the rank of Apostle in St. Paul's opinion, I must proclaim that Jesus's death baptizes and redeems all according to God's unilateral new covenant (Jer 31:31).

Later, at the "Liturgy of the Eucharist," I read an introduction furnished by the authors of *Today's Missal*:

> *Christians* are baptized into the paschal mystery of Christ's death and resurrection for the forgiveness

> of sin and the fullness of salvation. This mystery is celebrated at every Mass, remembering Christ's loving deed and giving thanks and praise to God.

I added the underlined emphasis to indicate where you and I disagree on the definition of "Christian." Vatican II translates charitably to include all people as members of the Church of Christ who are saved solely by God's goodness regardless of our merit.

Thus, when I pray the "Intercessions for the Church," I pray for the global Church of Christ to make us grow in love. Also I ask *our Lord* to make my shepherds and the Roman Catholic Church grow in love for all the world. Recalling Jesus died to redeem the world, I prayed:

> LORD, remember your Church throughout the world; make us grow in love, together with Benedict, our Pope, Jaime, our bishop, and all the clergy.

As I prayed I imagined the Church of Christ extending in love God's Eucharist to all our neighbors unconditionally. Also, I prayed for us to specially love non-Catholics as Jesus demonstrated in his paschal message fulfilling God's new covenant (Jer 31:31ff.) in an open and all-inclusive Communion (1 Cor 11:23-26).

Yours in Christ,

October 11, 2011

Dear Holy Father,

I wrote of *Journal of a Soul* by Pope John XXIII and specifically his prayer "To Jesus In The Eucharistic Mystery" which he wrote as he waited to open the Second Vatican Council in 1962. Pope John and his gathered bishops, in council with the curia leashed to limit its intrusions, produced the ideal Church of Christ as one which subsists in the Catholic church, rather than "is" in the Catholic church, leaving it open for later defining. Fr. Karl Rahner felt the global church concept to be the best product of Vatican II. It was phrased to keep the matter open for later definition or development, but you define the true church both is and can only be, *fully* present in the

Roman Church. The indication of the church's new openness at Vatican II was evidenced in theologians and New Testament scholars, criticizing the exclusive church's Eucharist and contending it was meant by Christ to be open to everyone unconditionally. Here, too, you opposed our Bible experts on scriptural translations. (See Cardinal Ratzinger's *God Is Near Us*, pp. 59 and 60.)

Pope John's prayer "To Jesus In The Eucharistic Mystery" evidences John's thoughts later to be discussed and used by the council. In parts, he prayed: "O Jesus, our true Bread, and the only substantial food for our souls, gather all people around your table . . . (and) . . . Nourished by you and with you, O Jesus, men will be strong in faith, joyful in hope, and active in the many and varied expressions of charity. Our wills will know how to overcome the snares of evil, the temptations of selfishness, the listlessness of sloth." The prayer obviously calls for Eucharist to renew everyone.

It is no wonder that our theologians and New Testament scholars were launched by John's council to contend that *our Lord* instituted the Eucharist in the words of the Last Supper to be universal in effect as you so accurately pointed out in *God Is Near Us*, at page 29. The universality of the crucifixion and Jesus's words are "interdependent," meaning the death gives universal meaning to the words, without the death of Christ, the Eucharist is a mere meal for Catholics of bread and wine. You located the church's founding with the institution of the Eucharist, in Jesus's Last Supper words where Jesus links his fulfillment of the new covenant (Jer 31:31*f*) by reference, to sacrificing himself "for many" (Mk 14:24, Is 53). Interpreting "for many" in its most charitable translation, a standard also which you use, God meant for all his created peoples to be saved and share Eucharist. God's commandment of love prevents the true Church of Christ from being a select community of baptized believers who deny others Eucharist or condemn other people to eternal death, so you thought.

"Theology" is defined as "the study of God and his relation to the world," according to *Webster's* dictionary. It is a presumptious study since God teaches theology (see new covenant Jn 31:31-34). God places God's law within us and imprints it on our hearts so we no longer need a teacher on "how to know the Lord." Thus, I know by heart that God meant for the Eucharist to be shared by all people

God creates and God loves impartially. God creates us to be one with God in all things.

Yours in Christ,

October 13, 2011

Dear Holy Father,

Why would the curia scribes of Pope Paul VI desecrate the words of God by deleting them from the scriptural text of the new covenant (Jer 31:31-34) in our *Dogmatic Constitution on the Church*? They removed essential words of God, for instance, "for I will forgive their iniquity, and I will remember their sin no more." (Jer 31:34)

Luke's Gospel today had an apt sentence: "Woe to you lawyers! You have taken away the key of knowledge." (Lk 11:52). Where the *Gospel According to John* disregards the words of the new covenant in Jesus's words at the Last Supper, the Vatican followed suit and forged a new covenant more to their liking to rebut the concept of the Global Church of Christ, which subsists in the Catholic church as submitted by Pope John XXIII in council with his gathered bishops while the curia was restrained. Note the ideal church is recorded in Chapter 1, part No. 8, of *Lumen Gentium*, and the profanation of the new covenant text is immediately afterwards, at Chapter II, part No. 9, of the Vatican II documents to give us our *Antichrist* church.

As phrased by God, the new covenant reads as if the forgiveness by God of our sins caused us to know by heart all God requires us to know of God and God's law to be renewed as God's people in the blood of the Lamb. God knew not to trust men to define Christ's church.

I claim a Constitutional right of part No. 37 of *Lumen Gentium* to express my opinion on those things I have written about the Eucharist in letters to spiritual leaders. By reason of the knowledge imprinted in us by God "for I will forgive their iniquity," we are "sometimes even obliged" to express opinions on those things, which concern the good of the church. However, the duty is vested with a corresponding right of response. Attentive in Christ the fatherly advice from you may become hopefully "dialogue between" us. In this way, the whole church (Church of Christ or Roman Catholic Church or both), "strengthened by each one of its members may more effectively fulfill its mission for the life of the world."

Being an experienced lawyer, I was struck with the awareness that God's new covenant (Jer 31:31*f*), as directed from heaven by our Glorified Lord (1 Cor 11:23-26), is a unilateral agreement, not a bilateral one requiring contribution by its beneficiaries and is fulfilled. The good news according to Jesus is contained in these cited passages. However, the gospels according to men, especially John's, took away from us our key of knowledge and, No. 9 of *Lumen Gentium* evidences the church's *Antichrist* stance that results. Another squeezed out dropping of the Roman Church is our exclusive Eucharist's denial of God's gift to most people.

Yours in Christ,

October 14, 2011

Dear Holy Father,

I was reflecting on the words of Jesus at the Last Supper, wondering why I believe that I am receiving the real presence in the consecrated Eucharist at mass. Jesus holds out a piece of bread and a cup of wine for us to take and to consume, saying "this is my body, which will be given up for you," and, "this is the cup of blood, the blood of the new and everlasting covenant. It will be shed for you and for all so that sins may be forgiven."

What he says is unreasonable, it is absurd, but we accept it as true because of who is speaking and the context in which he speaks those words is convincing. It is Jesus who speaks, and we believe he speaks with authority, speaking the words that he believes his Father instructs him to state or we believe because he is Jesus Christ our *Lord* God speaking surreal words of mystery that changed bread and wine into the body and blood of Jesus Christ, while he is on his way to die horribly on the cross.

Jesus believes so convincingly in his mission according to scripture (see Is 53 and Jer 31:31*f*) that he freely presents himself to be crucified, to suffer such a horrible and shameful death so that humankind's sins are all forgiven to live with God forever. Shedding his blood fulfills God's unilateral performance of the new covenant (Jer 31:31-34) renewing all of humankind by the death and words of

Jesus Christ (1 Cor 11:23-26).

God is Love. In caring for us all impartially, God, by covenant, forgives and forgets our evildoings to save each and every one to be loved forever, and God teaches us to know by heart the knowledge of God and God's law of love, so we need no other teachers and even the least of us know enough to be at peace to joyfully reciprocate with love. Of course, being human, we will continue doing evil and selfish things because it is natural to follow our instincts; however, knowing God constantly forgives us and loves us anyway as most of our mothers do, we can spontaneously love God and each other if we want. Once with the beatific vision, we likely cannot not love God, and this may be our best and only way to favor God with gifts of our love.

So when Jesus says, "Take this all of you and eat it . . . Take this, all of you and drink from it . . ." and "Do this in memory of me," we take Jesus at his word, and the real presence becomes intimately within us, to love us as sinful as we are and help us love others.

Yours in Christ,

October 17, 2011

Dear Holy Father,

Jesus Christ, from heaven, extended God's new covenant benefits and relationship to every human creature (1 Cor 11:23-26), and those new covenant terms, fulfilled in the death and resurrection of Jesus, included God imprinting the knowledge of God and God's law of love so we know by heart all we need be taught (Jer 31:31-34).

Statements "On The Primacy Of Conscience," which God imprints in us, are quoted at page 7, *NCR* 9/20/11, from Vatican documents and from Joseph Ratzinger, in part, as follows:

> Deep within his conscience man discovers a law which he has not laid upon himself but which he must obey. Its voice, ever calling him to love and to do what is good and to avoid evil, tells him inwardly at the right moment do this, shun that. For man has in his heart a law inscribed by God. His dignity lies in observing this law and by it he will be judged. His conscience is man's most secret core,

> and his sanctuary. There he is alone with God whose voice echoes in his depths. By conscience in a wonderful way, that law is made known which is fulfilled in the love of God and of one's neighbor. (*Guardium et Spes*, no. 16)
>
> Over the pope as expression of the binding claim of ecclesiastical authority there stands one's own conscience which must be obeyed before all else, even if necessary against the requirement of ecclesiastical authority. This emphasis on the individual, whose conscience confronts him with a supreme and ultimate tribunal and one which in the last resort is beyond the claim of external social groups, even the official church, also establishes a principle in opposition to increasing totalitarianism. (Joseph Ratzinger, *Commentary on the Documents of Vatican II*, 1967)

God's words instituting the Eucharist for everyone to consume is voiced by Jesus at every *Lord's* Supper, and God remains really present in the meal consumed to transform the life and faith of every human fed. However, churchmen who cling to human traditions and disregard God's law of love imprinted in us deny, others God's gift out of vincible ignorance of knowledge we all possess.

Yours in Christ,

October 20, 2011

Dear Holy Father,

René Descartes' thinking is famous for the reflection "I think therefore I am" which I believe Descartes argued that subjective thought alone undoubtedly proves the fact of his being. He implies that all objective views or other judgments are cast in doubt. Being Catholic, however, Descartes deductively reasoned to a Benevolent God in the perception given him and trusts God would not want to deceive him. He supposed this acquiring knowledge of God is based on deductive reasoning and perception. Being Catholic of his time, he overlooks God's new covenant imprints of knowing God.

God imprints knowledge of God in us and knowledge of God's law in our minds and hearts, even of the least of us, so we need no other teacher, and, by the experience of Jesus Christ's death and resurrection Descartes too knew of God loving us. Christ's death fulfilled God's covenant and extends it to Jews and Gentiles, news to all humanity (1 Cor 11:23-26 and Jer 31:31ff.). We and Descartes, thus, know what God wants us to know. It may be only news that God loves us in unilaterally saving all of us as loving mothers do.

Maybe we are not to know God subjectively or objectively, until God lifts our veils of ignorance, other than God is Love to us. God wants us to love each other as we love ourselves here on earth. God loves us no matter what evil we do. God knows we will love God for eternity, later when we cannot help loving God. But now, I think, God would rather have us love each other and not suffer celibacy, and so on, for God. So God teaches us of God Unknowable, and the fact God cares for us impartially. The passion and death of Jesus, in context of the new covenant, for which he expressly sacrificed himself out of love for us is enough knowledge of God for us to know. Consequently, God meant for Holy

Communion to be shared with every human being to proclaim Jesus's loving death and have God's real presence further transform lives by renewing a God of love within us.

Yours in Christ,

October 21, 2011

Dear Holy Father,

Yesterday I wondered how Cartesian knowledge in modern philosophy dealt with God's new covenant impressing us with knowledge of God and God's law. Today is St. Paul of the cross's feast day. The Passionist Fathers' founder resolved to think of nothing, but Jesus Christ crucified as the wisdom of God. I suggest that René Descartes' subjective perception of our Benevolent God is imprinted in him and all human beings by the spilled blood of the Covenant, and we are unaware or unappreciative of this fact of God recreating us unless God awakens us to the fact. A means designed by God to transform our faith and lives is God's Eucharist, the institution of which is "interdependent" as you wrote in *God Is Near Us* with the death of Jesus that redeems the world. Still, the Catholic church got it wrong until Vatican II.

God evidenced love of each of us in the saving action of Jesus Christ crucified and this saving action in history is defectively reported by humans. Christ correctly announced it from heaven (1 Cor 11:23-26 incorporating Jer 31:31ff.) to record the event in the New Testament. Later human hearsay and biased opinions negating the evidence of God's new covenant's saving action in history have tried to tell the good news in human ways.

You have played a major part in obscuring the truth of God's salvation of humankind. You too ignore the fact that God forgives everyone's evildoing in the baptism of blood Jesus shed on the cross. As a result of your ignorance or worse, the enlightening of Vatican II, which involves Pope John XXIII's Church of Christ which subsists in the Roman Catholic Church and its followers and New Testament scholars' efforts to include all human beings to share an open Eucharist have been negated by your clinging to human tradition. Specifically, you use *Sacramentum Caritatis* to uncharitably deny God's real presence in the Eucharist to most every human being thus depriving them of God personally to transform them. Your Catholic church disregards God's covenantal cleansing and baptism in Christ's blood, to insist on church reconciliation and baptism sacraments, as though they are improvements on the cleansing of God and Jesus, as preconditions to receive the body and blood of Jesus Christ.

Yours in Christ,

October 24, 2011

Dear Holy Father,

The New Yorker, 7/25/05, had an article "Reading Ratzinger" concerning Benedict XVI, the theologian, by Anthony Grafton. It pointed out the different way you read the historical text of Vatican II's *Lumen Gentium* ("Light of the Nations") Chapter 1, No. 8, which explained that the true church "subsists in the Catholic church, which is governed by the successor of Peter and by the bishops in communion with him. Nevertheless, many elements of sanctification and of truth are found outside its visible confines." You wrote in 1964 enthusiastically of the church's new openness, qualifying the traditional exclusivity that Catholics alone are members of the mystical body.

Yet decades later you read the same text differently. You applied a noun—*substantia*—to explain the terms "subsists in" (from Latin *Subsist in*). The noun, you argue, is related to the verb *subsist* that the council fathers used. *Substantia* meaning "substance," refers to the essence of a thing (as in "transubstantiation"). You argued the council used the verb "subsists" to state strongly that the true church "both is and can only be, *fully* present" in the Roman Church, with all its hierarchies. The writer Grafton reviewed the historical circumstances of the text and saw that nowhere was the noun "substance" mentioned, and attributed the misrepresentation to your ideological partisan bias.

Hans Küng also argued that you subvert the council's teachings. He wrote Msgr. Gerard Philips, the secretary of the theological commission, to ask why they replaced "subsist in" for the preliminary text's "is," and, he replied that "we wanted to keep the matter open" (see *NCR*, 11/12/10).

Rene' Descartes would have argued against your use of "substantial" (as in transubstantiation). A main part of his philosophy rejects the analysis of corporal substance into arguing matter and form. Thomism based on Aristotalienism argued metaphysics concluded on Eucharistic transubstantiation. However, the arrogant presumption of Roman Catholic doctors of theology who delved into the mystery of God in Jesus, or God in Scripture, or God in Eucharist, based on Greek thinking of matters of faith, would have us love Pure Act. Critically thinking person should find Cartesian thought more reasonable, and so it prevails today in education, science, and theology because it fits God's imprint of common sense.

God our Creator "spoon-fed" us evidence beyond reasonable doubts of God's saving action in human history. God promised the terms of the new covenant (Jer 31:31-34) and fulfilled it in Jesus Christ (1 Cor 11:23-26). An interdependent part of Jesus's death includes an all-inclusive Eucharist instituted during the paschal mystery. You have known the true church is based on love and cannot exclude anyone from our Eucharist since your doctoral dissertation. But you hypocritically negate love of others by your *Sacramentum Caritatis* (see Mk 7:1-13).

Yours in Christ,

October 31, 2011

Dear Holy Father,

God's pledges in the new covenant (Jer 31:31ff.) are incorporated by reference in the paschal mystery of Jesus's death. They are intended to benefit every human creature by *our Lord*'s unilateral performance and announcement of fulfillment from heaven (1 Cor 11:23-26). Thus, God imprints in each individual conscience the knowledge of God and God's law of loving each other at or before our birth. *Gandium et Spes*, a document of Vatican II, reads that "Deep within his conscience men discover a law which he has not laid upon himself but which he must obey. Its voice, ever calling him to love and do what is good and avoid evil, tells him inwardly at the right moment do this, shun that. For man has in his heart a law inscribed by God."

Jesus's words at the Last Supper, reported by St. Paul and later by the synoptic (but disregarded by the author(s) of the Fourth Gospel), gave meaning to Jesus's crucifixion as an execution of God's promises in God's new covenant. In the blood of the covenant, God teaches each of us, even the least of us, so we need no other teacher and, in the same instant, forgives our evildoing and remember our sin no more (Jer 31:34 and Mk 14:24, Mt 26:28, Lk 22:20). By the blood of the covenant, God recreates human beings, as Jesus redeems the world, to save us existing as we are.

However, an *Antichrist* tradition exists in the tradition of Christianity that is evidenced in the Gospel according to John and in many other thoughts of well meaning humans, including our reigning Pope Benedict XVI while clinging to human tradition. An example of this conduct amounting to blasphemy exists in Vatican II writings promulgated by Pope Paul VI and his scribes, to wit, No. 9, Chapter II, of our *Dogmatic Constitution on the Church* (*Lumen Gentium*). Therein, these writers fit the hypocrisy Jesus prophesied about. They remove God's expressed pledge in the new covenant promised to us, which I quote again: "for I will forgive their evildoing and remember their sin no more" and uncharitably cling to man-made tradition (see Mk 7:1-13).

Pope Benedict and his mentor Saint Augustine also disregarded God's pledge and insist on church baptisms to make people worthy to receive God's Eucharist and God's salvation. As Cardinal Ratzinger, the Pope wrote in opposition to New Testament scholars influenced by Vatican II's openness to make our exclusive Eucharist inclusive of everyone. As Jesus prophesized, *Sacramentum Caritatis* as used by the Vatican also artfully sets aside God's law of love to have us cling to the Pope's human precepts negating God's relationship of love for humanity.

Yours in Christ,

November 1, 2011

Dear Holy Father,

It is too bad that St. Augustine did not face the hindsight we now have in the Catholic church. He, however, fit into Constantine's militant church, and his original sin theory resulted in becoming a primary dogma.

Unfortunately, we have a Pope who is bound by traditional teaching of the church, at least since the Council of Trent, even though it was reinterpreted when we learned of the advance knowledge about human origins. The modern evolutionary world view had overwhelming evidence that man evolved. We see God wisely created man to be pardoned by God, and, in time, first promised salvation in new covenant (Jer 31:31*f*) to the Jews but unilaterally extended in the Blood of the Lamb (see Mk 14:24 and 1 Cor 11:23-26) for all mankind.

Saintliness is being bestowed on Pope John XXIII because of his showing a love for all humanity as members of the Church of Christ. The honor of sainthood might have been laid on Pelagius, a member of Christ's Church globally, in concluding mankind was not evil. Or, on another of Pelagius' global church, members Julian of Norwich (c. 1342-1416), the earliest woman writer on Christ in English because she subscribed to the notion of "universal salvation"—the idea that God saves everyone, and the human spirit is somehow identical with God (*Commonweal*, 11/4/11, p. 28).

Our diocesan bishops were handed the saintly opportunity to distribute God's gift of Eucharist to all humanity in *Sacramentum Craitatius* (Sacrament of Charity), but I know of none who dared contest your edict in Vatican documents sent to their Synods ordering no Communions to be distributed to non-Catholics. How accurately Jesus prophesized about your hypocrisy! (See Mk 7:6-10). Not one diocese has law based on Christ's teachings. They choose to follow you.

Yours in Christ,

November 2, 2011

Dear Holy Father,

I received a booklet entitled *A Guide To The New Translation Of The Mass* and was concerned with the liberties taken to bind us to your personal opinion of the Eucharist to require people to accept God's gifts of salvation in Christ similar to your insistence on receipt of the Eucharist to be only for those "who have let themselves be reconciled by

God" (see page 60, *God Is Near Us*). The *Guide* at page 16 mentions concerns that the new words "For many" substituted for prior words "For all" give the misimpression that Jesus did not die for everyone created. Hence the text of the *Guide* emphasizes: "The new translation points to the realty that while Jesus died for all, not everyone chooses to accept this gift."

The quote from the *Guide* is immediately followed by a teaching of Joseph Ratzinger heard at Tübingen. Professor of Theological studies at St. Louis University, Ronald Modras, wrote an article using typescripts of his professors lectures in 1968/1969, when you taught him that Jesus links the themes of the new covenant (Jer 31) with the suffering servant who gives himself up "for many" (Is 53) so that "for many" (Mk 14:24) prevents the church from becoming a select community of the righteous, a community that condemns the wayward masses to perdition (*Commonweal*, 4/21/06, p. 13).

The Ratzinger of 1968 and the referred to *Guide* both acknowledge that some Catholics misconstrue the Mystical Body of Christ to be identified with the Roman Catholic Church even though we know historically the Church of Christ does not "subsist in" the Catholic church when it uncharitably fails in loving every human being impartially. But again your hierarchy proved the prophecy of Jesus to be correct in disregarding God's commandment of love and translating the text to cling to your traditional views, to wit, "Each individual must choose to welcome the gift of salvation in Christ and live according to that grace so that they may be among "the many" who are described in this text."

Jesus said you "hypocrites" (Mk 7:6-13) disregard God's law of love imprinted in each of us by God's new covenant (Jer 31:31ff.) blood. You negate God's order of salvation and exclude those ignorant of Christ or fail to choose god's gift of salvation. How can you consent to a choice the knowledge of which you are not fully informed? God in goodness unilaterally performs the new covenant for all created humans and, unlike the church, requires only that you be created "for God forgives our evildoings and forgets our sins forever" (Jer 31:34 and 1 Cor 11:23-26).

Yours in Christ,

November 4, 2011

Dear Holy Father,

I am also reading *A Biblical Walk Through The Mass* by Edward Sri, in company with the *Guide* book the (topic of my last letter to you), and both books make clear that *our Lord* has a universal mission that announces salvation to all humanity (e.g., Is 42:1-10, 49:6, 52:10). However, the books and the program of the Catholic church to establish a new mass ritual are deviously coached only to give lip service to the evidence of God's commandment, God's new covenant and God's saving action in human history. To negate either is a blasphemy again the Spirit (see footnote Mt 12:31ff.). Jesus accurately prophesized of hierarchies making a fine art of keeping their traditions and disregarding God's law of loving everyone (Mk 7:1-13).

Only a scintilla of comment does author Edward Sri give to Jesus Christ's expressed purpose for his mass sacrifice to fulfill God's new covenant (Jer 31:31-34). St. Paul wrote he received from the *Lord* in heaven and handed on to Jews and Gentiles, every human being in effect, that the blood being shed is Christ's "new covenant in my blood" (1 Cor

11:23-26). Instead, Sri's *Gospel According to John* negates mention of God's new covenant in the words of Christ at his Last Supper. Jesus's words which you yourself wrote were "interdependent" with the death on the cross, giving universal meaning to both death and Eucharist. The death and word's purpose both redeem humanity by the unilateral action of our loving God solely performing God's Covenant through Jesus Christ.

The *Gospel According to Jesus* is written in his blood and cleanses without Holy Communion, every human being created. It tells us God alone teaches all we need know and forgives all the evil we do by the terms of the new covenant (Jer 31:31*f*). My old Missal's introductory paragraph to the Eucharist liturgy gives us the mass' purpose: "We are here to bless God and to receive the Gift of Jesus's body and blood so that our faith and life may be transformed" (see p. 624 of *New Saint Joseph WEEKDAY MISSAL*). God thereby is constantly renewing all who consume God within them, although all people are recreated before birth in the blood of the covenant.

Yours in Christ,

November 7, 2011

Dear Holy Father,

I must apologize for assuming that you or your Vatican are trying to bind us to your personal opinion of the Eucharist in presenting us with *A Biblical Walk Through the Mass* and *A Guide To The New Translation of The Mass* program presently in our parish. Layman Edward Sri, from Colorado with his books bearing the imprimatur by the Archbishop of Denver, proclaims and shows his own lay opinions on the mass and its changes.

I am concerned about Sir's mass explanations and, of course, as you may know through my writings (not approved by you or any imprimatur), hereby contend that Sri's disregard of God's "new and everlasting covenant" (Jer 31:31*f*) of our Eucharistic Prayers is blasphemy. He nowhere in his teachings refers to the covenant words of the Last Supper, repeated from heaven (1 Cor 11:23-26) and in every mass commemorating Jesus's words and death as are expressed in the scripture of God's new covenant salvation. "Jer 31:31-34" is cited in our *Dogmatic Constitution on the Church* (*Lumen Gentium*,

Chapter II, No. 9), a Document of Vatican II, promulgated by His Holiness, Pope Paul VI on 11/21/64 but, ignored by Sri.

God in Christ performed the new covenant, promised by God in the Old Testament (Jer 31:31ff) and fulfilled it by Jesus in his blood and new testament Mk 14:74, 1 Cor 11:23ff., etc.). The words of the Last Supper explaining Jesus's sacrifice on the cross and sacrifice at every mass are expressly in context of performing the covenant solely by God in Christ (Jn 12:49,50). As you taught, Jesus's words and death are "interdependent," giving both mutual meaning (*God Is Near Us*, p. 29). Also instituted by the words, in context of Jesus's death and God's covenant, is the Eucharist as the church meal to share God's real presence with everyone created, an essential part of Covenant and Redemption, it appears.

I have recently discovered that it was not your doings, but that of well-meaning laymen who want to serve the church, that brought this incompetence and confusion to our parish. Unfortunately, with the church's lack of explaining the new covenant to we laity, and my one-sided correspondence, I jumped to an unwarranted criticism. *Mea Culpa*. I'm sorry.

RSVP,

November 9, 2011

Dear Holy Father,

Recent Mass reading had Jesus violently disturbing the routine of the temple to make a point. I too feel that I disturbed the class being conducted in our church who were involved in the learning of your new mass changes as taught by lay professor Edward Sri, PhD. His doctorate was from Rome's Pontifical University of St. Thomas Aquinas. The Vatican would appreciate Sri disregarded any teaching of the new covenant (Jer 31:31-34), which Jesus died to fulfill. His teachings, thus, border on blasphemy to the Spirit because he negates the evidence of God's solo saving action in history (see footnote Mt 12:31ff.). When our deacon asked if anyone of us questioned the program taught up to that point, I could not be silent and impliedly consent to the evildoing, so I spoke up to awaken the students.

I questioned the authority for the program and the competence of its author because I had discovered no clear authorization by you for the teachings of Sri. Our parish computer expert said they were relying on Sri's expertise as a theologian in teaching his own opinions on the changes. I questioned the opinions as theological truths since the knowledge of God is imprinted in each of us by God, so even the least of us knows by heart the knowledge, with the greatest of us. God has imprinted in our consciences, by the blood of the covenant, all have common knowledge of God. Thereby we no longer need to be taught how to know the *Lord*. "All from the least to greatest shall know me, says the LORD, for I will forgive their evildoing and remember their sin no more" (Jer 31:34). As God promised, the day came when Jesus bloodily fulfilled the new covenant and included Jews and Gentiles (1 Cor 11:23-26, Mt 26:28, Mk 14:24, and Lk 22:20) by shedding blood to his death.

The program as presented by my local lay members mean well, but Jesus's scathing criticism of the art of those who disregard God's commandment of love in translating the Bible, to cling to human precepts and church's traditions (Mk 7:1-13), is here deceitfully hidden by not mentioning that God does it all for all of us in God's new covenant. We need do nothing but be created to be cleansed and saved by God in Christ.

Yours in Christ,

November 10, 2011

Dear Holy Father,

As a lay Passionist, I read *Living Wisdom for Every Day* and today Father Ben Kelley, C. P., advises us not to try and picture God, quoting from Saint Paul of the Cross: "God is pure spirit and can never be comprehended by us since he is beyond our comprehension. We must adore him in spirit and in truth (Jn 4:23), and plunge ourselves into him in simplicity and humility and love in living faith, without trying too hard to picture what he is like."

I find this advice timely because Dr. Edward Sri has been presented to me as authority on his guide to the new mass changes that you proposed. He is offered as qualified by his education and as a professor of theology to discuss the changes. Theology being the study of God and God's relationship to us is not science but reflects on faith and mystery, far from the subject of mass changes and in a stretch might have subjective means to what God has already imprinted in our minds. A discussion on common knowledge or on a subject on which even the least of us has as much knowledge as does Dr. Sri needs no expertise.

Jesus incorporated by reference the new covenant which he died to perform. Sri suggests a new covenant other than Jeremiah 31:31ff. at page 109-110. He submits a Moses covenant which God expressly rejects in God's new covenant. Sri speculates that Jesus had some type of sacrifice in mind and "mysteriously anticipates his sacrifice on the cross." Sri claims Jesus is echoing what Moses said in the sacrificial ceremony at Mount Sinai that sealed God's covenant union with Israel as his chosen people (Ex 24:1-17). However, Pope Benedict XVI taught at Tübingen that Jesus referred to the new covenant at Jer 31:34 and, the Catholic Church's Dogmatic Constitution—(*Lumen Gentium*, Chapter II, No. 9) spells out that Jesus died to institute Jeremiah's new covenant (Jer 31:31-34) for all God's people.

I possess the New American Bible which has a footnote (Mt 12:31ff.) stating the author's views that blasphemy against the Spirit happens when one negates the evidence of God's saving action in history. I would think negating God's new covenant (Jer 31:31-34) as evidence of God's saving action, which Jesus died to establish, to save all sinners especially, as reported by Christ from heaven (1 Cor 11:23-26) would make us critically question Sri's opinion negating the evidence.

Yours in Christ,

November 12, 2011

Dear Holy Father,

If Jesus's words at the Last Supper and his death are "interdependent," giving mutual meaning of universality to each other, why do you now change the mass words "for all" with "for many." You cause what is clear to be unclear, even though you add your explanation that "for all" means "for many." People will think: "Maybe I am one of the few damned." Have a heart and keep "for all."

You correctly appreciate that people will take "for many" literally and read the words of Jesus to mean that not everyone's sins are forgiven, and Jesus redeems all but the few. In fact, adding Pope Paul VI's version of *Lumen Gentium* specifically Chapter II, part No. 9, only a small flock of people, "it does not actually include all men," are saved by Christ's shedding of the blood of the new covenant. Only those who believe in Christ and are reborn by baptism in water (cf. Jn 5:3-6) are saved according to the scribes. Hopefully, "the many" left to perdition will seek salvation by conversion to the Catholic church. It explains why the scribes deleted the ending provision of God's new covenant (Jer 31:34).

The deceit of the scribes in selecting a small flock of forgiving according to the forged terms of the *Dogmatic Constitution On the Church* (*Lumen Gentium*), a purported document of Vatican II, raises my suspicions on why you deliberately changed the clarity of "for all" to "for many." The change is obviously a less charitable translation of scripture and lends itself also to be used by churchmen to justify Eucharist not being intended "for all" but "for many." Your personal assurance that "for many" means "for all" is not persuasive in view of the Catholic church's historical failings toward veracity, for example, the art you practice in using the synod system to control diocesan bishops from freely judging *Sacramentum Caritatis*, thus, preventing non-Catholics open access to God's gift, was prophesized by Jesus (Mk 7:1-13).

Dr. Edward Sri adds his support to your change by writing at page 113, that although "Jesus died for all, not everyone chooses to accept this gift. Each individual must choose to welcome the gift of salvation and live according to this grace, so that he or she may be among the many who are described in this text." (*A Biblical Walk Through The Mass*). Again our self-asserted expert teaches an anti-God blasphemy because he negates the evidence that God alone, in Jesus Christ, forgives all Jews and Gentiles their evildoings forever as promised in God's covenant (Jer 31*f* and 1 Cor 11:23ff.).

Yours in Christ,

November 14, 2011

Dear Holy Father,

My dictionary defines theology as the study of God and God's relationship to us. In fulfilling God's new covenant (Jer 31:31-34) in his blood, Christ expressly teaches us in the words of Jesus's Last Supper, proclaimed in every mass today, and repeated from Heaven by Jesus glorified to St. Paul, to hand onto every Gentile and Jew (1 Cor 22:23-26), what God imprints in everyone's hearts and minds the knowledge of God and God's relationship law. Jesus performs God's pledges, the terms of the deal God makes with us, and, by Jesus incorporating by reference God's covenant, God clearly states in the strongest terms that any further teaching on the subject matter is unneeded because: "*All from least to greatest, shall know me, says the Lord, for I will forgive their evildoing and remember their sin no more*." (Emphasis mine.)

God, mysteriously in Jesus performs the new covenant unilaterally in Christ's blood. Jesus Christ expresses this fact in words at the Last Supper before his death and thereafter from heaven to Paul (Saul) when any veil of ignorance Jesus might have possessed was lifted. I believe that God is Love, and every human being is saved by God since we are assured by God and confirmed by trustworthy hearsay. Apparently, this is God's plan of creation, from the beginning to save us in the flesh of the Lamb. God "telegraphs punches" in remedying the problem of creating mankind with free will, knowing everyone will sin (do their own things and not God's will), by God pardoning God's evildoing creation from its start and in Jesus Christ demonstrably revealing God's design by words expressing love for everyone created and so dearly dying for us to suit his Father's plan. But the event in human history earned only a mention by Josephus. God, thus, included humanity consuming the Eucharist to spread God's news.

As part and parcel of the package of salvation, Jesus was instructed by God to institute the Eucharist, and likely servants, to distribute God's real presence to all humanity. Christianity, however, did not get the message correctly and had to do things their own way to improve on God's way. The church chooses to limit sharing Eucharist. Vatican II's, Pope John XXIII, and his bishops in council began correcting us and presented the ideal Church of Christ, a global church made up of all people created by God and an open Eucharist whereby God is actually within every human being to renew and transform them in teachings.

Yours in Christ,

November 15, 2011

Dear Holy Father,

I have been expounding on my concerns as though I know what I am talking about. But I am simply repeating God's words as charitably translated by me from the Old Testament of God's promised provisions in the new covenant (Jer 31:31-34). It was made significant in the New Testament by Jesus's death and words at the Last Supper (and from heaven) extending the covenant terms to benefit all Gentiles as well as Jews (1 Cor 11:23-26). Since I receive no response to my obligatory correspondence to you, I let my imagination run in search of motivating items. Sadly, I suspect that I am making no impression on my spiritual leaders, and I should leave it to God. Except for Vatican

II, *our Lord* seems unresponsive to my concerns.

I received a response, repeating the church's traditional pre-Vatican II teachings, from Bishop William Wiegand, by letter in August 2007. He told me that I was in error analytically and was in need of "obedience in faith" to the teaching of the church. That teaching was the erroneous one I too had learned since childhood trusting the church. You, too, agreed with Wiegand and answered the post-Vatican II scholars of the New Testament's contention with the prior traditional church teachings (*God Is Near Us*, pp. 59-60). But as Pope Benedict XVI, you had your Vatican artfully use the bishop synod system to force diocesan bishops cling to prior traditions and not the way of Christ toward an open Eucharist.

Because you did not rule outright for an exclusive Eucharist but released *Sacramentum Caritatis*, I retain hope in you. I feel hopefully that you see Christ's Church does not subsist in the Roman Catholic Church so long as the church uncharitably denies Eucharist to most of humanity. I feel there is hope in your deep-seated insecurity that seemingly flares up in 1968/69 from fright caused by the student's revolt. Hans Küng says it overwhelmed you to leave the camp of the stalwarts of Vatican II and attach yourself to church's traditionalists for comfort. Others say you sold your soul for power and to gain control of the Church and return it to the uncharitable traditions before Vatican II. I doubt if you ever read my correspondence so I write as I am "obliged" in hopes that *our Lord* might awaken you to love your neighbor as you should and let God have God's will with humanity's gift of Eucharist.

Yours in Christ,

November 22, 2011

Dear Holy Father,

Hans Küng has consistently held true to his progressive theological views and believes that your departure from the direction of the Second Vatican Council has placed the whole Roman Catholic Church system in question. At the root of your bishops' cover-ups of clerical sexual abuse, he sees, centralization, clericalism, and absolutism (see *NCR* 11/12/10, John Wilkins' "straight arrow") as disastrous results.

Here in the *United States,* we experience a similar crisis in our republic system of government. Our elected officials are no longer representing the people but answer to their respective party's, democrat or republican, campaign fund givers. It is the self-interests of individual politicians wanting to stay in office who seek funding that benefits the parties. Their political self-interests are so addictive and overpowering that the knowledgeable experts among us citizens feel a new constitutional convention is needed to redirect our civil servants to serve us instead.

Our US Constitution was created by our infant government to define the powers of the republic over the democracy of the people. The Whiskey Rebellion was about the home-made distillers' refusal to pay taxes on their income to the newly formed government. Somewhat like Pope Paul VI and the Curia overruling Pope John XXIII's progressives to reverse openness extending to a global church.

I submit that Pope Paul VI and his scribes drew up Chapter II, No. 9, of *Lumen Gentium*, in our *Dogmatic Constitution on the Church*, to protect against ideas like the global church of Christ idea membered with all humans created. Pope John had frightened the Curia by restraining their participation in debates and by threatening their role, if any, in the Church's future. So, while frightened, the bureaucratic hierarchy acted in extremes and forged God's words into a new relationship. Pope Paul's Vatican then made up its own version of God's words in covenant to negate evidence of God's unilaterally saving us. Now, baptized believers in Christ are saved, not solely by God, but by aid of humans in the Roman Catholic Church.

Today, you rule us as a dictator, and not a benevolent one. Where Christ impartially loves all human beings, Pope Benedict chooses to deny God's gift of life, meant for all humankind, to be shared only with those deemed worthy traditionally by human precepts.

Sadly yours,

November 23, 2011

Dear Holy Father,

Immediately after the Second Vatican Council, our New Testament scholars and the influenced theologians moved to share our Eucharist with everyone in the world. Neither baptism nor being reconciled from mortal sin was preconditions to receiving the real presence of God in Holy Communion (see *God Is Near Us* by Joseph Cardinal Ratzinger, p. 59). Such was the outcome of the ideal global Church of Christ *ressourced* by Pope John XXIII and his bishops in council (see *Dogmatic Constitution on the Church*, Chapter 1, No. 8) holding that "the unique church of Christ . . . subsists in the Catholic Church." At the time, Hans Küng was told by the secretary of the theological commission who was responsible for using "subsists in," rather than "is" as the preliminary text of the council had had it, that "we wanted to keep the matter open" (*NCR*, 11/12/10, p. 17).

Our noted Catholic theologian, Karl Rahner, said that the best idea that came out of Vatican II was the ideal global Church of Christ. Its membership is considered to be all of humanity. Thus, the New Testament scholars' *ressourcement* translated into Christ's intention to share Eucharist with all humanity cleansed by God in the blood of the covenant.

At Tübingen, you agreed with Küng that Jesus did not intend to found a church. You lectured that the church's foundation was based on the words of the Last Supper instituting the Eucharist for the redeemed world. Those words, being "interdependent" with the death of Jesus (see *God Is Near Us*, p. 29), included the Eucharist and its purpose to benefit all humankind. Jesus's paschal words linked his death and words from his understanding of scripture's paschal lamb (Ex 12), suffering servant "for many" (Is 53), and new and everlasting covenant (Jer 31:31ff.). Thus, his words recorded by the synoptic, for example, Mk 14:24: "This is my blood, the blood of the *covenant*, to be poured out on behalf of many" (emphasis mine) are proclaimed in Eucharist prayers.

In your ambitious rise from Tübingen to the Vatican, you seemingly forgot that the "for many" prevents the church from becoming a community of righteous who condemns the rest of humanity to perdition (see *Commonweal*, 4/21/06, p. 13) or to excommunication. Consequently, today with your condoning the exclusion of "many" from Eucharist and Church, the true Church cannot "subsist in" the Catholic Church, and the whole Roman system lacks the fundamental virtue of charity.

Yours in Christ,

November 30, 2011

Dear Holy Father,

It was reported in *The New Yorker*, 7/05/05, that you silenced Brazilian theologian Leonardo Boff and arrested his movement of "liberation theology." The movement tried to share the wealth more fairly with the poor; so the authorities, both governmental and the Roman Catholic bishops, likely will favor you in any reasonable request you now make to Brazil.

My daughter has a close friend, Adria Kibbe of 9362 Loma Rica Road, Marysville, California. Adria has been frustrated in learning the true circumstances of the death of her paternal uncle Fr. Ferdinand Azevedo,

S. J., age 72, who was murdered by means of a broken neck ("Intervertebral disarticulation" according to the US Department of State's Report of Death, 3/15/2011) in his room while on annual retreat at A V, Beira Mar, Janga in Paulista, Pernambuco, Brazil. The Society of Jesus and the local authorities have promised further details, but soon a year from death will elapse, and the authorities suspiciously are not reporting the circumstances of the January death and a cover-up of his homicide may be occurring.

You are aware of the troubled times to which our clergy and missionaries are exposed in Brazil. Male clerics are additionally subject to cover-ups of possible sexual scandals. This elderly Jesuit was found naked and a chain attached appearing to have strangled him. The fractured neck, however, cannot be self-inflected and evidences the homicide of an actively social Jesuit in troubled lands. Evidently Father Fred was silenced in his liberation efforts.

In truth and fact, Adria received holiday wishes as recent as two weeks of his death from "Uncle Fred." He was enjoying public activities and studies on behalf of Christian women in the state of Pernambuco. He added that his other activities continue, and he was always pressured to publish books and articles. He ended with "My health is good and I take care to see that it remains so. Love, Uncle Fred."

I believe your access to the civil authorities or the church authorities in Brazil can result in obtaining detailed information on the death of Father Azevedo. You may prove martyrdom and give us a local saint born and raised nearby to boast about.

In anticipation of your assistance, I remain.

December 1, 2011

Dear Holy Father,

You may know I am a daily communicant. I am presently experiencing the changes you made in the wording of the mass. I will be eighty years of age in April so I recall responding in Latin as an altar boy for many years and only by the weekday missal in hand did I have an inkling of what transpired. God alone, in the form of the wafer I consumed, enlightened me on the happening, I suppose. So with the wakening of *Lumen Gentium*, the light from Vatican II and the blessings of English to show what the priest was saying at mass, did Christ's good news reach my consciousness. Since the mid-1960s to date, I have followed along with *St. Joseph Weekday Missal* and was content.

Much like you, I too dislike new way that change the comfortable ways we become used to. My clinging to routine in use of the *Missal* has been shattered. I tried to pen and pencil in the changes in the liturgy, but my aged eyesight defeats me in reading my writing. More disturbing is in the rest of the mass that you changed to suit you. Many of our priests speak with foreign accents and reading the *Missal* along with them was a blessing. Like in my youth hearing Latin, I could read along and understand the priest. Tragically, this is no longer available to me. I am now distracted by the presiders' utterances as I try to read my altered *Missal* and am forced to buy new ones as you change their wordings.

I recall first opening a Bible in 1950, and it meant little to me. But after Vatican II, I became a disciple of Christ's good news, even to express concerns about their translations to Pope Benedict XVI. The only response was from Bishop Wiegand, my diocesan spiritual shepherd, who said I needed to obey my Catholic Church's teachings more faithfully. However, my obedience to the now understandable divine teachings that had existed in my conscience's faith convictions overruled the teachings of the church, particularly, on the Eucharist.

I am aware of your mental abilities and religious education far exceed my own, but I am convinced that the teachings of *our Lord* make us equal in knowing God and God's law of love. I also suggest that our egos differ, and mine is less self-ingrained in Catholic tradition. Even moreso, I cling to the conviction that each human being is created equal to you and I, and as Christians, we are obliged to serve everyone created impartially. At mass today I seem to hear a clashing cymbal from your involvements, which I pray to overcome by *our Lord* opening our hearts to do God's will moreso than our own.

Yours in Christ

December 6, 2011

Dear Holy Father,

You knew the real reason for your seemingly abrupt departure from Tübingen. Hans Küng suggests that the students' revolt frightened you away but also suggests you sold out the progressives to gain your present glory. I lean toward the latter opinion from speculating on your ego involvement during my years of watching you.

I have the feeling that you resented the position that all those more renowned theologians placed you in during the Second Vatican Council and afterward. My last letter reminded me of how difficult it might have been for you to be confronted with Hans Küng exchanging his viewpoints and those of Edward Schillebeecjx, Karl Rahner, Bernard Haring, and others who contradicted yours from being enlightened by Vatican II. They not only accepted the global Church of Christ, with its openness to non-Catholics and liberation theology satellites (see Chapter 1, No. 8, of *Lumen Gentium*) but criticized the uncharitableness of the Catholic Church's exclusive Eucharist.

I wonder which had the greater contributing cause to your change of attitude, the refusal to cling to Catholic church's tradition, or the opportunity you saw in clinging to the tradition and ride the coat tails of Karol Wojtyla. Once joined with the traditionalists and the power of the church hierarchy, the mentioned theologians were silenced and you rose to fame. The rise began with the death of Pope John and the release of the Curia to assist Pope Paul VI writing forgeries into Constitutional dogma (see Chapter II, No. 9, *Lumen Gentium*). Thereafter the New Testament scholars' contentions for an open Eucharist were silenced and, on attaining the papacy, you released *Sacramentum Caritatis* for your Vatican to control the episcopate and artfully manage the synod system to secure a Eucharist only for baptized Catholics and those well reconciled to think like you.

Somehow you must take comfort in what you have done as Pope Benedict XVI, knowing that you have deliberately denied most of the mystical body of Christ, who make up the global church of Christ, God's gift of Eucharist. God "spoon-fed" us, you especially, in knowing of God and god's law of love to benefit every individual created and renewed by God solely performing God's new covenant in the blood of Christ.

Yours in Christ

December 8, 2011

Dear Holy Father,

Common knowledge of God and God's law of love is imprinted in every human being created. As Christians tend to believe Mary was immaculately conceived, this feast day, human beings should accept they are redeemed from their ignorance and evildoing by the blood of the new covenant, even before their birth. Our God of Love created everyone in divine image and destines them to live forever and together with God. God creates us so I know by heart and so do you, but we can also trust on scripture's new covenant (Jer 31) with an open heart to perceive our own immaculate pardoning in redemption.

The moves you made in about 1969 to change your views from that of the progressive theologians of Vatican II were in keeping with the complexity of your personality. I think from what I perceive of your works, that you felt being disrespected in your opinions by your more listened to colleagues and contemporaries. At the same time, you witnessed the power of Pope Paul VI and the popularity of Karol Wojtyla in clinging to church's traditions. You saw your opportunity and grasped Wojtyla's trailing robes to climb the hierarchy. Once attaining the papacy, you do as Jesus prophesied in clinging to human precepts and tradition while disregarding God's commandment. Recently, you expressed your opinion on Jesus being "incarnate" of Mary and sided with human opinions conforming to the prologue of John's gospel establishing Jesus preexisted his birth of Mary. My diocesan bishop warned me in 2007 that I need "obedience in faith" to the teachings of the church, which I now assume are the teachings of the Roman Church and not that of the Church of Christ based on God's covenant.

You also recognize what God imprints in our conscience of teachings or knowledge that takes precedence over your church teachings. Vatican II concluded that we human beings, all created people of God, make up the Church of Christ. Its Catholicism is identified with Christianity from the beginning.

God's covenant relationship with humanity is guaranteed not for external torment of anyone but for everlasting love. All is God's good news in Christ. Jesus incorporates by reference God's new covenant in the words of the Last Supper, words of which are "interdependent" with Jesus's death for universal meaning and vice versa, those words, including the institution of the universal Eucharist, are defined by God in Jesus's paschal death. I can only see a touch of megalomania that prevents you from seeing the truth or doing what you know you ought to do. I suggest on your death that you use this psychiatric defense for your obstinacy toward negating God's design. Plead it in extenuation or mitigation.

Yours in Christ

December 9, 2011

Dear Holy Father,

I happened to open a book by J. P. Arendzene, D. D., entitled *Purgatory and Heaven*. I first looked to see Archbishop of New York, Francis Cardinal Spellman, had given it an Imprimatur of being free of doctrine or moral error. It was dated 1960, well before Vatican II.

I saw error at its first reading, for example, "no sooner has the soul left the body, but, if it was in mortal sin it is in hell; if it was without any stain or remnant of sin, it is in heaven; if it was in sanctifying grace, but with stains and remnants of sin, it is in purgatory" (pp. 9 and 10). For millenniums before this 1960 date, Jesus is proclaiming in contrast: "this is the cup of my blood, the blood of the new and everlasting covenant," indicating God forgives sin by Covenant on Jesus's death. Thus Jesus authentically incorporates by reference the new covenant (Jer 31:31-34) signifying God solely forgives each created person's evildoing. God's loving redemption proves the words of *Purgatory and Heaven* are false and a blasphemy of God's salvation.

The Second Vatican Council also opened our eyes to the truth of God's plan. Whatever Church of Christ Jesus established in the words of the Last Supper, it assured benefits to every human creature created with the tendency to do evil in exercising its free will, by a built-in pardon from God to guarantee everyone's salvation. God is love as Jesus demonstrated, and our life is blessed as objects of God's love, predestined to be in God's constant care no matter how unworthy we are in God's presence. This includes the real presence that God designed into the Eucharist. God makes a unilaterally performed covenant with God's people saved solely by God's goodness, regardless of any faith or good works from God's beloved in exchange.

You soon will die and face *our Lord*. Your time is running short to remedy the artful setting aside of God's commandment of love of neighbor, in the interest of keeping an exclusive Eucharist for Catholics alone. I suggest you are evildoing in condoning *Sacramentum Caritatis* negating of God's gift for salvation. Please take my concern as a caution to open your heart to reflect on what God has imprinted therein of God's law of love.

Yours in Christ

December 12, 2011

Dear Holy Father,

All weekend I was troubled by using the word "blasphemy" of God's salvation in describing the words of *Purgatory and Heaven* in my last letter. I was thinking of the term used in the New Testament's *The Gospel According to Mathew*, in footnote 12:31ff., referring to Jesus's response to the Pharisees' charge that he casts out demons by Beelzebub. Jesus answers us, according to Mathew, that blasphemy against the Spirit of God will not be forgiven. The author of the footnote explains that the Pharisees assign the sole work of God in Jesus to an evil principle making it anti-God. My use of "blasphemy" was based on the fact that a typical Roman Catholic, in 1960 as well as today, "negates the evidence of God's saving action in history" to needing our faith and good works to aid God to save us. Individuals, such as Arendzene, Spellman, and yours truly in 1960 believed we need faith and works to be saved. Blasphemy charged by me lacks the element of willful irreverence to be the sin. That is not to say that those who know better today, who deliberately disregard God's new covenant and God's commandments of love, are not willfully or recklessly negating the unilateral action of God's redemption for everyone created. God's pledge to forgive and forget sin includes blasphemy simply because God loves us and is perfect in action.

I was wrong to charge "blasphemy" so generally because in 1960 I too was as ignorant as every other Catholic. Those who spoke up at Vatican II gave us the true history of God in Christ's saving action of all humanity in God's new covenant. The two passages of the Bible I keep citing; to wit, Jeremiah 3:31ff. and 1 Corinthians 11:23-26 are all the evidence we need to prove God's saving action. All the rest of human writings, that is, Bible, Koran, Book of Mormon, and so on, are mere commentary on these cited words. The bases for my opinions are what I know by heart, as I am within the range of the least and the greatest of us who are imprinted with the Covenantal knowledge of God.

Our Vatican II Constitution states that the Church of Christ subsists in the Catholic church. I write of the concerns that I am obliged to express by it to my spiritual leaders. But the same Constitution assures me I am to receive from you advice correcting me if I error. Your silence admits my truth.

Yours in Christ

December 13, 2011

Dear Holy Father,

On the feast of the Immaculate Conception, I wrote that we human beings should learn that we are immaculately redeemed from our ignorance and evil freewill doings by God's new covenant (Jer 31:31-34). What gives the covenant words veracity is the fact that Jesus Christ incorporated them by reference at the Last Supper, the words which he dies for. Their meaning gained too on the crucifixion (see Cardinal Ratzinger's *God Is Near Us*, p. 29); also they are made authentic by Jesus voicing them at a most acutely significant time, confessing they are not his but God's words and repeating them from heaven to make sure St. Paul reveals the covenant's coverage to include all Gentiles and Jews (1 Cor 11:23-26).

I suggest that the references to the new covenant passages of scripture are the most divinely significant communications ever, and all the rest of the religious writings are commentary on these words to us of God.

In truth, some of the most treasured writings of human precepts, for example, *The Gospel According to John,* deliberately negate evidence of God's saving arrangement with humankind. The author(s) of this fourth Gospel are likely of a cult from Ephesus who brought the Helenist gods of Homer to bury God's new covenant relationship and substituting their own where we humans must contribute faith and good works to earn our salvation. God's new covenant and Jesus Christ's motive to fulfill it are disregarded, to establish a human Christology that the Roman Catholic Church identifies with today. Note: the new covenant is not mentioned in this *Antichrist* news.

Our Creator designed us to be far more influenced by the instincts of self-preservation than by God's law of love that was imprinted on our hearts and minds at birth. Too often, we prove that we will deny our neighbor something that is to our own advantage not to share. Only influenced by God after considering

God's commandment of loving neighbors, might we serve strangers. However, on sharing Eucharist, the real presence of God in form of a wafer of bread or a sip of wine will transform our life and faith to do better.

Yours in Christ,

December 16, 2011

Dear Holy Father,

Today's Gospel (Jn 5:22-27) was surprisingly educational on the subject of my monologue. Jesus told the Jews about John the Baptists' saving testimony lighting up the greater testimony Jesus possessed on his Father's behalf. John's testimony apparently points to the testimony Jesus had which *our Lord* God gave to Jesus to reveal in performing the new covenant and New testament. Jesus said also that "the least born in the Kingdom of God is greater than he," that is, John the Baptist (Lk 7:28).

It is obvious to me on basis of the common knowledge God imprints in all of us and from what Communion may have drawn out of me that Jesus died to perform the task given him. God's covenant forgives, teaches, and saves us all as revealed in the blood of the covenant (Jer 31:31ff., Mt 26:28, Mk 14:24, and Lk 22:20). Jesus likely errs in thinking he redeems only those born after John the Baptist dies. Our Loving God saves in Christ everyone impartially.

Imprinted in everyone created by God and recreated by God's sole performance of the new covenant is the knowledge God imprints to cause us to know by heart God and God's law of love. It is from that common feature of our humanity that the words of Jesus conform, to my faith contentions. The author(s) of the Fourth Gospel also quoted Jesus claiming that ". . . Since I know that his commandment means eternal life, whatever I say is spoken just as he (His Father) instructed me." (Jn 12:50). Of course, when Jesus calls us Gentiles "dogs" that is the Jew in Jesus and not God instructing him to say the uncharitable slur.

That leads me to question what Jesus's thoughts were when he felt abandoned on the cross. His exclamation, "I thirst" likely indicates the symptoms of his bleeding to death, and as his loss of blood affects him mentally, the basic animal instincts of self-preservation may turn him to *Psalm 22* "My God, my God, why have you forsaken me . . . Rescue my soul from the sword, my loneliness from the grips of the dog. Save me . . ." It is apparent that Jesus died, handing over his spirit to God who he trusts is there to care for him. Having persevered in faith, over reasonable doubts, it is credit to Jesus that his loving action glorifies and serves us all eternally.

I quoted your first encyclical words (see letter 3/22/06; or, *God's Gift To You* p. 21) that Communion draws you out of yourself toward *our Lord*. You should realize that God baptizes all humans in the blood of the covenant into the Church of Christ, and they should have the same experience as you. We all are recreated, thus, to be worthy Christians by God Almighty. Accepting the testimony of Christ, you should order your diocesan bishops to reapply *Sacramentum Caritatis* charitably and return the Catholic Church to a true church status by excluding no one from the sacrament (see your doctoral dissertation).

Yours in Christ,

December 20, 2011

Dear Holy Father,

The greatest news ever told us is that of the paschal mystery of Jesus's death and resurrection in the context of God's *new and eternal covenant*. You know it by heart; yet, you persist in negating evidence of it in a maintained Vatican II document written by the curia scribes for Pope Paul VI to promulgate. I refer to Chapter II, No. 9, of *Lumen Gentium*, obviously made to rebut Chapter I, No. 8, wherein the global Church of Christ, consistent with the new covenant, is mentioned.

The Roman Catholic Church purports to write for a *Dogmatic Constitution on the Church* in No. 9 by distorting terms of the covenant pledges promised by God and irreverently deleting God's words that establish we no longer need be taught how to know God and God's law or be forgiven by the church "for I will forgive their evildoing and remember their sin no more" (Jer 31:31-34). The covenant makes plain we need no Catholic church to teach, forgive, or rule Catholics because God accomplishes all we need in the global Church of Christ, which merely subsists in the

Catholic church when the latter is true to God's law of loving everyone as equals. Simply read the blatant lies of No. 9, for example, claiming "*this*" (forgery) is the "new covenant, New Testament," that Christ instituted by his death and resurrection is *Antichrist*. Pope Paul VI and his scribes so deviously change the words of God in the eternal new covenant to deny its coverage benefiting all humanity created as Jesus Christ told St. Paul from heaven (see 1 Cor 11:23-26).

Pope Paul VI and company's blasphemy negates the evidence of God's saving covenant, planned from the beginning as God sees humanity's persistent evildoings require God's pardon for justice sake and God's love for each one of us. Pope Paul VI and his people may be ignorant of the evil they did, but the same does not hold for you. You tried since to identify the Church of Christ and the Catholic church in essence and "artfully passed the buck" to diocesan bishops to deny most everybody access to Eucharist. Likely, you will answer to God for your self-centered efforts unless you remedy the wrong soon.

Yours in Christ,

December 21, 2011

Dear Holy Father,

Translate, please, by a charitable standard the words of Jesus at the Last Supper, when he instituted the Eucharist by taking the cup for (1) "all of you must drink from it, for this is my blood, the blood of the covenant, to be poured out in behalf of many for the forgiveness of sin" (Mt 26:27-28), (2) "This is my blood, the blood of the covenant, to be poured out on behalf of many" (Mk 14:24), or (3) "This cup is the new covenant in my blood, which will be shed for you" (Lk 23:26). Then translate (1), (2), and (3) interdependently with the death of Jesus redeeming the world. It translates that everyone created is supposed to share in the Eucharist as they share in redemption. Jesus died to tell us that in the blood of the covenant, the blood we drink in Eucharist inserts the real presence of God within us. Jesus died to fulfill God's unilateral performance of the new covenant, establishing God's teaching us all we need know about God and God's law of love "for I will forgive their evildoing and remember their sin no more" (Jer 31:31-34). To emphasize that the new covenant beneficiaries included all Gentiles with the Jews, Jesus Christ spoke to St. Paul from heaven (1 Cor 11:23-26). Thus God of Love, out of goodness, solely cleansed every human creature, designed with free will to sin, to be eternally worthy and be with God.

Today's Gospel (Lk 1:15) Gabriel told Zachariah that, while in Elizabeth's womb, John was filled with the Holy Spirit. Jesus said everyone born in the Kingdom of God, brought about by Jesus's fulfillment of the new covenant, is equally worthy to John (Lk 7:24). God according to your strained interpretation, however, wastefully deals with the death and resurrection news of Jesus by limiting Eucharist to a few. The "many" for whom Jesus died might never hear of him if it was not for God's plan of Eucharist proclamations and God's presence therein. Much human success has extended the Catholic church's influence throughout the world. But God's real presence in an all-inclusive Eucharist and God's actual influence in the bowels of all created humanity will transform everyone's life and faith by God-self perfecting salvation.

You must realize and appreciate that your artfully concocted Church's Eucharist, manipulated by your Vatican in controlling diocesan bishops through the hypocrisy of

Sacramentum Caritatis, is the major negating blasphemy of the evidence of God's saving action. By God solely performing the new and everlasting covenant, no matter how evil, stupid, and *Antichrist* you and we might be, God saves everyone. Think of this, we lose so much in old age that you may not know what God is doing, and the rest of the Vatican may not be interested to help you against their interests. A younger, more charitable and objective pope may do God's will.

For love of God and all humanity, would you consider retiring?

Yours in Christ

December 21, 2011

Dear Holy Father,

Translate, please, by a charitable standard the words of Jesus at the Last Supper, when he instituted the Eucharist by taking the cup for (1) "all of you must drink from it, for this is my blood, the blood of the covenant, to be poured out in behalf of many for the forgiveness of sin" (Mt 26:27-28); (2) "This is my blood, the blood of the covenant, to be poured out on behalf of many" (Mk 14:24), or (3) "This cup is the new covenant in my blood, which will be shed for you" (Lk 23:26). Then translate (1), (2), and (3) interdependently with the death of Jesus redeeming the world. It translates that everyone created is supposed to share in the Eucharist as they share in redemption. Jesus died to tell us that in the blood of the covenant, the blood we drink in Eucharist inserts the real presence of God within us. Jesus died to fulfill God's unilateral performance of the new covenant, establishing God's teaching us all we need know about God and God's law of love "for I will forgive their evildoing and remember their sin no more" (Jer 31:31-34). To emphasize that the new covenant beneficiaries included all Gentiles with the Jews, Jesus Christ spoke to St. Paul from heaven (1 Cor 11:23-26). Thus God of Love, out of goodness, solely cleansed every human creature, designed with free will to sin, to be eternally worthy and be with God.

Today's Gospel (Lk 1:15) Gabriel told Zachariah that, while in Elizabeth's womb, John was filled with the Holy Spirit. Jesus said everyone born in the Kingdom of God, brought about by Jesus's fulfillment of the new covenant, is equally worthy to John (Lk 7:24). God according to your strained interpretation, however, wastefully deals with the death and resurrection news of Jesus by limiting Eucharist to a few. The "many" for whom Jesus died might never hear of him if it was not for God's plan of Eucharist proclamations and God's presence therein. Much human success has extended the Catholic Church's influence throughout the world. But God's real presence in an all-inclusive Eucharist and God's actual influence in the bowels of all created humanity will transform everyone's life and faith by God-self perfecting salvation.

You must realize and appreciate that your artfully concocted Church's Eucharist, manipulated by your Vatican in controlling diocesan bishops through the hypocrisy of *Sacramentum Caritatis*, is the major negating blasphemy of the evidence of God's saving action. By God solely performing the new and everlasting covenant, no matter how evil, stupid, and *Antichrist* you and we might be, God saves everyone. Think of this, we lose so much in old age that you may not know what God is doing, and the rest of the Vatican may not be interest to help you against their interests. A younger, more charitable and objective Pope may do God's will.

For love of God and all humanity, would you consider retiring?

Yours in Christ

December 22, 2011

Dear Holy Father,

Today is the darkest day of the year, our winter solstice. We look forward to the sun enlightening our world the rest of the year. With that anticipation let me tell you of my law partner's experience with Catholicism and the light he shines for me.

John Trezza is a Sicilian-American born to a family of fourteen siblings. He was raised by immigrants dependent on fishing. John was a cradle Catholic but ceased attending mass after his confirmation. He was the first of the family educated in higher learning and intelligent enough to be in Korea as one of the US Army's intelligence soldiers. He was given a jeep and traveled the hills of South Korea during that campaign. He met an Irish priest who was stationed in a parish of no congregation since about 1937, and they had many discussions. A topic was John's nonchurch attendance, and the priest told John that *our Lord* did not insist upon him attending mass if he chose not to do so. John has never sought a second opinion and doesn't receive Eucharist at the few funeral masses he attends.

John and I have been law partners and close friends for one-half century. He knows of my concerns written to you but, like you is not persuaded to respond by changing his ways. My concern is not for his everlasting wellbeing. I personally perceive John's conduct and in open discussions conclude he is loving God by serving his fellow men and women impartially. He does not suffer hypocrites well and knowing my good and bad sides will not be persuaded by me to change his faith convictions. He is a year older than I and feels the wiser but, being familiar with me, also has contempt unfortunately to acknowledge much truth in what I say. He likes what God has imprinted in his heart and mind so he needs no other teacher, appreciating what the Irish priest confirmed, of what he already knew by heart, to love others equally without any church teaching him better or worse.

God needs no help to do good. John does good likewise not for God or for merit but because his conscience tells him what he ought. He's actively doing probate work, for rich and poor impartially, while I write these useless letters to you. I once did good works seeking merit and obedience to the Church, and now I do them because I do not know what is better to do. John is content with the use of his work and life, but I need you to have a heart and at least read my writings to make me a useful servant of God.

Yours in Christ

December 27, 2011

Dear Holy Father,

At Mass my missal has the Liturgy of the Eucharist read:

> Christians are baptized into the paschal mystery of Christ's death and resurrection for the forgiveness of sin and fullness of salvation. This mystery is celebrated at every Mass,

> remembering Christ's loving deed and giving thanks and praise to God. By this action the 'sacrifice of the Cross is continuously made present in the Church. (*Sacramentum Concilum*, No. 47)

"Christians" in the sense of members of the global Church of Christ which subsists in the Catholic church, when it is true to Jesus Christ over its own traditions, are those baptized into the blood of the covenant. In other words, "Christian" means human being. The mystery of Christ's death and resurrection has this meaning given by God instructing Jesus to explain his paschal sacrifice made in context of the new covenant (Jer 31:31-34) and Jesus's words were repeated from heaven (1 Cor 11:23-26) and in every mass since to clarify God means that every human being created is a Christian cleansed by God's covenant pledges and fulfilled in the blood Jesus shed in baptizing us all Christians. The death on the cross and the words at every Lord's Supper repeat the invitation of God to share God's real presence in the body and blood of Jesus crucified in order to have God within each human person to transform us to love each other as brothers and sisters in Christianity.

The hypocrisy in you and your consorts in the hierarchy artfully excluding most people from Eucharist on clinging to uncharitable church's traditions that only baptized believers in Christ are to be saved or invited to share Eucharist was prophesized by Jesus (Mk 7:1-13). You taught that the "for many" of those saved, according to scripture (Mk 14:24 and Is 53) prevents any church from becoming a select community, condemning the non-baptized and nonbelievers to perdition (see *Commonweal*, p. 13, 4/21/06).

The New Testament scholars who criticized your exclusive Eucharist and proclaimed God intended the Eucharist for all humanity was opposed by you, but I felt "half-heartedly" (See *God Is Near Us*, pp. 59-60), and you passed the responsibility to your hierarchy to use the synod system to control diocesan bishops to apply *Sacramentum Caritatis* uncharitably.

Yours in Christ,

December 28 2011

Dear Holy Father,

The reading of the Epistle today was from the first letter of John who writes that "God Is light," meaning God is knowable because God-self reveals God as love in Jesus Christ. Our Advocate with God is Jesus and

> He is expiation for our sins, and not for our sins only, but for those of the whole world. (1 Jn 2:2)

The quotation is consistent with God solely performing the new covenant (Jer 31:31ff.) in the bleeding to death of Jesus for all Jews and Gentiles (1 Cor 11:23-26). Jesus is expiation (pays the penalty for our evildoing) for every human being's sin.

Our memorial mass of the redemptive sacrifice of Jesus was, today, also the feast day of the Holy Innocents. *Mathew*'s story has traditional conversion values for Jews to have Jesus come out of Egypt. The traditional church has problems with the innocent as Adam's heirs thanks to St. Augustine's idea of original sin, and the church has to stretch its credibility to make the infant's innocent because they weren't church baptized.

After Pope John XXIII's death, you were confronted and opposed the New Testament scholars' criticism of our church's exclusive Eucharist and their contention Christ meant Eucharist to be open to everyone even the unbaptized, as his death was interdependent with the words instituting Holy Communion. Had God's real presence been allowed to nourish everyone created, most of us might be practicing Christians today as God originally intended. Practicing what God teaches us of God's law of love in the new covenant, the extermination of millions caused by traditional Christianity should not have occurred in your Germany.

Realizing the error of our ways, *Sacramentum Caritatis* as it is being controlled by your Vatican is causing greater evil to human beings on earth than the killing of them in infancy or the exterminating them in showers because they are not church baptized or deemed worthy. God is constantly forgiving the evildoings of all created peoples in God's new covenant's relationship. Wake up! You can still correct your wrong by correcting conduct toward those God's pardoned.

Yours in Christ,

December 30, 2011

Dear Holy Father,

Jesus died trusting his Divine Father would rescue him from death, and we are to do the same. Jesus's death gave meaning to words at his last supper. He believed his death was to ransom every human being created from their own everlasting deaths. Thus he died out of love for us. He also felt he was fulfilling God's new covenant promised in scripture (Jer 31:31ff.), which made every person worthy to receive God's actual presence in Holy Communion or in heaven forever more.

God allowed Jesus an excruciating and shameful death on the cross but was always there to receive Jesus's spirit and glorify him. Jesus rose in three days as he predicted and appeared to his followers who he assured would see him again. From heaven, he appeared to Saul (Paul) and repeated the words of the Last supper ordering us all to take of the Eucharist, the blood of which baptized each human individual born in the new covenant kingdom the least of whom Jesus assured us is to be greater than St. John the Baptist. We know by common knowledge God imprints in us that we all are created or recreated as equal brothers and sisters of *our Lord* crucified. We are all God's children and entitled to impartial treatment from each other.

I intend to publish a book entitled *The Good News According to God*. It sounds presumptuous, but its contents are the faith convictions I have gained in these years of writing you. I believe I am "obliged" to write by part No. 37 of our *Dogmatic Constitution on the Church* (see my *God's Gift To You* and *A Sequel* efforts, both lodged with the Library of Congress and available online.) The new book is to express opinions that I am obliged to express to the members of the Church of Christ, which includes every one created by God and renewed in covenant. I pray that as I write to my fellow brothers and sisters in Christ, I may strengthen the whole Church of Christ to more effectively fulfill its mission for the earthly and heavenly life of the world.

Presently, everyone has a God-given right to share God in Eucharist and hereafter.

The good news is also that God in Jesus Christ saves each human individual from eternal death, simply out of God's goodness and love. It is a true gift without making any demands on we humans. God saves us all in Jesus Christ, whether or not God finds us in evildoing, simply because God creates and loves us as we are.

Yours in Christ